Studies in Zoroastrian Family Law

CNI PUBLICATIONS 28

STUDIES IN ZOROASTRIAN FAMILY LAW

A COMPARATIVE ANALYSIS

BY BODIL HJERRILD

THE CARSTEN NIEBUHR INSTITUTE OF NEAR EASTERN STUDIES

UNIVERSITY OF COPENHAGEN 2003 · MUSEUM TUSCULANUM PRESS

BODIL HJERRILD: STUDIES IN ZOROASTRIAN FAMILY LAW
CNI PUBLICATIONS, 28

Cover design by Thora Fisker
Set by Anders Brüel
Printed in Denmark by Special-Trykkeriet, Viborg

ISBN 87 7289 807 0
ISSN 0902 5499

The publication of this book was made possible through grants from
The Danish Research Council for the Humanities
Davids Fond og Samling

Denne afhandling er af Det Humanistiske Fakultetsråd ved Københavns Universitet antaget til offentligt at forsvares for den filosofiske doktorgrad.

København, den 2. oktober 2001 John Kuhlmann Madsen
dekan

Published and distributed by
Museum Tusculanum Press
University of Copenhagen
Njalsgade 92
DK-2300 Copenhagen S

Orders and catalogue:
www.mtp.dk

Contents

PREFACE

The present book is the result of my interest in Zoroastrian law, family law, in particular, which goes back more than twenty years.

One fascinating aspect of Zoroastrian family law is that while, in a certain measure, the spirit of the law remained the same, the interpretation of the letter of the law seems to have changed to quite a remarkable degree between the Sasanian and the post-Sasanian era.

This curious fact drew my attention and aroused my curiosity right from the beginning of my work with the Middle Persian law texts, one of the results of which is the present comparative analysis. My purpose in this study has been to compare Sasanian laws with laws instituted at a time when Zoroastrianism was no longer the state religion, and also to analyse and compare laws drawn up at two different post-Sasanian periods.

I wish to acknowledge my debt to The Danish Research Council for the Humanities for a grant enabling me to concentrate on these difficult manuscripts from 1980-83. So far, this work has resulted in various articles on the present and related topics. The idea of making a comparative analysis was carried out in 1989-91 thanks to a generous grant from The Carlsberg Foundation for which I am sincerely grateful. Thanks are also due to The Danish Research Council for the Humanities for their financial support to the revision of the English text of my treatise.

The publishing of this book has only been possible thanks to the extremely generous support from The Danish Research Council for the Humanities and C. L. Davids Fond og Samling.

I wish to express my gratitude to the late Professor Jes P. Asmussen for first drawing my attention to this subject, and for his never failing help and encouragement. I also want to thank Ass. Prof. Hanne Carlsen for revising the English text and for her ability to turn the highly condensed Middle Persian law texts into readable English, and Anders Brüel for his very competent help with the computer setting.

Last but not least, I want to thank my family for their never ending patience and understanding.

INTRODUCTION

The Choice of Sources and Institutions

As material for my examination of the four institutions in Zoroastrian family law, *sardārīh, cakarīh, ayōkēnīh,* and *x*ᵛ*ētōdah*, and for the comparative analysis of the Sasanian and post-Sasanian regulations I have used the *Mātiyān ī hazār Dātistān* (*MHD/MHDA*), The *Pahlavi Rivāyats of Aturfarnbag and Farnbag Srōš*, (*AFS*) and *The Rivāyats of Ēmēt ī Ašavahištān* (*REA*). The choice of a Sasanian law text has been easy inasmuch as the *MHD* is the only extant law codex from Sasanian times, which we possess. It dates from the first half of the 7th century, judging from the fact that the last king mentioned in the text is *Khosro II* (591-628 A.D.). Reference is made to a protocol (of inquiries) drawn up in the 26th year of his reign, and there is no mention of Arab supremacy *(MHD 100.7)*.
The author of the book presents himself by name: *Farrox*ᵛ*mart ī Vahrāmān* (*MHD 79.17*), but does not give further information of himself. It is to be inferred, however, that he must have been a jurist. We do not know where he was born, but he must, at least for a time, have lived in the district of *Artaxšēr-X*ᵛ*arrah*, since he quotes from the archives there, (*MHD 78.3*), which means that he must have had access to them. The *Mātiyān ī hazār Dātistān*, i.e. "The Book of a Thousand Judicial Decisions"[1] is a compilation of cases and lawsuits, real and fictive, of decrees and commentaries by different jurists.
The sources of the compilation are manifold. Sasanian law was based upon the Zoroastrian religion and ethics; like all ancient and some modern laws, it was the social expression of religious ideas, or seen from the opposite angle, the social regulations made necessary by the religion which everybody must obey in order to obtain his just reward in the hereafter. The legal *Nasks* of the *Avesta* were still in use in the Sasanian epoch, and are referred to in the law book, but changes in society in the course of history had demanded commentaries, new interpretations, and the institution of new rules. These works (*cāštak* "doctrine, precepts") are often quoted with mention of their authors. Some of the theologians/jurists (*dastavars*) formed veritable law schools and in many cases, their differences of opinion are cited in the law code[2]. Besides the commentaries, the author had access to other collections of judicial decisions; he cites for instance one *Dātistān nāmak* (*MHD 11.2, 36.2, 44.3, 44.14, 62.10 ff.*). Furthermore, he must have had access to court protocols, court decisions, wills, and decisions by influential persons as for instance the memorandum of the *magupatān magupat*, *Vēh-Shāpūr*, (*MHDA 35.14-16*) and the famous Prime Minister *Mihr-Narseh* (*MHDA 35.16-36.3*). Furthermore, the author has used the "Book Regarding the Special Duties of *magupats*", *X*ᵛ*ēškārīh-nāmak ī magupatān* (*MHDA 26.15*), and the "Book about the special

1. M. Macuch, in *Rechtskasuistik und Gerichtspraxis zu Beginn des siebenten Jahrhunderts in Iran. Die Rechtssammlung des Farrohmard i Wahrāmān*, Wiesbaden 1993, p. 10-11, has rightly pointed out that the title ought to be "A Thousand Judicial Decisions", because the sentence in which the book is named (*MHD 79.3*) runs as follows: *īn mātiyān hazār dātistān x*ᵛ*ānēnd*, "they call this book A Thousand Judicial Decisions". There is no *ezāfe* between *mātiyān* and *hazār*.

2. cf. A. Perikhanian: *The Cambridge History of Iran*. Vol. 3 (2), Cambridge 1983, p. 629.

duties of officials", *X^vēškārīh-nāmak ī kārframān ī šahrīhā* (*MHDA 38.16-39.1*). He also includes certain decrees by Sasanian kings.

This very important work exists only in one manuscript. This has been made available for scholarly research thanks to the work of J.J. Modi, the eminent Iranologist who published a facsimile edition of the greater part of the manuscript (*MHD*) in 1901[1].

In 1912 followed an edition of the rest of the manuscript (*MHDA*), also in facsimile, edited by T.D. Anklesaria[2]. The first complete edition with a translation of the text was made by Bulsara[3], but the scholarly standard of this edition leaves much to be desired. The first really outstanding contribution to the understanding of Sasanian law was made by Ch. Bartholomae[4], much of whose work still stands. In 1973, A. Perikhanian published an edition with a translation of the whole text into Russian[5], an achievement that has constituted the basis for much later work. Since then, M. Macuch has edited the *MHDA* and later the *MHD* with a transliteration, translation and exhaustive commentary[6]. Many other Iranologists have investigated selected themes from the law book. These will be referred to in the analysis of the text.

This vast body of scholarly investigation has contributed signally to our understanding of the Sasanian law codex and its complicated juridical terms, which it has helped define. The present study naturally takes as its starting point the results presented in the seminal work of the above-mentioned scholars.

The *Rivāyats* are texts of quite a different nature. They take the form of a dialogue with questions and answers. The subjects cover a wide field of the social, religious, ritual, and legal customs and rules of the Zoroastrian minority communities under Arab rule. Both texts stem from manuscripts in the library of the Anklesaria family. The *AFS* were made ready for publication by the eminent scholar Behramgore Tahmuras Anklesaria, and through the endeavour of Dastūr Dr. Kaikhusroo M. Jamaspasa[7]. The *AFS* consists of 147 questions put to *Aturfarnbag ī Farrox^v-zātān* together with his replies, and 5 questions put to *Farnbag Srōš ī Vahrām* of whom we know nothing but his name. *Aturfarnbag*, son of *Farrox^vzāt*, held, as the first one known to us, the office of *Hudēnān pēšōpāy*, i.e. leader of the faithful. He lived during the reign of the Caliph *Ma'mun* (813-833), but the precise data of his

---

1. J.J. Modi: *Mâdigân-i-Hazâr Dâdistân*. A Photozincographed Facsimile of a MS. belonging to the *Mânockji Limji Hoshang Hâtariâ* Library in the *Zarthoshti Anjuman Âtashbeharâm*, Poona 1901.
2. T.D. Anklesaria: The Social Code of the Parsis in Sassanian Times or Mādigān i Hazār Dādistān, Part II, Bombay 1912.
3. S.J. Bulsara: The Laws of the Ancient Persians as found in the "Mâtikân ê hazâr Dâtastân" or "The Digest of a Thousand Points of Law", Bombay 1937.
4. Ch. Bartholomae: *Über ein sasanidisches Rechtsbuch*, Heidelberg 1910; *Zum sasanidischen Recht I-V*, Heidelberg 1918-1923; "Beiträge zur Kenntnis des sasanidischen Rechts": *Mitteliranische Studien* IV, *WZKM* 27 (1913), p. 347-74.
5. A. Perikhanian: *Sasanidskij Sudebnik*, Erewan 1973; English translation: *The Book of a Thousand Judgements*, Costa Mesa & New York 1997.
6. M. Macuch: Das sasanidische Rechtsbuch "Mātakdān i hazar Dātistān" (Teil II), Berlin 1976; M. Macuch (1993).
7. B.T. Anklesaria: *The Pahlavi Rivāyat of Aturfarnbag and Farnbag Srōš*, I (Text and Transcription). II (Introduction and Translation), Bombay 1969.

life are unknown. He was the first of the authors of the *Dēnkart,* and the author of a theological disputation, real or imaginary, (*Gujastak Abāliš*) claimed to have been held at the court of *Ma'mun* where he is said to have defended the Zoroastrian faith[1]. He is also known from a letter to the Zoroastrians of Samarkand in which he gives answers to a question concerning a *dakhma*[2]. The text may then, fairly safely, be dated to the first half of the ninth century.
The *Rivāyat ī Ēmēt ī Ašavahištān* was prepared with a transcription, translation and critical notes by Behramgore Tahmuras Anklesaria, but remained unpublished until after his death. Thanks to J.C. Tarapore, volume I (Pahlavi text and transcription) was published in 1962[3]. The second volume has never appeared in print. The text comprises 44 questions posed by the disciple *Atar-Gušasp ī Mihr-Ataš-ī Atur Gušnasp* to *Ēmēt*, son of *Ašavahišt*, together with his replies. *Ēmēt* descended from the same family as *Aturfarnbag*[4], and also held the position of high priest. He can be placed in the first half of the tenth century[5] according to de Menasce's convincing dating. The only complete translation of the text has been done by N. Safa-Isfehani[6].
The *Rivāyats* have not been the object of as comprehensive a research as has the *MHD.* Thorough commentaries, like M. Macuch's on the *MHD* do not exist, and there are only comparatively few articles treating selected themes. Especially with regard to the *AFS* very little work has been done.

These two post-Sasanian texts have been chosen for several reasons. They are both concerned with the daily life of a Zoroastrian family. Besides clarifications of problems regarding various religious rules, they include very clear instructions about how a family should act in matters of marriage, inheritance, succession etc. The ever-recurring problems of regulation of the family's internal affairs are reflected here, as is also the uncertainty of the community with regard to the correct procedure. The answers are comprehensive and rich in detail.
The authors were both high priests, leaders of the Zoroastrian believers, and their words must have been normative for the Zoroastrian communities. Their answers were not debatable; they were given with firm authority and were based on a specialized knowledge of Zoroastrian law. Furthermore, the texts are complete entities in the sense that they are throughout expressions of a firm, authoritative Zoroastrian attitude towards establishing and maintaining the standards that would help preserve the Zoroastrian minority communities in adverse conditions. Precisely their focus on the legal problems was a means to ensure that laymen knew the

1. See J. Duchesne-Guillemin: *Religion of Ancient Iran*, Bombay 1973, p. 43-5; also M. Boyce: *Zoroastrians*, London & New York 1979, p. 153.
2. B.N. Dhabhar: *The Persian Rivāyats of Hormazyar Framarz and Others*, Bombay 1932, p. 104-5.
3. B.T. Anklesaria: *Rivâyat-î Hêmît-î Ašavahištân*, Bombay 1962.
4. See the genealogy of both in B.T. Anklesaria (1969) p. 21.
5. See J.P.de Menasce: "La Rivāyat d'Emēt ī Ašavahištān", *RHR* 162 (1962), p. 69-88; J.J. Modi: "The Mobadān Mobad Omîd bin Ashavast, referred to by Hamzā Isphahâni. Who was he?", *Studia Indo-Iranica, Ehrengabe für Wilhelm Geiger*, Harrassowitz/Leipzig 1931.
6. N. Safa-Isfehani: *Rivāyat-i Hēmīt-i Ašavahistān*, Harvard Iranian Series Vol.II, 1980.

rules and by acting according to them could keep up their particular culture and create a demarcation line, so to speak, between themselves and the surrounding Muslim society[1].

The difference in time between the texts affords us the possibility of discerning the differences in the rules governing family law that reflect the changes in the political environment.

To compare and analyse the changes in the law I have chosen four institutions in the field of family law, *sardārīh* (guardianship), *cakarīh* (the marriage by which a wife produced an heir to her first husband), *ayōkēnīh* (the daughter's marriage to produce a child for her father or brother), and x^{v}*ētōdah* (marriage between close relations). The reason for choosing these institutions is that they afford a possibility to gain an insight in the relations, responsibilities, and rights of family members inside the close family circle. Because of the detailed instructions of the texts regarding the relations between fathers, mothers, wives, sisters, brothers, and children it is possible to focus upon the internal structure of the family and get a comparatively clear picture of how the family ties worked. Guardianship was not exclusively used inside the close family circle (a man might for instance be guardian of a holy fire), but on the other hand, guardianship is an indispensable factor in the analysis of the family relations, because its presence or absence was always a decisive component in marriage or paternal relations. My aim has been to shed light upon the family in the modern, narrow, sense, because even in this tightly bound structure there were radical changes within the space of time that is treated here. The evident manipulations are striking manifestations of desperate measures to safeguard a dwindling community. The conservatism of marriage and inheritance law is known also in our own times, and therefore the development in this sphere is a sure sign of social changes.

The texts are all composed in the Pahlavi language. All parts of the texts treated in my exposition will be presented in transcription following the model of H.S. Nyberg[2], but I have rendered the actual spelling in cases where variant spellings occur, e.g. *cakar/cagar*. Photocopies of the Pahlavi text are included so as to make it possible to compare my transcription with the Pahlavi original and thereby enable the reader to judge for himself whether my interpretation of the text is correct; the more so because my attitude towards the texts in this treatise is that of a historian rather than that of a philologist. As to the translation, it has been my endeavour that it should make comparatively easy reading; the Pahlavi sentences and expressions are often, especially in the *MHD/MHDA*, very difficult to interpret due to the complicated syntax and the very compact, almost abbreviated form, which is used to frame the rules. To convey the meaning in understandable English, the translation cannot always be word-by-word. It also means that Pahlavi expressions are not necessarily translated with exactly the same words every time they occur. The juridical *termini technici* will be rendered in many of the cases by their Pahlavi word, because there are no equivalents in English. For that reason a list of the most commonly occurring terms with explanation of their meaning is included in the book.

---

1. cf. J.P. de Menasce: "Problèmes des Mazdéens dans l'Iran Musulman", *Festschrift für Wilhelm Eilers*, Wiesbaden 1967, p.220 ff.

2. H.S. Nyberg: *A Manual of Pahlavi*. Part I (Texts), Wiesbaden 1964, Part II (Glossary), Wiesbaden 1974.

Historical Background

Sasanian imperial Iran was a state built on a firmly rooted idea of national unity, with Zoroastrianism as state religion, one universal law, and a strongly centralized power structure. The Sasanian empire subsisted, despite external wars and internal upheavals, for 400 years, the Sasanian dynasty providing rulers to succeed one another, beginning with *Artaxšēr*'s rise to power and ending with defeat under the Arab invasion[1]. To begin with, the Sasanian rulers maintained power after the principle of *divide et impera*, depending on petty kings and great feudal lords, but during the sixth and seventh century the power became centred around the court, supported by a strong bureaucracy and lesser landowners. The period saw widespread settlements and a considerable expansion of land brought under cultivation, accompanied by urbanization endeavours, reaching its peak in the sixth century[2]. This is highly concordant with the Zoroastrian goal of creating life and expanding the cultivation of land.

The secular administration and the religious institutions cooperated, but we do not know in detail how this cooperation worked. We know, however, that the *magupats*, the Zoroastrian priests, were concerned with legal affairs as jurists or judges, and that the laws of the Sasanian state were based upon the *Nasks* of the *Avesta*, made, upheld, and administered by the clergy. The law was not a holy law in the sense that it was revealed by God, but it was, nevertheless, based on the religious texts, and as such the legal expression of the Zoroastrian creed and ethics. The law of succession, inheritance, and marriage, the theme of this book, was expressly designed to fulfil the Zoroastrian principle of perpetuating the family line until the end of time, and to bring forth sons to perform the obligatory services for the soul, and maintain the family altar.

On the worldly side, the family law served to keep possessions in the family and to hinder land from falling into disuse. There are strong indications, although this is not specifically stated in the preserved law-texts, that if no male successor existed, or was expected to come into existence, so that the family could fulfil its obligations to the state, then the land would revert to the crown. This means that the possession of land may have been a kind of conditional possession[3].

Iranian society was divided into four estates or castes after *Khosro I*[4]. The estate of scribes was added to the already existing estates of priests, warriors and the people, consisting of peasants, artisans, and tradesmen. Although this division of the citizens into castes must, obviously, have had great significance for the individual who only rarely succeeded in passing from one estate into another, there is no mention of the fact in the law text. We must therefore assume that the rules of the law must apply to everybody in principle, although the landed classes had the

1. R.N. Frye: *The Golden Age of Persia*, London 1975, p. 7.
2. See P. Christensen: *The Decline of Iranshahr*, Copenhagen 1993, p. 67-9.
3. See A. Perikhanian (1983) p. 631; G. Widengren: "Recherches sur le féodalisme iranien", *Orientalia Suecana* Vol.V (1956), Uppsala 1957, p. 111-5; R.N. Frye: *The Heritage of Persia*, London 1962, p. 196.
4. See R.N. Frye (1975) p.18; A. Christensen: *L'Iran sous les Sassanides*, Copenhague 1936, p. 92-5.

greatest interest in the inheritance laws as a means to preserve the property (*dast-kirt*) on family hands[1].

We possess a fair amount of historical facts of the period, but virtually none about the social life of the citizen of Sasanian Iran. The *MHDA* is therefore, apart from its factual importance, an extremely valuable source of information on family structure, inheritance, and succession, and on rules about marriage. Presumably, the rules regarding inheritance and succession must apply specially to families with some fortune, invested in land, business, trade, or buildings, but the rules regarding marriage must have been in general use. How the lower orders of society, and the very highest, for that matter, organized their family life we still do not know.

The rise of Islam and the subsequent unity of the Arabs resulted in the conquest of Iran, and the downfall of the Sasanian state. The islamization of the Iranians took its beginning. The Zoroastrians, as a whole, were not persecuted. They were counted as the "people of the Book", which meant that they might adhere to their religion, but were required to pay a poll tax, *jizya,* just like Christians and Jews. The status of the Zoroastrians was not specifically stated in the *Koran*, but was made in accordance with the practice of Muhammad[2].

The Sasanians had demanded payment of land tax collectively of village or town, and the Arabs adopted this, as they adopted the Sasanian bureaucratic system. This meant that if a person converted to Islam and left his village and his land, the tax burden would not be eased for his village. This became a serious problem as more and more people converted. The central administration tried to solve it by requiring the convert to pay his land tax, and, at some point, even going so far as to forbid conversion. Gradually the poll tax became the main distinction in tax obligations between Muslim and non-Muslim. New problems arose later when many converts left their land uncultivated to move to the large city centres[3].

Consequently, the Zoroastrians found themselves in a position where they had to pay extra tax, but they were definitely not persecuted. Actually, we know of a case of infringements by subordinate officials upon Zoroastrians in Sogdiana around 840, which was punished by the government. On the other hand, we also have a few recounted instances of abolition of fire temples[4].

However, the explanation of the steadily growing number of people who converted to Islam must be sought in other circumstances: For instance, a wish to achieve a higher social position in the new empire, or a wish of the bureaucratic leaders to win favour with the new masters, the wish of the lower estates to be freed from the trammels of the caste system, and for everybody the wish to escape the poll tax.

To all this might be added the collapse of the idea of Zoroastrianism as state religion, and the resulting disinstitutionalized state of the believers. The formerly so

---

1. See M. Macuch: "Herrschaftskonsolidierung und zoroastrisches Familienrecht: zum Verhältnis von Kirche und Staat unter den Sasaniden", *Iran und Turfan*, Harrassowitz 1995, p. 159 ff.; W. Skalmowski: "On Middle Iranian *dstkrt(y)*", *Medioiranica, Orientalia Lovaniensia Analecta*, Leuven 1993, p. 157-62.

2. See B. Spuler: *Iran in früh-islamischer Zeit*, Wiesbaden 1952, p. 184; On the development of *jizya* see J. Bæk Simonsen: *Studies in the Genesis and the Early Development of the Caliphal Taxation System*, København 1988, p. 44 ff.

3. R.N. Frye (1975) p. 70.

4. B. Spuler (1952) p. 185.

powerful and government supported Zoroastrian clergy were, unlike Christians and other minority religions, wholly unaccustomed to having to fight for their belief. Moreover, the Zoroastrian church towards the end of the Sasanian epoch was undoubtedly pestered by the priesthood and their demands of payments for religious services. Of course, there were many good priests, but a powerful church would also have attracted people who were governed by ambition and greed; accordingly, many laymen must have preferred to get rid of the burdens put upon them by the clergy[1].

In addition, some aspects of the Zoroastrian religion must have appeared troublesome, especially for poor and hardworking people. The purity laws, for instance, must have been a bother. It cannot have been easy for every family to do without the work of the housewife for five days of the month when she had to be isolated because of her menstruation. Islam must have appeared easier to live with in one's everyday life[2].

Nevertheless, for many Zoroastrians the new religion did not give the same satisfactory answers to the great questions of life and death. Many became followers of the 8th century Shi'ite movement which evolved many ideas that made Islam more “Iranian” and thereby more acceptable, inasmuch as it incorporated concepts known from Zoroastrianism. The concept of a saviour at the end of time, for instance, has a parallel in the Zoroastrian *Saoshyant.*

The centres of Zoroastrianism were, apart from localities in the Caspian provinces, Fars with Kirman and Yazd, but also Ray and Isfahan continued to have fire temples and worshippers. Around the middle of the tenth century, during the reign of the Buyids, the Zoroastrians enjoyed a brief spell of better times, but this ended abruptly in 979 when a battle between Muslims and Zoroastrians in Shiraz caused heavy losses among the Zoroastrians, many of whose houses were burnt down[3].

Nevertheless, one must not forget that, despite harassment and apostasy, the communities that continued to exist during the eighth, ninth and tenth centuries were allowed to live and to worship as required by their religion. They were permitted to keep their own family law and arrange their succession according to the creed. Not even the custom of *x*^{v}*ētōdah* (marriage between near relations) was prohibited, although this particular custom must have seemed an unnatural sin in the eyes of the Muslims.

The Family Structure

A vital tenet of the Zoroastrian creed was to increase life. It was a holy duty to create life and to care for it, by raising cattle, by cultivating the earth, and by bringing forth children. As in many other cultures, it was a sin to stay single; a man had a religious obligation to marry, beget children, and procure heirs/successors. There was, naturally, also a secular side to this, namely the wish to keep the family possessions in the family. If, as mentioned above (p. 13), land would be forfeited to the crown in case no male successor could be installed to

---

1. Cf. A. Christensen (1936) p. 432; M. Boyce (1979) p .143-4.
2. M. Boyce: *A History of Zoroastrianism*, Brill 1975, p. 307 ff.
3. M. Boyce (1979) p. 159.

shoulder the obligations towards the state, it would be of paramount importance for the family to establish a succession.

To this end, the Zoroastrians created a family law of incomparable complexity. They instituted rules that made it virtually impossible for a man to die without a successor. These rules presupposed a certain amount of property, so we must assume that the indigent were allowed to die without heirs.

After the Arab conquest, the succession laws took on new importance. The government was a foreign occupying power, and it became of vital importance always to be able to present an owner to a piece of land so that Zoroastrian owned land should not diminish.

The family pattern we find described in the law texts, both Sasanian and post-Sasanian, shows an extended family with a paterfamilias, *katak-x^{v}atāy*, and a *materfamilias*, *katak-bānūk*. The master of the house is guardian, *sardār*, of his wife/wives, his minor children, unmarried daughters, and minor siblings. In reality, the family structure was, however, rarely as simple as that. Because Zoroastrian inheritance law does not recognize the principle of primogeniture the master of the house, probably the eldest of the brothers, shared his position and inheritance with his brothers, and consequently the brothers shared the administration of the income from the family property. In the cases where brothers lived jointly off the family property, they would enter into partnership, *hambāyīh*, which might also sometimes include sisters. Of course, this arrangement would serve the purpose of avoiding a splitting up of the family fortune into small unprofitable units. Thus, the only difference between an elder brother, or one who had been given the position of *katak-x^{v}atāy*, and the younger brothers was the former's function as legal guardian to the minor members of the family. This, however, meant that he would be in temporary control of a greater part of the inheritance than would any of his brothers.

The very complexity of the marriage laws was designed to secure the succession. The principal type of marriage is the *pātixšāy*-marriage. In this, the woman will be married with her guardian's consent, and will come under her husband's guardianship. She becomes mistress of the house, she and her husband will inherit one another, and their children are the legal heirs to their parents' property, the sons being successors of the father. A man might have more than one *pātixšāy*-wife, one instance of two is recorded (*MHDA 1.3*), and it was possible to divorce a *pātixšāy*-wife[1].

This type of marriage was the simplest way of procuring heirs, but if this failed there were other possibilities. A man's *pātixšāy*-wife might contract another marriage, either while the husband was still living or after his death. This marriage was entered by a special contract and was called a *cakar*-marriage. The issue of this marriage was the legal heir and successor of the woman's *pātixšāy*-husband, and the natural father, originally, had no claim on the children. A woman was not allowed to live with more than one man at a time.

Another way of procuring heirs for a man without male issue was to let this man's daughter or sister contract a marriage of which the issue was the legal heir of her father or brother. In this case, the woman was called *ayōkēn*. In such a marriage as well as in a *cakar*-marriage, the couple did not inherit one another, and the man who was assigned the role of begetter did not assume guardianship of his wife.

---

1. B. Hjerrild: "Zoroastrian Divorce". *Acta Iranica* Vol. XII, Brill 1988, p. 63-8.

The succession was direct, which means that in case a *pātixšāy*-son did not exist the succession and inheritance would not automatically go to male relatives of a testator following the agnatic model (see p. 147). If the succession was secured by a wife or daughter/sister who procured an heir, the production of this successor was a result of the duty these women owed to their closest male relations: husband, father, brother. In case these measures were to fail there existed two other possibilities; one could either adopt a son or install a *stūr*, a proxy, whose function was to provide the man for whom he was *stūr* with an heir, and to be curator of the property that went with this function. When a son had been born and had come of age, he would be the successor and heir to the *stūrīh*-property.

A *stūr* could be either a man or woman provided he/she was of fertile age, but a man was allowed to contract several *stūrīhs*, a woman only one[1]. This difference reflects the fact that a woman could live with only one man at the time, no matter what kind of marriage contract she had, while a man might have several wives and so be able to produce not only heirs for himself with his *pātixšāy*-wife, but also heirs for other men with a wife/wives under the required types of marriage contracts.

The laws mention three types of *stūrs*: The natural, *stūr ī būtak*, which includes the *pātixšāy*-wife and –daughters[2], the *stūr ī kartak*, designated by testator's will, and finally *stūr ī gumārtak* which is the term for a *stūr* appointed by the authorities. For any type of *stūr* the same rule applied: they were temporary successors and the connecting link to the sons who eventually would become the legal successors and owners of the *stūrīh*-property. In case no children were born, the stūrīh had to be transferred until an heir was provided. The property involved had to amount to the minimum sum of 80 *stērs*[3], invested for instance in land or cattle so that it was interest bearing.

The institution of *stūrīh* is closely linked with the obligation to secure the continuation of a man's name, as can be seen in the *MHD 45.2-5* which relates how a man institutes a *stūrīh* on the fortune of 80 *stērs* in order to secure the continuation of his name (*pat nām dāštan*). In order to be certain that this would actually happen, a man could institute *stūrīhs* although he was already blessed with *pātixšāy*-children, as M. Macuch points out[4]. Contrary to the institutions of *ayōkēnīh* and *cakarīh* the *stūrīh* gave a testator the opportunity of instituting several successorships (e.g. *MHD 105.5-10*) provided he was affluent enough, of course. By doing so, he would safeguard himself against a deficiency of successors in times when the mortality rate was high. If he could only spare the money for one *stūrīh*, he might increase the chances of success by appointing two persons who enjoyed the property in alternating years. The first child born to one of them would then be the successor (e.g. *MHD 46.10*).

Stūrīh differs from *ayōkēnīh* and *cakarīh*, in that it was not confined to daughters, wives, and sisters. As mentioned above, men could be installed as *stūrs*, not only

---

1. MHD 43.8-11, 50.6-7.
2. *MHD 46.15 – 47.2, 90.8-14*; see M. Macuch (1993) p. 355.
3. 1 *stēr* = 4 *drahm*. The value varied in Sasanian times. H.S. Nyberg (1974) p. 65 gives the value of 1 *drahm* as 4.25 gr. of silver, while it is given as 3.99 gr. of silver by J. Harmatta in "Inscriptions des Vaiselles Sassanides", *Mémorial Jean de Menasce*, Louvain 1974, p. 194-5.
4. M. Macuch (1993) p. 320, 337 ff.

male relations although these were preferred, but even men from outside the family circle.
So, although the aim of the institution of the *stūrīh* is essentially the same as that of the *cakarīh* and *ayōkēnīh* there are several aspects of it which differ widely from these and thus does not fall within the scope of the present analysis, which deals with the closest family ties only[1].

It is apparent that women were expected to perform the duties of providing heirs, which might lead to the misapprehension that women were oppressed. This is far from the case, as will be shown later. Women had certain rights, one of them being that for a marriage to be legal the woman must give her consent to it, and also a woman might enter into a perfectly legal marriage with a man of her own choice. This type of marriage was called *x^{v}asrāyūn*, but in the *MHD,* the usual term is *gātār kartan*, "to take a lover"[2].
One of the most conspicuous features of the marriage law is that near relatives could marry. No incest taboo existed, so sisters could marry brothers, daughters fathers, mothers sons. This type of marriage was named *x^{v}ētōdah* and will be treated in chapter 4.

The aim of the present book is to give a comparative analysis of four institutions of Zoroastrian family law, *sardārīh*, *cakarīh*, *ayōkēnīh*, and *x^{v}ētōdah.*
To use law texts as sources of information about the life of a society in a given historical period, obviously, presents certain problems. The law is the expression of the type of society, which the authorities want to establish, and thus a regulator of the existing conditions. If a government wishes to change society, it employs the law to effect this change. At the same time, however, the law is conservative, old rules existing alongside the new ones, although nobody adheres to them any longer. So the law does reflect aspects of the life of a people, and I will, in the following, attempt to show how the social conditions and internal family economy with its power balance are reflected in the rules of the *MHD*, and that the differences apparent in the *Rivāyats* are not accidental, but form a pattern, yet always within the bounds of the Zoroastrian creed. I will demonstrate how they were caused by the changing social conditions, and that the law was changed in order to help preserve the Zoroastrian minority communities in adversity under Arab rule.

1. About *stūrīh* see M. Macuch (1976) Anm. I.9, II.10, 14 et passim; M. Macuch (1993) passim; F. Schirasi-Mahmoudian: *Rechtsnormen der Vormundschaft und der sekundären Erbnachfolge im sasanidischen* "Rechtsbuch der tausend Entscheidungen", "Mātagdān-ē hazār Dātastān" ("Mādayān-ē hazār Dādestān"), Diss. Berlin 1975, p. 167-185; A. Perikhanian (1983) p. 652-5; J.P. de Menasce: *Feux et fondations pieuses dans le droit Sassanide*, Paris 1964 III.

2. See also M. Macuch (1976) p. 20.

SARDĀRĪH

In Sasanian family law the term *sardārīh* is a frequently recurring one, often in connection with the terms *cakar*, *ayōkēn*, and *x^{v}ētōdah*, the objects under discussion in this treatise. It is necessary therefore to examine the term more closely. In the following *sardārīh* will be translated as "guardianship". In certain cases, it corresponds to the Latin *manus*, but it has a wider meaning; it may for example denote the guardianship of a sacred fire[1]. In the following, I propose to determine the implications of *sardārīh* as it applies to and affects various types of marriage contract, inheritance, and orphans, and to analyse the changing denotations of the term as they reflect the changing social reality.

The notion of guardianship has its origin in the Indo-European patriarchal family structure, as we know it from Indian, Greek, and Roman law, and from the mention of family relations in ancient Persia in Greek texts. In early Roman law, the *patria potestas* was unlimited. Nevertheless, the Roman wife in her capacity of *materfamilias* occupied a highly respected position. However, there was a gradual diminishing in the authority, *manus*, of the Roman *paterfamilias* over the members of his family and their income, so that after the Republic a marriage contracted with *manus* became quite rare[2], although *manus* was not formally abandoned until the reign of Constantine.

Justinian's laws were contemporary with the decrees in the *MHD*. Zoroastrian family legislation, however, is far more complicated. One reason for this must be sought in religious differences. Christianity had become officially established as state religion in the Roman Empire in 391-92, during the reign of Theodosius. Hence, the rituals in connection with the ancestor cult were no longer officially observed, nor were there any ideological basis for legislation intended to secure the continuation of the family[3]. In Zoroastrianism, however, the continuation of life and of the family, and the observance of rituals for one's ancestors were central tenets of faith. Continuity was also the core of the social, economic, and military life of the community. The extended farming family constituted the cornerstone in Sasanian social structure and must as such be upheld. Special inheritance laws ensured that property was never left without an owner.

Mātiyān ī hazār Dātistān (MHD)

A thorough examination of the *MHD* enables us to estimate the extent of authority of the head of the family over its members, but only to a certain degree. It is, however, the only possibility we have of shedding light on this aspect of Sasanian social life. In the text the term *sardārīh* is not explicitly defined, and it is assumed that what is involved is familiar. It has therefore been necessary to draw conclusions about the reality stipulated in the law from what seems to be implied in the term in each case. The same applies to the term *pātixšāy* (authorised), which is

1. J.P. de Menasce (1964).

2. D. Tamm: *Romerret*, København 1980, p. 187 ff.

3. E. Sachau: *Syrische Rechtsbücher* III, Berlin 1914, p. 155.

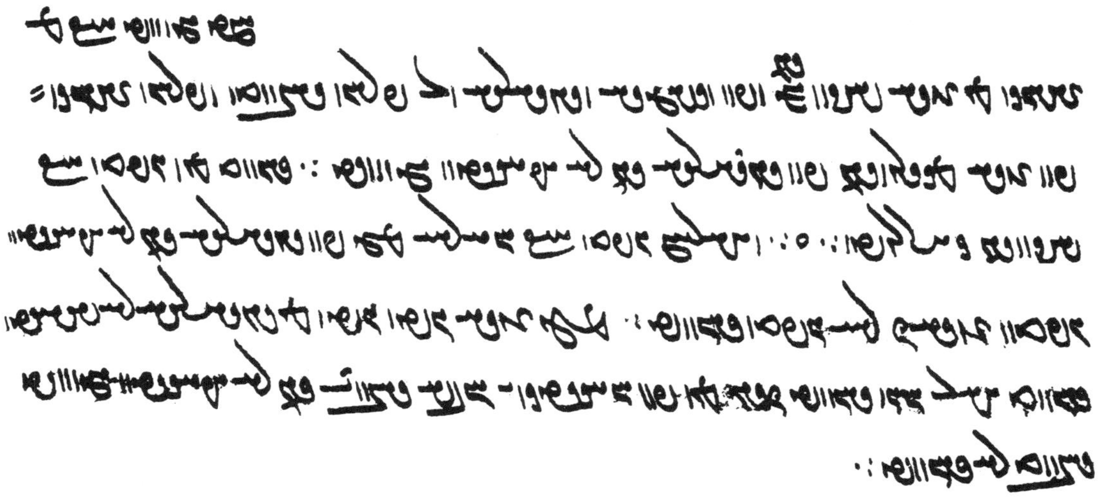

used about the marriage contract that is always concluded with *sardārīh*[1]. *Pātixšāy* is an adjective that may be applied to "husband", "wife", "children", and "marriage".

In the following, I propose to analyse a number of paragraphs in the *MHD* with the intention of determining the actual meaning of the term and the implications of guardianship with regard to economy, the privileges and responsibilities of men and women, and the guardian's and ward's rights and duties.

MHD 4.14 – 5.3

ka gōbēt kū-m ziyānak hac zanīh hišt u pat zanīh u sardārīh ō Farrax^v dāt u Farrax^v ziyānak pat zanīh patigīrēt pat sardārīh andar nē apāyēt gōbēt. būt kē guft kū hišt kār nēst. Vahrām guft kū ē rād cē pat sardārīh andar nē apāyīt(an) guftan zanīh-ci rād guft bavēt. cē zanīh yuvat hac sardārīh nē šāyēt būt. pas ōgōn bāvēt cigōn kē pat x^{v}āstak ī aviš dahēnd andar nē apāyītan gōbēt dāt nē bavēt.

If he (the husband) says: "I have released my young wife from marriage and given her in marriage and guardianship to *Farrax^v*[2]", and *Farrax^v* contracts a marriage with her but declares the contract of guardianship unnecessary (then) someone has declared the divorce[3] invalid. *Vahrām*[4] says: "This (*Farrax^v*'s) declaration concerning the guardianship, "it is not necessary" will also apply to the marriage. For marriage and guardianship are inseparable." In such a case, what applies is identical with (what happens) when someone wishes to give a person something and the latter declares that it is not necessary; that is to say, the object will not be presented.

This paragraph gives us certain information apart from the one intended about divorce, one of the issues being *sardārīh*. The case concerns a man who gives up his guardianship over and marriage with a woman, and gives her to another man, *Farrax^v*. *Farrax^v* evidently wants to have her as wife, but for some reason he does not want to take over the guardianship. The jurist, *Vahrām*, forwards the opinion that, in that case, *Farrax^v* has not married the woman, as marriage and guardianship are inseparable. The point is, however, that since this case is being debated there must have been some doubt as to the inseparability of marriage and guardianship. *Farrax^v* was evidently not aware of the consequences when he declined the guardianship, and jurists had to decide whether his marriage to the woman was valid or not.

A marriage in which the husband has the guardianship over his wife is called a *pātixšāy*-marriage[5], but this connection is not put forward in a specific legal claim. We may deduce this by implication only, as for instance, in the following text:

---

1. C. Bartholomae (1910) p. 8: "Welche besondere Bedeutung es hat, dass hier und 3.16 *sardar* mit *patexsah* verbunden wird, ist mir nicht deutlich."
2. This name is often used to signify any man.
3. B. Hjerrild (1988) p .66.
4. The author of a work on legal decisions which was evidently one of the main sources used by the author of the *MHD*.
5. On *pātixšāy*-marriage see also M. Macuch (1976) p. 18 ff; A. Perikhanian (1973) p. 510 ff.; F. Schirasi-Mahmoudian (1975) p. 118 ff.

MHD 49.3-6

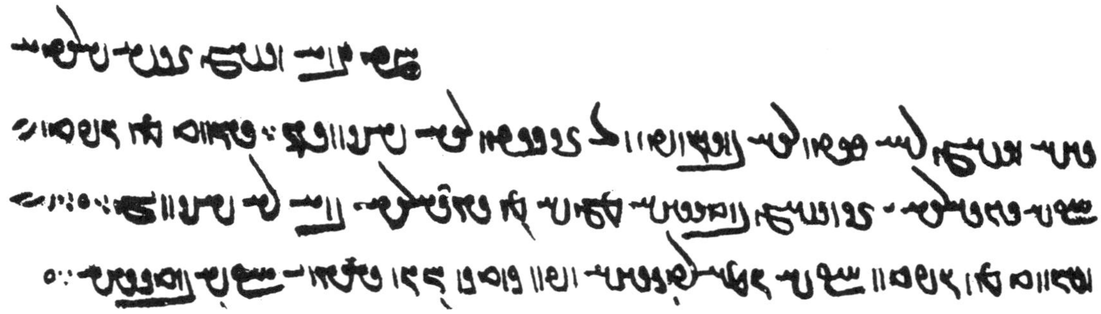

MHD 87.5-9

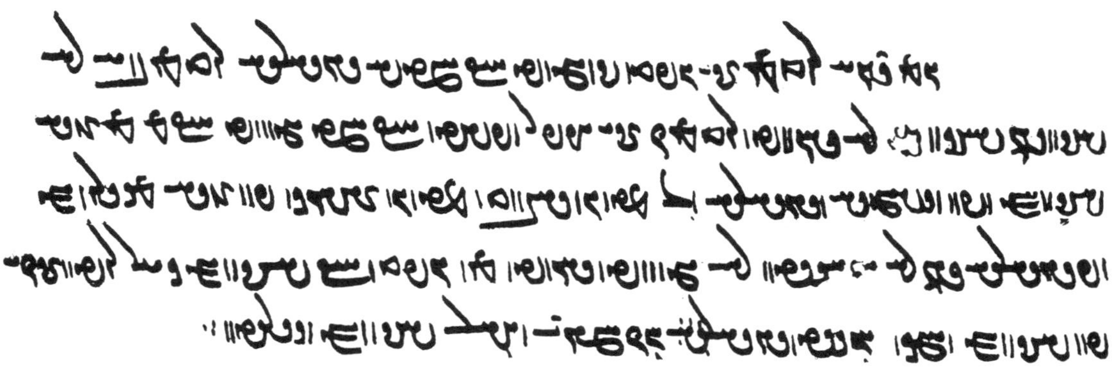

MHD 49.3-6

ka mart zan ī-š pātixšāyīhā zan rād stūrīh xᵛāhēt ō ān stūrīh hilēt. būt kē guft kū-š sardārīh ī ān zan būtakīhā cē-š hac sardārīh bē nē hilēt/hilāt. u būt kē guft kū-š gumārtakīhā u pat kartak ōgōn dārēnd kū-š būtakīhā.

When a man wants his *pātixšāy*-wife to assume *stūrīh,*[1] he releases her (from marriage) to (be able to undertake) that *stūrīh.* One (jurist) said: "The guardianship of this woman is a natural one[2] because he does not release her from his guardianship." Another (jurist) said that the guardianship is the appointed one. According to the general practice of the law[3] this guardianship is considered the natural one.

According to one jurist then, and apparently also according to common legal practice a husband might retain guardianship of his wife after he has divorced her, so that she can undertake a *stūrīh*. This means that the couple still has economic relations, while the dissolution of the marriage means that her offspring will belong to another man. The phrase *būt kē guft* shows clearly that we are here dealing with the opinion of one jurist, an opinion that is at variance with statements found elsewhere, e.g.

MHD 87.5-9

Ēn dātistān apāk ān ī guft ēstēt kū ka-š sardārīh apāk bē nē hilēt hišt nē bavēt u apāk-ic ān ī hacapar nipišt kū ka gōbēt kū-m hac zanīh hišt u pat zanīh u sardārīh ō Mihrēn dāt u Mihrēn ziyānak pat zanīh patigīrēt u pat sardārīh andar nē apāyītan rād gōbēt bavēt kē guft kū hišt kār nēst u ān-ic ī pat hišt nāmak naxᵛist[4] sardārīh hanjāmēnd pas hišt nikērītan.

This decision is to be observed[5] together with that which has been said: "If he (the husband) does not give up the guardianship (of his wife) as well, the divorce does not come into being", and together with that, too, which is written above: "If he (the husband) says: 'She is divorced from marriage with me and given to Mihrēn in marriage and guardianship', and Mihrēn takes the woman in marriage and says of the guardianship that it is not needed/ desired, then one (jurist) stated that: 'The divorce is not effectuated'", and

---

1. See also F. Schirasi-Mahmoudian (1975) p. 118 ff.

2. According to *MHD 26.10-12* natural guardians are: *Pātixšāy*-son, adopted son, an appointed *stūr* and a brother who is a business partner (*hambāy*).

3. *Kartak*: The legal practice as opposed to the canonical law, *cāštak*; Cf. M. Macuch (1976) p. 241 ff.

4. MS does not have the initial *n*, and might therefore read *ōst* "firm, reliable" (D.N. McKenzie: *A Concise Pahlavi Dictionary*, London 1971, p. 61); J.J. Modi (1901) p. 15 corrects to *naxᵛist* and is followed in this by A. Perikhanian (1973) p. 253, M. Macuch (1993) p. 561, and F. Schirasi-Mahmoudian (1975) p. 87.

5. M. Macuch (1993) p. 209 explains this use of *nikērītan* and gives references to other instances in the *MHD*.

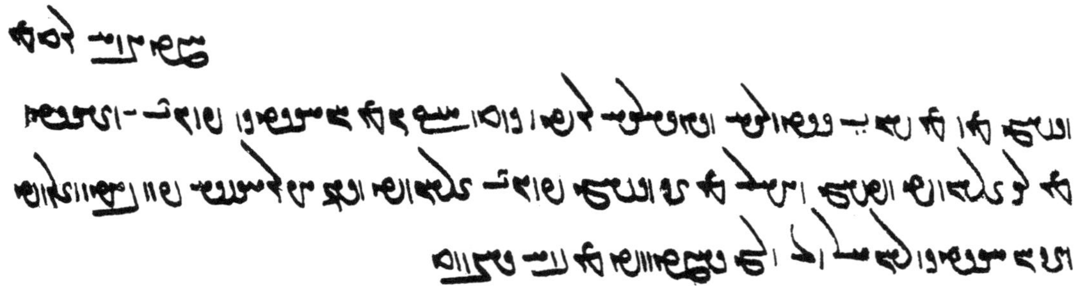

also that which (is) in The Book of Divorce[1]: "First they bring the guardianship to an end and then they carry out the divorce".

In this case, the *pātixšāy*-husband does not retain *sardārīh* over his wife in case of divorce. Another example of this is found in *MHD 4.9-10*, but in *MHD 49.3-6* it says that a husband can retain guardianship over his former wife because he is her natural guardian, *sardār ī būtak*, but that an appointed *sardār* might have the same claim. In other words, the difference between the various forms of *sardār* is diffuse or non-existent here. A *pātixšāy*-marriage contract normally means that a husband holds guardianship over his wife. The relationship between a *pātixšāy*-marriage contract and *sardārīh* was, according to these juridical statements, such that if these two are both present there will be a *pātixšāy*-marriage in which the couple lives together with all that this entails; the children will be heirs of the husband and the husband will administrate the wife's fortune. The situation that is treated in the MHD 4.14-5.3 means that the husband wished to give his wife in a *pātixšāy*-marriage to *Farrax*^{v}, because here the guardianship and marriage are inseparable. *MHD 87.8-10* states the same, but also points to the fact that guardianship and a *pātixšāy*-contract are two distinctly separate things, as the dissolution of these institutions has to be done separately, first one and then the other. M. Macuch[2] maintains that it is the guardianship of a woman that makes her children belong to the man who is her guardian, but this assumption makes the rules illogical, because if guardianship meant that the children became those of the guardian, no jurist, surely, would propose that a woman undertook a *stūrīh*, while under the guardianship of another man. *Stūrīh* was a means of procuring heirs, so there would be no point in acquiring a *stūr* whose children would belong to her guardian. The problem is also illustrated by the fact that a man who wants his wife to conclude a *cakar*-marriage dissolves his guardianship over her, but not the *pātixšāy*-contract (see p. 83).
The flexibility and complexity of contracts between man and woman is further illustrated in:

MHD 19.12-15

ka mart apāk zan kē hac šōd[3] stūrīh u sardārīh nēst kart kū ēn x^{v}āstak frazand ī nazdist hac tō zāyēt x^{v}ēš u pas hac ān zan frazand zāyēt u andar apurnāyīh pat baxt šavēt u ān x^{v}āstak apāc ō ōi rasēt kē[4] bē dāt.

When a man enters into a contract with a woman who is not a *stūr* for a husband and who has not got a *sardār* with the following stipulation: "This property shall belong to the first child you bear", then, if the woman later bears a child who dies a minor, the property goes back to the man who gave it.

---

1. M. Macuch (1993) p. 563 translates to "Entlassungsurkunde". *Ibid.* translates *hanjāmēnd* to "wird...beurkundet". See also M. Macuch (1993) p. 80-1 and (1976) p. 246 about *nāmak* "Protokol". F. Schirasi-Mahmoudian (1975) p. 88 translates to "Buch der Scheidung". I prefer the last translation, as it seems that this is a general statement.
2. M. Macuch (1993) p. 74-6 and p. 359.
3. Sometimes spelled *šōy*.
4. Emendi MS *MN* to *MNW*.

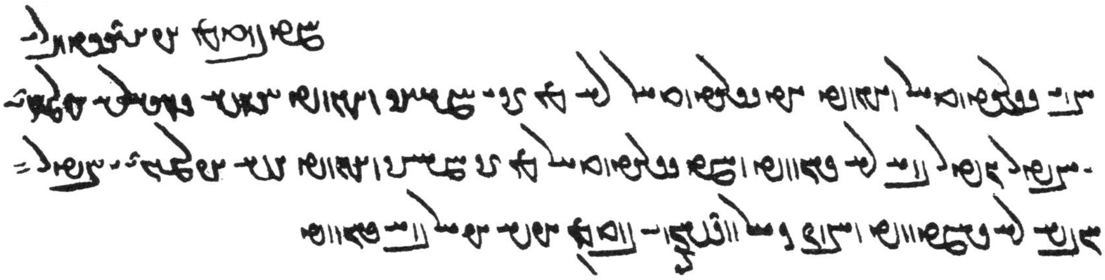

This reveals some interesting features. That the woman must not be *stūr* for anybody is, obviously, important; if she were, her children would then belong to the man for whom she was *stūr*. The fact that the woman has no *sardār* is even more interesting, as this is the only passage in the *MHD* in which this fact is explicitly stated. There is no mention of her status, whether she is a widow or divorced. The only fact we learn from the passage is that she was under no obligation to produce children for the sake of securing heirs for a former husband or for her father or brothers. She was in reality free. Whether this was an advantage or not must to some extent depend on her having private means or not. If she had not, she could support herself by agreeing to a contract like the above-mentioned, according to this passage in the *MHD*. On the other hand, the agreement will not benefit the man if the forthcoming child is not his legitimate offspring who can be his heir and continue his lineage. The agreement between him and the woman must thus be a kind of marriage contract which is, however, conditioned by the birth of a child and this child's survival until its fifteenth year, the age of majority.

I consequently conclude that at the time of the *MHD* there were different types of marriage contracts that were not totally regulated, as became the case later on. Rather it was possible to operate with a variety of contracts and also with different combinations between marriage contracts and guardianship. This view seems to be supported by the case in which a girl or woman takes a husband without her guardian's consent, e.g.

MHD 24.7-10

ka duxt apēdastovar ī pit gātār kunēt hakar gātār nē hac ān ī hamēīk kunēt adak-iš sardārīh (u) aparmānd ī pitar yuttar bē nē bavēt u ka gātār hac ān hamēīk kunēt ā-š aparmānd ī pitar aviš nē rasēt u pit-ic kār vindišn ī duxt hac-iš apar bē bavēt.

When a daughter enters into cohabitation with a man without her father's permission, her inheritance and the father's guardianship will remain unchanged if she does not live with the man for ever. If she continues living with the man for life she will not inherit her father and the daughter's earnings will not benefit her father.

Thus, the daughter's union with her self-chosen lover is certainly legal inasmuch as it can have legal consequences and involves legislation. Here I disagree with Shaki who calls these unions unlawful or irregular[1]. The union in question must be a kind of marriage in which the children are legitimate. In the above passage two possibilities are stated: Either the union will last for a certain, not explicitly defined, length of time, or it will last for life. In the first case the father will continue to be his daughter's guardian and she will consequently inherit him in due time. In the second case, the guardianship will be cancelled with a consequent dissolution of all economic relations between father and daughter.

This passage affords us an important insight in the nature of *sardārīh*; it emerges as a relationship in which the father has the right to dispose of his daughter's earnings, and she, in return, has the right to inherit him. In a way, it resembles our insurance systems: We pay over a number of years and receive the returns later. The daughter may break the "contract" by withdrawing from the guardianship of her

1. Cf. M. Macuch: "Die Zeitehe im Sasanidischen Recht", *Archäologische Mitteilungen aus Iran 18*, 1985, p. 197.

MHD 36.2-4

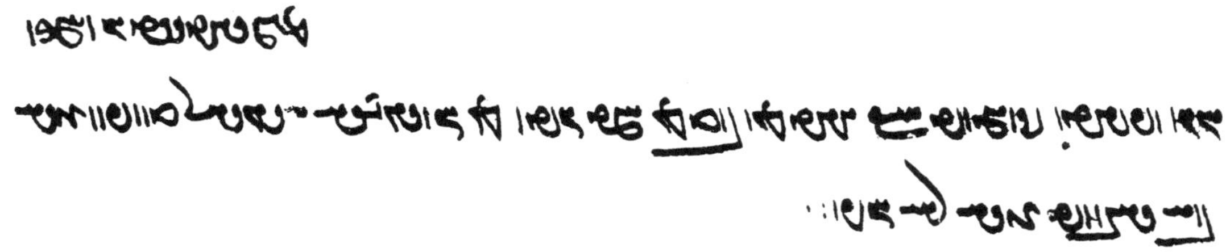

MHD 36.12-16

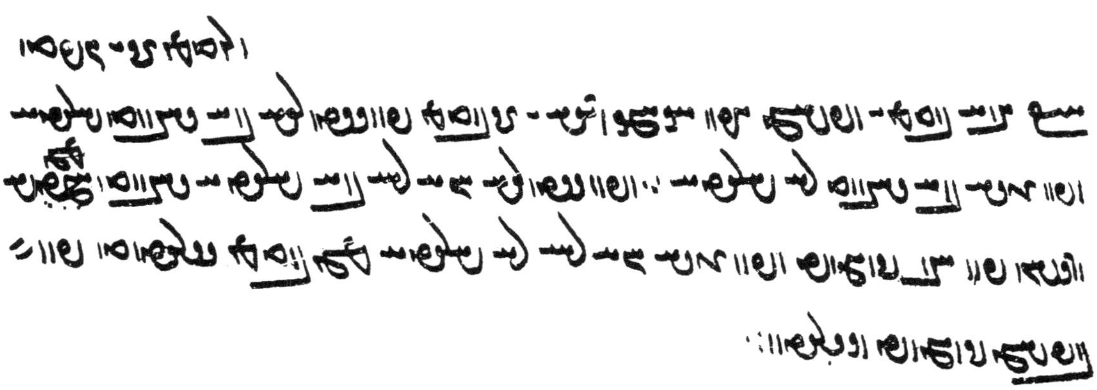

father and from her economic relationship with him. This means, of course, also that she denounces the security she enjoys, but the withdrawal does not entail any other sanctions, legal or otherwise, and it is not a sin in the religious sense.
We have no testimony to show that a father could do the same. He seems to be stuck with his guardianship unless he transfers it to someone else. We do not know whether the guardianship over the daughter is transferred to her self-chosen husband, or whether she remains independent like the woman in the *MHD 19.12-15*. However, we do know that the marriage thus contracted was legal since children of this type of marriage were legitimate. The validity of such a marriage is ratified by the law in

MHD 36.2-4

apar dātistān nāmak ōgōn nipišt ēstēt kū x^{v}ah u duxt ka yuvat hac x^{v}ansandīh ī sardār tan pat zanīh bē dahēt zanīh rād xūp.

In the Book of Laws is written thus: "If a sister or a daughter without her guardian's consent gives herself in marriage, that marriage is valid in law."

Shaki's emendation of *l'd* to *L', (rād* to *nē*) alters the meaning. He reads:

x^{v}ah ut duxt kē yut hač hōnsandīh i sardār tan pat zanīh bē dahēt, zanīh *nē xūp...

If a sister or daughter gives herself in marriage without the guardian's consent, that marriage is not valid[1].

This should probably be seen as an attempt to make the passage fit into his own conception of lawful and unlawful marriages. The text has, clearly and quite unmistakeably, *l'd*.
That the woman was free to shape her own destiny is confirmed by

MHD 36.12-16

u apāk ān-ī guft kū mart duxt ī x^{v}ēš pat akāmakandīh ī ān duxt pat stūrīh bē dāt pātixšāy u pat zanīh bē dāt nē pātixšāy. u pat stūrīh ēt rād bē pātixšāy dāt cē-š vindišn pat pit ēstēt u pat zanīh ēt rād nē pātixšāy cē duxt gāt pat x^{v}at ēstēt nikīrītan.

And together with that which is said, it is to be observed[2]: "A man is authorised to give his daughter in *stūrīh*, but not in marriage against her wishes. He is authorised to give her in *stūrīh* because her earnings belong to her father, but he is not authorised to give her in marriage for the reason that a daughter's sexual life is her own affair."

This passage provides us with invaluable information about the extent of a father's, and consequently a guardian's, rights. On the basis of this, and on the information on economic relationships given in *MHD 24.7-10* I feel justified in concluding that a father's guardianship over his daughter had, primarily, economic significance, as also the guardianship of anybody else, including a wife. It entailed the right to benefits and the duty to provide for those under guardianship. In the

1. M. Shaki: "The Sassanian Matrimonial Relations", *Archiv Orientální* 39, 1971, p. 323 ff.; M. Macuch (1993) p. 269.
2. See M. Macuch (1993) p. 272.

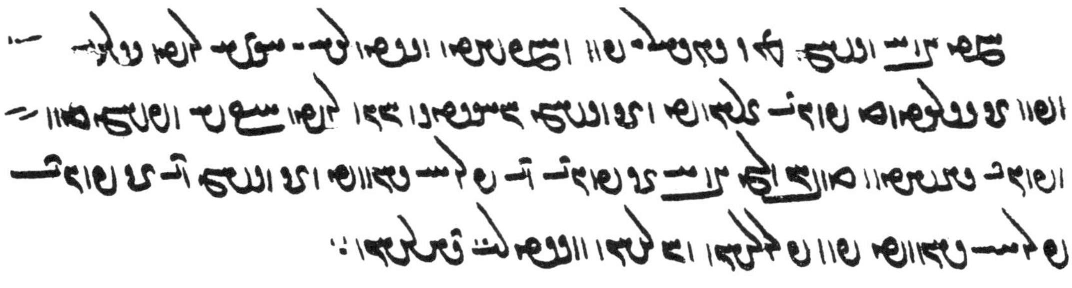

extended family, the father, or the head of the family administrated the incomes of the various members of the family. In return, daughters were securely provided for, either by inheritance, or by having suitable husbands procured for them. It is evident from the law-texts, however, that the father had no legal right to force a daughter into marriage against her wishes. She had a statutory right to decide for herself. A question that immediately suggests itself is, of course, whether reality corresponds with the intention of the law. Some fathers may have imposed their wills by force, but at least the law supported the woman's right to choose for herself, and the woman who married against her guardian's will was protected by the law.

Furthermore, a woman who had no guardian, and who had no income from being *stūr* to somebody, i.e. having specified income from a property in return for producing heirs to a man, enjoyed much greater protection from the law than European women of the last century.

MHD 36.6-9

> ka mart zan kē sardār ī pat nāmcišt u stūrīh ī kas nēst gāyēt u pat ān gāt frazand zāyēt u ān zan x^{v}āstak ōgōn nēst kū-š x^{v}ēš tan u frazand dāštan tuvān ōi mart ān frazand tāi purnāy bavēt u ān zan tāi ān frazand purnāy bavēt pat parvarišn u x^{v}arišn u vastarak dārišn.
>
> If a man lies with a woman who has no *sardār* in particular, and who is not *stūr* to anybody, and if she bears a child as a result of the intercourse, and she has not enough property to support herself and the child, then the man must provide the woman and the child with food and clothing until the child comes of age.

This passage speaks for itself: Once paternity is established, mother and child must be provided for by the man. The passage also throws light on the remarkable fact that nowhere in the *MHD* is there any reference to illegitimate children: Illegitimate children simply do not exist[1]! Nor is there any question of adultery in the above-mentioned case. As long as a woman has but one man at a time, she does not commit adultery. The child was not branded as illegitimate, and the only concern of the law was to emphasize the father's duty to support his offspring and the mother for a period of fifteen years until the age of majority.

The above paragraph also supports my former statement that there was a great variety of legally acknowledged, sexual relationships. This is in consonance with one of the central Zoroastrian concerns: The continuation of the line. According to this, it would be sinful waste if a child's parentage were not known so that he, in his turn, should not be able to contribute to the continuation of the paternal line. Therefore, every child has a recognised father, and every woman and her offspring are accepted as members of organized society.

In the *pātixšāy*-marriage in which the husband is *sardār* for his wife problems about *sardārīh* will only arise in case of divorce, as discussed above. The *MHD* gives but scant information about the *pātixšāy*-marriage in practice, but from the following text, we glean a few facts about the economic relationship between *pātixšāy*-husband and wife:

---

1. See C. Bartholomae (1923) p. 7; M. Macuch (1993) p. 271, speaks in connection with this passage of "ausssereheliches Kind".

MHDA 6.14-16

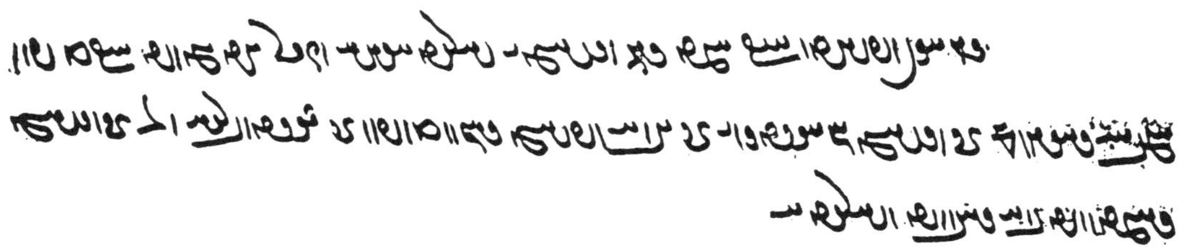

MHDA 5.15 – 6.1

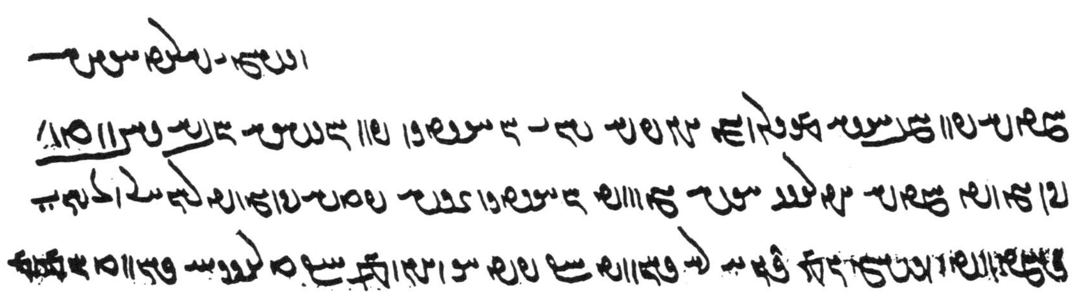

MHDA 6.14-16

giyāk 1 nipišt kū ka andar zan ī pātixšāyīhā vicīr āvašēt kū-t pat hambāy dārom ān zan x^{v}āstak ī ān mart x^{v}ēš bavēt pat ān dastavarīh ō ān zan rasēt (u) bē dāt pātixšāy.

In one passage it is thus written: "When concerning his *pātixšāy*-wife he seals the decision: 'I take you for my partner', the man's property becomes that of his wife; i.e. by that decision it belongs to the wife, and she is authorized to spend it."

The decision to enter into a business partnership is that of the husband, but once the decision is made he cannot change it, it is legally binding (*dastavarīh*). The wife has been made partner with equal rights in the management of their joint property[1]. The only reason accepted by the law for the dissolving of the partnership is the wife's alleged disobedience:

MHDA 5.15 – 6.1

zan ī pātixšāyīhā ka-š pat hambāyīh patigrift aivap-iš šōd x^{v}āstak pat x^{v}ēšīh aviš dāt ēstēt ka-š atar...kīh[2] gōbēt x^{v}āstak ī-š patiš ēstēt apāc ō šōd rasēt u zan ēn dātistān nē bavēt kū paitāk kunēt kū tarsakāy būt hom.

If a husband has taken his wife for business partner or has transferred property to her name, the property goes back to the husband if she is disobedient according to what he says; but if she states: "I have been obedient", the decision is made invalid.

It appears clearly from the text that the wife is protected against false accusations from her husband; presumably her misdemeanour must be common knowledge or of a fairly blatant order for the husband to be able to carry through the dissolution of the partnership.

The notion of husband and wife as business partners is an interesting one, and the above-mentioned reference to such a relationship is by no means the only one. It seems safe to assume that there must have been weighty reasons for a man, and head of a family, to enter into business partnership with his wife, and thus renounce complete control over the family property. One reason might be that the husband was obliged to stay away from his home for long stretches of time, either to go to war, to serve his king, or to go abroad on business. In such cases it would certainly be in his own interest to leave the management of the family property in the hands of the person who was as nearly concerned as himself in the thriving of the fortune.

The fact that women could be taken into business partnership with their husbands also throws light on the education of women. One would presumably not entrust the economic management of property to a person who had been taught the so-called female duties only. The girls must have been schooled in basic economics; they must have learnt to manage property, to do business, and to act in their own person in a legal sense[3].

---

1. C. Bartholomae (1918) p 27 takes *ī* as I do, whereas M. Macuch (1976) p. 169 reads it as a relative pronoun.
2. M. Macuch (1976) p. 191, suggests *atarsakāyīh*, and I agree with this solution.
3. *MHD 57.2-12* bears witness to the fact that girls did receive some measure of education.

MHDA 30.10-12

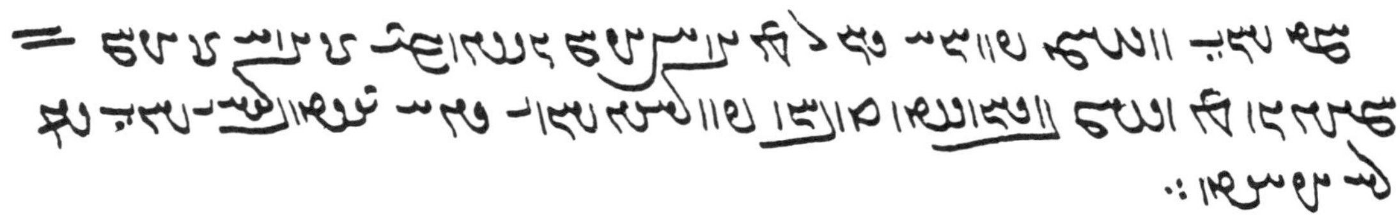

MHDA 1.2-6

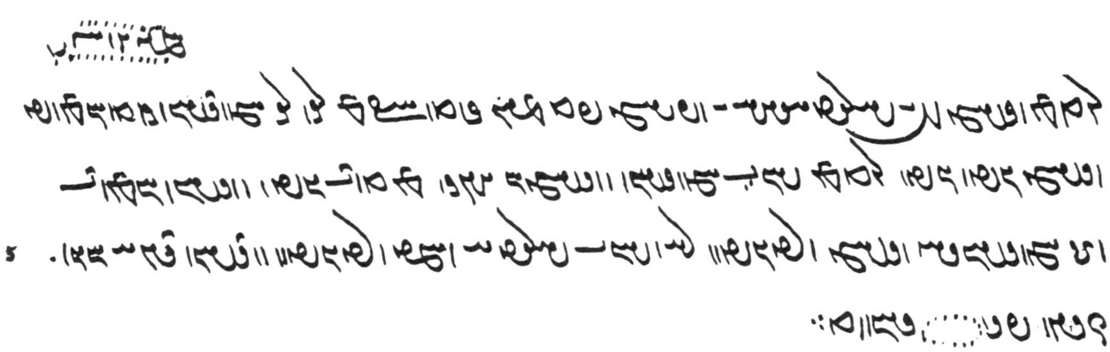

MHDA 2.17 – 3.1

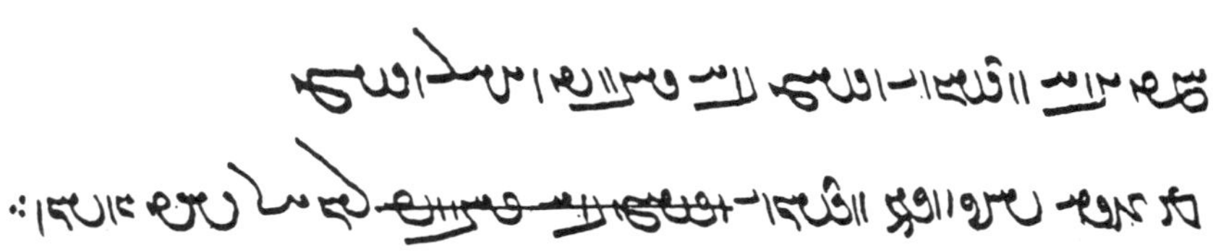

In support of this assumption, we find an allusion in

MHDA 30.10-12

ka šōd u zan pat ē yāvar hac mart 1 āpām stānēnd ān mart ān āpām hamāivēn hac zan x^vāstan tuvān u pat rāyēnišn ī datistān dastavarīh ī šōd andar nē apāyēt.

If a husband and wife together raise a loan from a man, the said man may demand the debt paid by the wife; an authorization from the husband is not necessary for the managing of the case.

I agree with Bartholomae[1] that this passage indicates that a woman is a person in a legal sense. She is evidently entitled to negotiate affairs concerning their common property, and, as the text implies, to appear in court.
Just as the initiative to enter into partnership with his wife rests with the husband, the right to dissolve it is his alone.

MHDA 1.2-6

ka mart 1 apāk zan 2 ī pātixšāyīhā ī x^vēš patmān kart kū-m tō hamvindišn kart hēt zan yuvat yuvat apāk šōd hamvindišn u zanān ēvak hac dit yuvat vindišn hēnd u ān hamvindišn zan vartēnītan nē u šōd pātixšāy u ka vartēnīt vindišn dātistān ōgōn cigōn pē(š) būt.

If a man has entered a contract with both his *pātixšāy*-wives (stating): "You and you are made my business partners", then each of the wives separately enters into partnership with the husband, and the wives' businesses are kept separate, and the wife has no right to alter this partnership, only the husband, and if he dissolves it, the rules which pertain to incomes also apply here.

The text clearly implies that if a husband does not enter into partnership with his wife she would normally have her own income, which again indicates that they would have separate property.
A particularly interesting feature of this passage is that it furnishes us with evidence that a man might marry two women by a *pātixšāy*-contract. At the same time, it is clearly stated that the two wives have completely separate incomes. Unfortunately, we have no information as to whether they lived in separate houses, but it seems safe to assume that, at least, they lived in separate quarters.
Apart from the privilege of being able to institute or dissolve business partnerships with his wife (wives), the *pātixšāy*-husband had other advantages as well:

MHDA 2.17 – 3.1

ka mart vindišn ī zan bē dahēt u pas zan hac zanīh hilēt vindišn ī ~~zan bē dāt~~ apāc avarišn.

If a man uses his wife's income, and later dissolves their marriage, he must give her back her income which has been used.

In his capacity of *sardār* the husband, evidently, has a certain right to dispose of his wife's income, but only as long as the marriage lasts. A wife has, by law, a right to her own property, and the right to take her accumulated fortune out of the

1. C. Bartholomae (1918) p. 26.

MHD 26.7-8

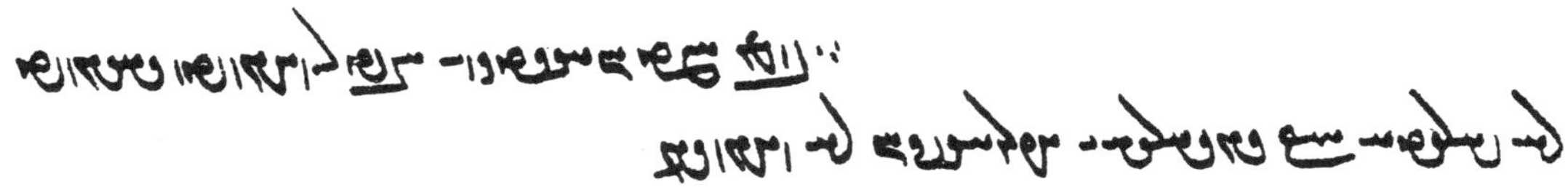

MHD 26.8-12

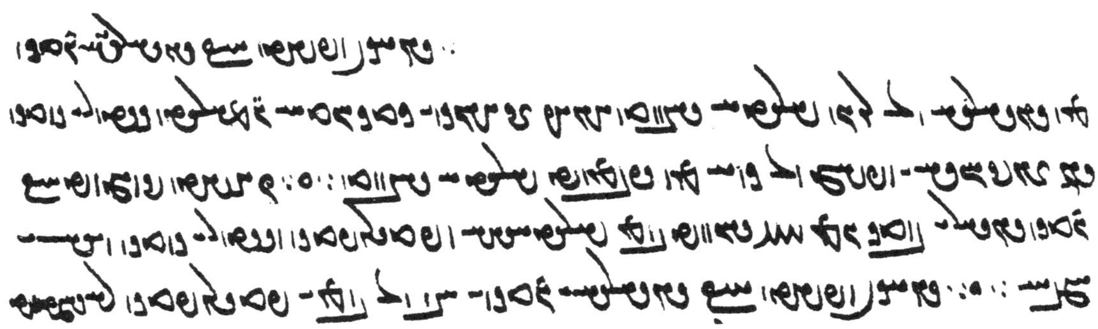

marriage, i.e. the legal protection of women's economic rights seems to be fairly comprehensive. These rules must have prevented quite a few divorces, and must have ensured especially older women their position as mistresses of their households.

The *pātixšāy*-husband and -wife held the position in their household of *katak-x^{v}atāy* and *katak-bānūk* ("master of the house" and "mistress of the house"). It seems reasonable to assume that in the extended family, which was the usual family pattern in the country, at least, one couple, presumably the eldest, enjoyed these titles with their attendant privileges and responsibilities while the married sons and their wives, one way or another, had to submit to their decrees. Zoroastrian law does not recognize primogeniture, not even in the succession to kingship.

When the head of a family dies, one of his sons is appointed, according to rules as yet unknown to us, *sardār* for the female members of the family, and the sons who are still minors. He becomes then automatically also *katak-x^{v}atāy*. There is ample evidence to show that the internal economy was carefully regulated by the law. To be the head of a family, and administrator of the family fortune carried with it not only privileges, but heavy responsibilities as well:

MHD 26.7-8

pus ka x^{v}āstak ī pitar gīrēt u dārēt nē pātixšāy kū sardārīh ī apurnāyīkān nē kunēt.

If a son assumes and keeps his father's property he is not authorized to denounce the guardianship of the members of his family who are still minors.

It seems likely, in this case, that the son's taking over the property and the guardianship happens in connection with the demise of his father. It also seems natural to suppose that the son would automatically succeed his father as guardian for the members of the family. According to Sasanian law, however, this is not always so:

MHD 26.8-12

giyāk 1 nipišt kū sardārīh ī dūtak kē sardārīh ō pēš pātixšāy dāt ēvāc ān ēvāk ī katakx^{v}atāy gumārēt stūr ī kartak andar zindakānīh x^{v}ēš ō har kē kāmēt pātixšāy dāt. cāšt ēstēt kū dūtak sardār ī būtak ēn 4 bavēt pus pātixšāyīhā u patigriftak u stūr ī kartak u brāt ī hambāy. giyāk 1 nipišt kū sardārīh ī dūtak ī pit ō pus ī patigriftak nē rasēt.

It is written in one place that the guardianship over a family can only legally be passed on to someone else if the head of the family has entrusted it to someone; a *stūr ī kartak* is entitled to pass it on to whom he may wish during his lifetime. It is taught that there are four kinds of *sardār ī būtak* (natural guardians): The *pātixšāy*-son, the adopted son, the *stūr* who is appointed by will, and the brother who is business partner. Some hold the view that the guardianship over the father's family must not be entrusted to the adopted son.

The most remarkable aspect of this passage is the fact that guardianship may only be passed on to another person if the deceased head of the family has personally entrusted this person with it; a *stūr ī kartak*, i.e. temporary steward of the family property, may only do so while he is still alive; he cannot do it by will. Another noteworthy fact is that guardianship may be assumed by persons who have more distant associations with the family. The order in which the types of guardians are

MHD 26.5-7

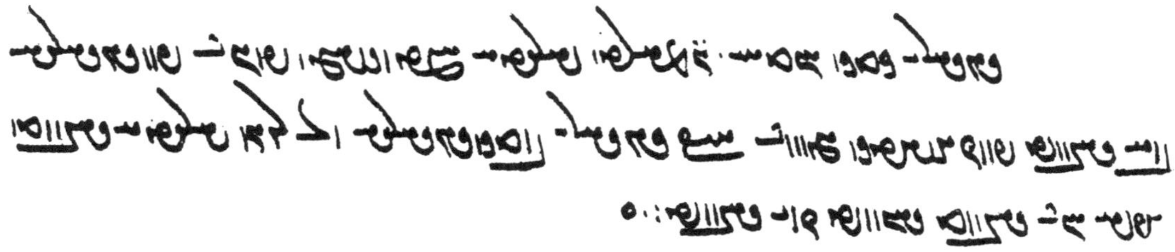

MHD 28.9-11

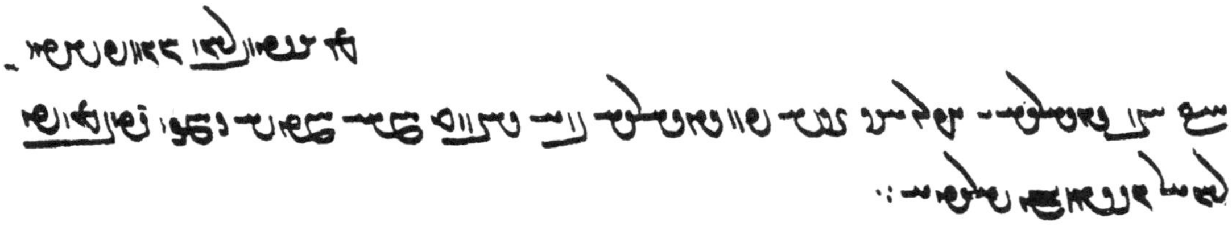

mentioned does not seem to reflect any kind of priority, cf. number two, the adopted son, who is obviously a questionable candidate according to some.

It seems highly probable that the master of the house, in his will, appointed a person whom he trusted to take over the guardianship. If the taking over of the guardianship takes place in connection with the death of the father, and one of his sons having reached majority assumes responsibility for the family property, the said son will have to take over the guardianship as well. The son will not get any extra share of the inheritance in return for this responsibility, whereas if another person is appointed *sardār* that person will receive a salary (*MHD 26.12*).

The possibility of passing on the guardianship is treated in the following passages:

MHD 26.5-7

sardār ī katakx^{v}atāy gumārt pātixšāy ka zan u frazand pat sardārīh bē dahēt pat cāštak gōbēnd kū sardār ī būtak sardārīh ō pēš pātixšāy dāt u-š and dāt bavēt cand dahēt.

If the guardian who is appointed by the master of the house passes his wife and children on into *sardārīh* (of another person) it is said according to the doctrine that the natural guardian may legally pass on the guardianship, and he gives as much as is given him.

MHD 28.9-11

hac dastavarān ōgōn nipišt kū pit sardārīh ī apurnāyak ān-iš pat sardārīh bē dāt hamē ka-š kāmak kāmēt apāc stat pātixšāy.

The jurists have written down that a father who has passed the guardianship of a minor on (to another) has the right to take it back, if he so wishes.

These paragraphs contain interesting information: Both a father and a natural guardian are entitled to entrust guardianship to others. Of course, this should be done according to the decrees of the law, but, apart from this, they seem to have had a fairly free hand in choosing a guardian.

This, in itself, is not particularly astonishing, what is remarkable, however, is that the rules concerning this are so extremely specific. This fact suggests that the passing on of guardianship must have been fairly common. It is difficult to imagine that a father or brother who live in the same household with their wards would wish to resign their guardianship. It seems reasonable to conclude that a guardian who was forced to leave his household for a considerable space of time would want to safeguard his family by leaving it in the custody of another guardian, chosen by himself. Life was a risky affair, travelling was fraught with dangers, and so, obviously, was the life of a soldier. The possibility for the appointed guardian to pass on the guardianship to a third person ensured that the affairs of the family would always be in the hands of somebody reliable.

MHD 28.9-11 could be interpreted the same way, but what it actually says is that a man may retrieve his guardianship over those members of his family who are minors, which in reality excludes his wife. This is perfectly logical since the man would automatically have renounced his claim on his wife's fortune the moment he gave up his guardianship over her. The law foresees the possibility that a father may want to resume guardianship over his own child; thus the father who has entrusted his son to another family, and thereby passed on the guardianship over him, will at any time be able to claim his son for his own again. One of the reasons why a father might want to send his son into another family could be for edu-

MHD 15.10-11

MHD 16.5-10

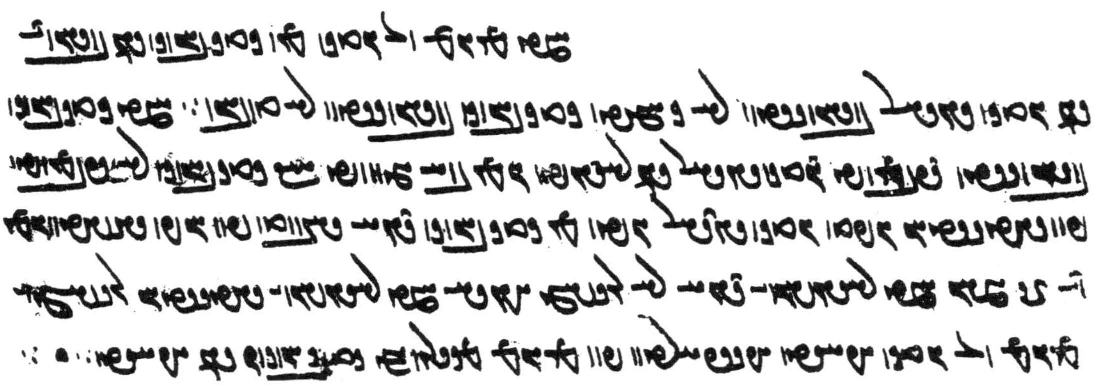

cational purposes. We know that young boys served as pages to members of the aristocracy just as they did in Europe during the Middle Ages[1]. It is possible that girls too could be sent into the care of another family. The exchange of children between the families would serve to strengthen the bonds between influential families, thus securing their position in society.
It cannot always have been an enviable task to be *sardār* for a family if one did not happen to be the father. The appointed guardian was supposed to manage the estate together with the mistress of the house, and, as we have seen, the *pātixšāy*-wives had a great deal of independence, so the collaboration cannot always have been running smoothly.

MHD 15.10-11

ka dūtak sardār [u] pus katakbānūk pat pēšēmārīh ī u pasēmārīh ī hīr ī dūtak ō dātistān nē x^{v}āhišn.

If the guardian of the family is a son, the mistress of the house does not have to be present in court in connection with a complaint being lodged against the (manager) of the family property.

We may conclude that if a *pātixšāy*-son is the guardian of the family, the mistress of the house does not have to represent the family in court. This implies that if the guardian is anyone else her co-operation is required in matters concerning the family property, which confirms my former statement that women were persons in their own right vis-à-vis the law.
This is also confirmed by

MHD 16.5-10

ka ciš ō dūtak kē katakbānūk andar x^{v}āhēnd andar dūtak sardār x^{v}āstan nē kāmēt katakbānūk x^{v}āstan nē tūvān. ka katakbānūk x^{v}āstan kāmēt dūtak sardār andar rāyēnītan ēn bē gōbēt kū katakbānūk nē kāmēt pat dātistān guft dūtak sardār yūvat hac katakbānūk dātistān dāt pat xūp dāštan ēn tāi ān zamān ka rāyēnišn ī dātistān nē sar ēnyā ka rāyēnišn ī dātistān sar ciš ō dūtak apāyēt apispārtan pat ciš patigrift katakbānūk-ic andar apāyēt.

If something is claimed on behalf of a family in which there is a mistress, but the guardian of the family does not wish to pursue the claim, then the mistress of the house cannot do so either. If the mistress of the house wants to claim the thing, and the family guardian while carrying on the lawsuit states that the mistress of the house does <u>not</u> want the thing, it is stated by the law that it is held as right that the family guardian shall conduct the case separately from the mistress of the house, and this shall continue as long as the case is running. If the result of the lawsuit be that the thing shall be handed over to the family, the mistress shall accept it.

This passage deals with the relation between the mistress of a house and the family guardian in a case where the family has a claim on some kind of property. The mistress was apparently obliged to abide by the guardian's decision, if he held to it. But the peculiar phrase about the guardian stating in court that the mistress does

1. J.M. Unvala ed.: *King Xusrav and his Page*, Wien 1917; see also C. Bartholomae: "Die Frau im sasanidischen Recht", *Kultur und Sprache* 5, Heidelberg 1924, p. 8.

MHDA 13.5-7

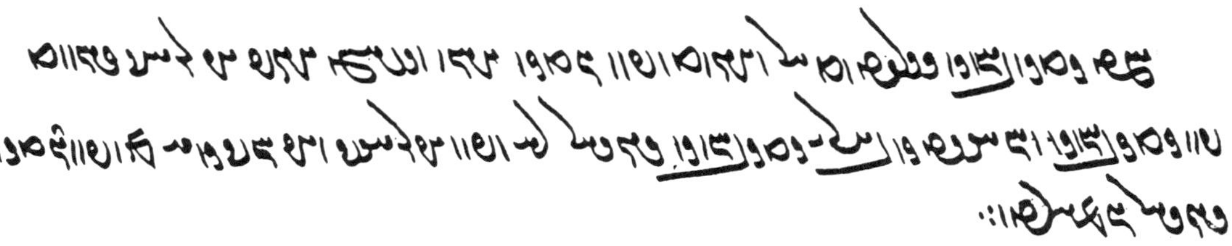

MHDA 31.5-8

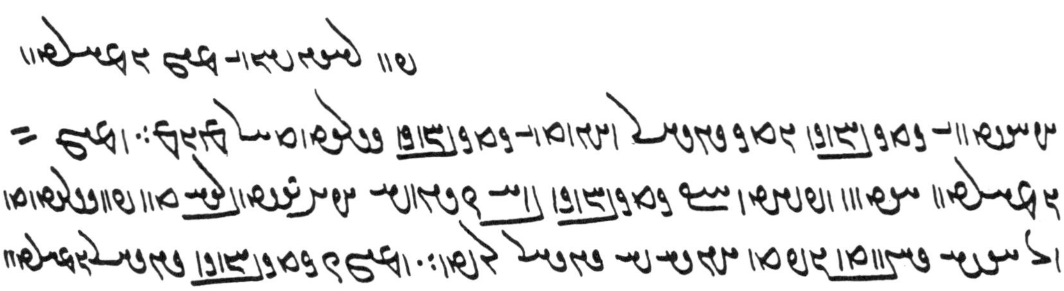

not want to stake the claim, when it has been declared that she does, is difficult to explain.

M. Macuch[1] has given the probable solution that it might be a kind of formal way of relieving the mistress from appearing in court. The passage as a whole, however difficult to interpret in detail, shows that there were definite rules for the relationship between family guardian and mistress in the handling of differences of opinion. Even if the mistress had to submit to his decisions, she still had some authority; for instance, it was necessary that she should accept the thing, i.e. accepted that it was equivalent to the claim.

If, after her husband's death the mistress of the house does not want to have a *sardār* appointed she may avoid this by employing the following tactics:

MHDA 13.5-7

> ka katakbānūk gātār kart u pat dūtak ani zan ayāp apurnāyīk būt, pat katakbānūk u x^{v}āstak bahr ī katakbānūk sardār nē u pat apurnāyīk u apārīk har kē pat dūtak sardār gumārtan.
>
> If the mistress has taken a lover, and if another wife or child under age are members of the household, no *sardār* will be appointed for the mistress of the house and her share of the family property, but only for the child who is a minor and everybody else in the family.

The same is stated in

MHDA 31.5-8

> pat rāyēnišn ī apar gumārtan apāyistan ī katakbānūk dūtaksardār kart ī katakbānūk gātār tiš apar gumārtan ētōn nipišt kū katakbānūk bē cigōn-iš apēdastovarīh tan pat gātan (or gāt) ō kas dāt guft ēnyā-š sardār nēst u aparic katakbānūk sardār gumārtan.
>
> In the case where the mistress of the house takes a lover while the necessary process of appointing a guardian for her is going on, the law states the following: "Unless the mistress of the house declares that she has taken a lover without authorization, she has no *sardār*, and a *sardār* must be appointed for her."

This must mean that the mistress of a house may choose a man for herself and enter into co-habitation with him. This type of marriage is denoted by the term: *gātār kartan*, elsewhere known under the name *x^{v}asrāyūn*; whatever the term, the woman may choose a man for herself. The advantages gained by this procedure are obvious: The woman avoids an appointed guardian who would probably have been a member of her husband's family, and she acquires a partner who is dependant on her goodwill to remain so; he may even be dependant on her income as well. Thus, she is in complete control of her own economic situation without any male interference. The chosen partner seems to be *sardār* of the woman, but since she has chosen him herself, she will probably be able to arrange matters to suit her own ideas. This paragraph demonstrates the freedom of choice that women enjoyed. The term *gātār kartan* in the *MHD* is used to signify marriage contracts according to which a woman chooses a man for herself. The term *x^{v}asrāyūn*, used in

---

1. M. Macuch (1993) p. 149, translation of the passage p. 143; Cf. F. Schirasi-Mahmoudian (1975) p. 28.

I

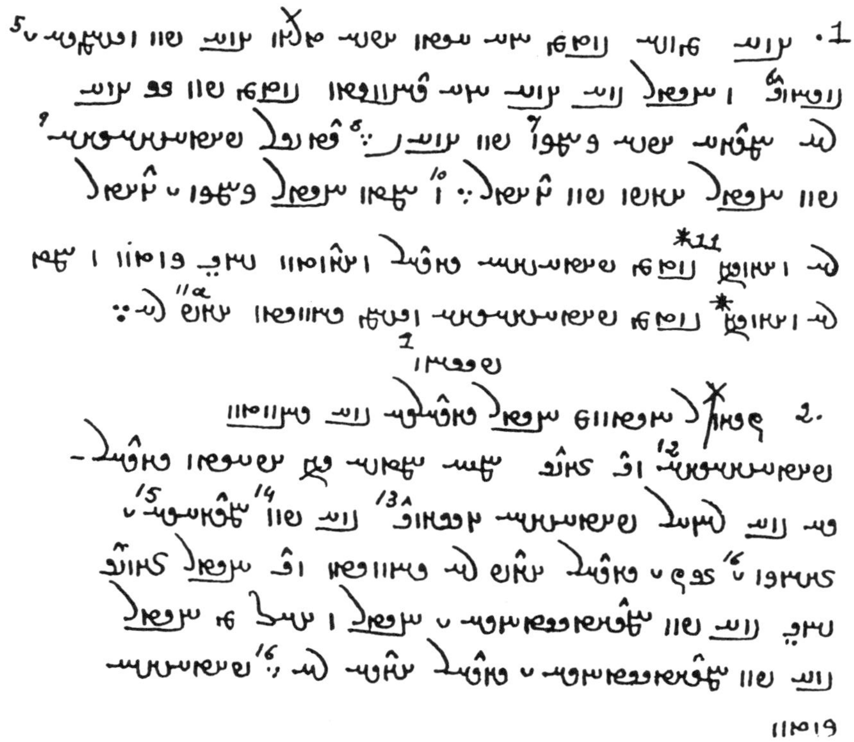

I 1. Written with red ink in TD_2. 2. G torn; thus TD_2 for [illegible] 3. G [illegible] 4. TD_2 [illegible]. 5. At the end of the line in TD_2; better om. . 6 TD_2 [illegible] . 7 TD_2 [illegible] . 8. Thus TD_2; G torn; better [illegible] 9. Thus both; better [illegible]. 10. TD_2 omits

11** TD_2 omits; the last two words missing in G as it is torn.} 11a. G [illegible] 12. Better [illegible]; G torn. 13. Thus TD_2; G torn; better [illegible]. 14 G omits (?). 15 G ....[illegible]. 16 Better om.

later law-texts to denote this type of union, is found only once in the *MHD* (*41.10 f.*). Throughout the *MHD*, guardianship is defined in relation to family economy and the administration of fortunes. Guardianship in connection with children is the right to make decisions as to their upbringing, education, and their eventual marriages. The *MHD* also shows that a marriage might be contracted without the consent of one's guardian, and that women might live independent lives without a guardian.

The Pahlavi Rivāyat of Aturfarnbag and Farnbag Srōš (AFS)

After the Arab conquest of Iran and the subsequent fall of the Sasanian Empire the greater part of the population was converted to Islam. Some did this of their own accord; others were prompted by prospects of an easier economic life, since non-Muslims were taxed much more heavily than Muslims. The Koran states that *ahl-al-kitāb* = people of the Book, i.e. Jews, Christians, and Zoroastrians should not be killed for their religious beliefs, consequently, the Zoroastrians were welcome to practise their religion provided they pay the required tax. However, concurrently with the dissolution of the institutions of government the religious institutions deteriorated, the two having always been intertwined, which was probably one of the main causes why the people who converted to Islam very soon outnumbered those who stuck to the old faith.

The strict Arabic-Islamic rule of the Umayyads made it exceedingly difficult for the Zoroastrians, by now without a strong spiritual leadership, to uphold their old traditions. However, about a hundred years after the Arab invasion, during the reign of the Abbasids, in which period the Iranians had regained considerable cultural influence, the Zoroastrian religion flourished once more under the strong spiritual leadership of the *Hudēnān pēšōpāy*.

This title was given to *Aturfarnbag*, son of *Farroxᵛzāt*, the author of *AFS*. *Aturfarnbag* has devoted considerable space and effort to the question of *sardārīh*, and his deliberations on the subject make up a section of his book:

AFS 1-10, 17-19

pursišn 1:

mart kē-š duxt ē hast u-š dō mart pat zanīh [ī] xᵛāhēnd u pitar pat[1] mart ē dahēt duxt, pat ān mart nē hamdātistān u-š kāmak pat mart 1. ditīkar pātixšāyīhā pat pitar aivap pat duxtar. u ka pitar kāmak ī duxtar nē kunēt, duxt pātixšāy sardār griftan šōd kartan u ka nē gīrēt duxt pātixšāyīhā zan bavēt aivap nē?

passaxᵛ 1:

cigōn man dānam: pitar sardārīh bē dātan pātixšāyīhā tāi zindak hamē, ka-š andar apāyēt sardārīh bē apāc pātixšāy stānēnd[2] bē pat hamdātistānīh ī ziyānak ī[3] ān-ic ī sardār aivap nē bavēt, tāi pitar zivandak šōd bē pat hamdātistānīh ī pitar u pas hac pitar bē pat hamdātistānīh ī sardār ēnyā nē pātixšāy kartan.

---

1. MS: *BR' (bē)*. In New Persian *pat* became *bē*.
2. B.T. Anklesaria (1969) emendit to *stātan*.
3. B.T. Anklesaria (1969) omits *ī*.

Question 1:

A man has a daughter whom two men wish to marry. The father gives his daughter to one of the men, but the daughter does not consent to marriage with this man, her mind being set on the other. Does the decision rest with the father or with the daughter? If the father does not comply with his daughter's wishes, is the daughter then entitled to take a (new) guardian and take a husband? And if the daughter does not take a guardian, will she then become *pātixšāy*-wife or not?

Answer 1:

As I understand it: The father is authorised to pass on the guardianship as long as he lives. If it should become necessary, he may (MS 3. plur.) take it back, but only with the consent of the woman and that of the guardian, otherwise it may not be done. As long as her father lives she is entitled to take a husband with her father's consent only, and after the death of the father with that of her guardian.

Superficially, *answer 1* does not seem to supply the answer to *question 1*. The question attaches most importance to the problem of a daughter's independence, whereas the answer stresses the authority of the father, without going into details. A close examination of question and answer reveals, however, that there is a correlation between them, but also that the answer is left deliberately vague.

The question pinpoints an essential uncertainty as to the extent of a daughter's right to decide her own fate. The author must have posed the question in order to give voice to the difficulties experienced in a community in which adherence to strict and universally accepted rules of conduct were no longer taken for granted.

The first sub-question about the choice of husband, and the right to decide could easily have been answered according to the rules set down in *MHD 36.12-16* which states that the daughter has a right to decide whom she will marry. The next sub-question puts forward the supposition that the father refuses to give his consent to his daughter's marrying the husband of her own choice, and then goes on to ask whether, in that case, she may choose a guardian and husband for herself. The phrasing is ambiguous, and it is difficult to determine whether the daughter takes the husband of her own choice whereupon he becomes her guardian (i.e. a *pātixšāy*-marriage), or whether she finds herself another guardian who is willing to give her in marriage to the man she wants; the last sub-question seems to imply that the latter interpretation is the correct one, since she cannot be a *pātixšāy*-wife without her husband being her guardian, and the question would thus be meaningless, unless it is taken to mean: Can she be a *pātixšāy*-wife if there is no guardian to give her away in marriage? This interpretation makes sense of the answer. The first part of the answer is then seen to be directed towards the last part of the question: No, she may not herself substitute another guardian for her father, but he can pass on the guardianship to someone else, which leads to the following unexpected amplification: If the father has passed on the guardianship over his daughter he cannot take it back without his daughter's consent.

The last part of the answer is directed at the first part of the question: A father has the right to choose his daughter's husband in his capacity of guardian. This means that she can only marry as *pātixšāy*-wife with his consent, but it is not stated that he can force her into a marriage against her wishes. On the other hand, the possibility that she should refuse to comply with her father's wishes is not touched upon either. If we compare with the *MHD,* we must conclude that the rules here seem intended to strengthen the authority of the father. The idea that a daughter should be entitled to choose a guardian for herself would, obviously, have far-reaching,

II

[illegible][1]

1. [illegible][1a] [illegible]
[illegible][2]
[illegible][3] [illegible][4] [illegible][5]
[illegible][5a] [illegible]

[illegible][1]

2. [illegible]
[illegible][5b] [illegible]
[illegible]

III

[illegible][1]

1. [illegible]
[illegible][2a]
[illegible][3]

[illegible][1] [3]

2. [illegible]
[illegible]
[illegible][8] [illegible][2]
[illegible]
[illegible][5] [illegible]
[illegible]
[illegible][6] [illegible][7] [illegible]
[illegible]

II 1. Written with red ink in TD$_2$. [1a. G [illegible], better omit.] 2. Added above the line in G. 3 G omits, 4. TD$_2$ omits. 5. TD$_2$ [illegible]. 5a. G [illegible]

III 1. Written with red ink in TD$_2$. 2. TD$_2$ adds [illegible]. 5b. G omits

2a. G [illegible].

3. TD$_2$ omits. 4. TD$_2$ [illegible]. 5. TD$_2$ [illegible] 6. For [illegible]. 7. For [illegible]. 8. G [illegible].

even revolutionary, consequences, resulting in the complete dissolution of the principle of guardianship, and although the question reveals doubts and discussions current at the time, the author firmly dismisses it, heavily underscoring the power of the guardian. The principle of guardianship seems to have been of much greater importance than in the Sasanian era, presumably, because it was felt to be vital to secure a faithful Zoroastrian as husband for one's daughter.

> *pursišn 2:*
> mart ē ka duxtar ē bē ō mart ē dahēt, ān mart anēr bē bavēt, ān zan rād sardārīh bē pat kē? u ka šōd kunēt pātixšāy zan bavēt aivap nē?
>
> *passax^v 2:*
> yuvat yuvat dātistānīh ī pat-iš bavēt kē guft hē. kē-š zan kunēt pātixšāy zan bavēt kē guft hē x^{v}asrāyūn[1].
>
> *Question 2:*
> If a man gives his daughter to a man, and this man turns renegade, to whom will the guardianship of the woman be passed on? And if she marries, will she then become a *pātixšāy*-wife or not?
>
> *Answer 2:*
> There are different views on this subject: There is one who said that the woman becomes *pātixšāy*-wife to the man who marries her; there is one who said that she will become *x^{v}asrāyūn*-wife.

Despite the guarded wording, this question and answer, nevertheless, reveal the brutal fact that defection was a very real threat. Zoroastrian society had no law of retaliation against defectors from the faith; the community could only make the position of the woman as attractive as possible with a view to secure her, and her reproductive powers within the Zoroastrian community. Naturally, in case of her husband's defection, she immediately obtains a divorce, and his guardianship over her ceases, but she must be suitably provided for if she is to remain a member of the community. The most attractive position that the community could offer her, in this situation, would be that of *pātixšāy*-wife; but one learned jurist had stated that, in a case like this one, she should only be allowed to marry as *x^{v}asrāyūn*. There is no explanation of this term in the text, but it seems likely that it denotes the same type of marriage as the *x^{v}asrāyūn* of the *MHD*. Here it is usually termed *gātār kartan*, "to enter into cohabitation with", i.e. a woman takes a lover of her own accord and lives together with him. *Question 3* and *answer 3*, however, make it abundantly clear that the opinion of the above-mentioned jurist must have been fairly unique:

> *pursišn 3:*
> dūtak ē ka-š martom hamāk anēr bē bavēnd bē zan ē ān duxt pātixšāy zanīh bavēt aivap x^{v}asrāyūn?
>
> *passax^v 3:*
> cigōn man dānam: ka hēc kas kē-š patvand šāyēt x^{v}ašmurtan hac pitarān im vēhdēn nēst pēš ratān aivap magupatān aivap dastavarān sardār ē gumārišn aivap kart ē pat-iš bē kunišn pat šōd bē dahišn. ka rat, dastavar nē mat ēstēt

1. *ōθrāīn* in Avestan script.

IV

[illegible]

1. [illegible]
[illegible]
[illegible]

[illegible]

2. [illegible]

[illegible]
[illegible]
[illegible]

IV 1. Written with red ink in TD_2. 2. G [illegible]. 3. TD_2 [illegible]. 4. G omits. 5. TD_2 \|. 6 TD_2 omits. 7 TD_2 [illegible]. 8 Thus both; better [illegible]

ān ī andar šahr pat dātistān frāc vicastārtar u u-š apastāk u zand vēš ōi[1] sardār ē bē paitākēnišn ān sardār pat šōd bē dahišn, dātan pātixšāy.

Question 3:
If every member of a family turns renegade except one woman, can this woman then enter into a *pātixšāy*-marriage, or will she have to become *x^vas-rāyūn*?

Answer 3:
As I understand it: If no relative of the ancestors of this true believer can be found, then a guardian shall be appointed or instituted for her in the presence of the *rats* or the *magupats* or the *dastavars*[2] and she shall be given to a husband. If no *rat* or *dastavar* be present, a guardian must be procured by the person in the province who is learned in law and has the best knowledge of the *Avesta* and the *Zand*. This guardian shall give her away to a husband: He is authorized to give her away in marriage.

This question and answer show that society employs every effort to secure a stable life for the woman who decides, against the pressure of her entire family, to remain alone within the Zoroastrian community. She may have a guardian appointed for her by the priests or by a learned man who is proved to be well versed in the holy law, and this guardian can then arrange a marriage for her. One may well imagine the bustle of activity entered into by everybody to find an appropriate guardian before the poor woman becomes desperate, and therefore willing to follow the rest of her family in their defection.

pursišn 4:
mart ē hac gētāh bē šavēt u-š zan ē u duxt ē hast pas hac ān anēr bē bavēt aivap hac gētāh bē šavēt ān duxt dātistān cē?

passax^{v} 4:
cigōn man dānam: ka zan frazām bavēt u-š ān duxtē ī nēst frazand ān duxt zivandak ī pitar, u ka zan ī pātixšāy, u duxt zivandak u zan pat sardārīh šōd kunēt pātišāyīhā zanīh xūp.

Question 4:
A man dies; he leaves a wife and a daughter; his wife turns renegade after (his death), or she dies. What are the rules regarding his daughter?

Answer 4:
As I understand it: If the wife dies and if the surviving daughter has no issue, and if she is able to enter into a *pātixšāy*-marriage, and marries a husband under *sardārīh*, then this *pātixšāy*-marriage must be regarded as legal.

The meaning of *question 4* is rather obscure, but if my interpretation is correct the question deals with a widow with one daughter; if this widow turns renegade or dies (the same thing to the Zoroastrian community) the daughter, even if she has no guardian, will be able to contract a *pātixšāy*-marriage. In that case, it is to be supposed that her father's lineage has been secured without her help.

---

1. *ᶜLH* (Ms). B.T. Anklesaria (1969) emendit to *nlm* (*narm*).

2. *rat* "spiritual chief", *magupat* "priest", *dastavar* "authority, priest", D.N. MacKenzie (1971) p. 70, 56 ,25; See also M. Macuch (1988) on the different meanings of *dastavar*.

V

[illegible][1]

1. [illegible]

2. [illegible]

VI

[illegible][1]

1. [illegible]

2. [illegible]

VII

[illegible][1]

1. [illegible]

2. [illegible]

VIII

[illegible][1]

1. [illegible]

2. [illegible]

V 1. Written with red ink in TD_2. 2. TD_2 [illegible]. (2a. G [illegible].) 3. G [illegible].
4. Both om. [illegible]. 5. Thus TD_2; G torn; for [illegible]
6. TD_2 omits. 7. Thus TD_2; G torn; better om.

VI 1. Written with red ink in TD_2. (1a. G [illegible]) 2. TD_2 [illegible]. 3. G [illegible]. 4. TD_2 omits.

VII 1. Written with red ink in TD_2. (2. TD_2 omits. 2a. G [illegible].) 2 **. Repeated by mistake.

VIII 1. Written with red ink in TD_2. 2. TD_2 adds ∴. 3. Thus TD_2.
4. Better omit.

pursišn 5:
mart ē ka-š x^v^ah ē aivap duxt ē hast, ān mart anēr bē bavēt ōišān sardārīh pat kē? ka-š šōd kunēt pātixšāy zanīh bavēt aivap nē?

passax^v^ 5:
cigōn man dānam: ka-š x^v^ēšāvand vēhdēn hast ān ī hac pitarān nazdīk patvandtar, hakar x^v^ēšāvand nēst sardārīh pat ō mādsardārīh aivap ōi ī dēn ākāstar.

pursišn 6:
mart ē kē duxt ē pat duxtarīh pat ō mart dahēt, adak-iš sardārīh pat kē?

passax^v^ 6:
pat ōi kē-š aviš dahēt.

Question 5:
If a man has a sister or a daughter, and the man turns renegade, who then will be guardian of them (sister or daughter)? If they marry, will their marriage be *pātixšāy* or not?

Answer 5:
As I understand it: If they have relatives who are true believers the closest relative of the paternal line shall be their guardian; if there are no relatives, the guardianship will be taken over by the mother, or by one who is well versed in the faith.

Question 6:
If a man gives his daughter as daughter to a man, to whom will the guardianship belong?

Answer 6:
It belongs to the man to whom he gives her (as daughter).

In *question 5* and *answer 5,* it is extremely interesting to notice that the mother seems to hold the guardianship over her daughter. This was not possible according to the *MHD*. Here the principle of guardianship secured for the men the control over the fortunes of the female members of their families, to some extent, at least. At the time of *Aturfarnbag,* it had evidently become of far more vital importance to keep a tight rein on the religious activities of the remaining members of the Zoroastrian community. This might mean that, at times, it would be advantageous to let a mother take on the guardianship of her daughter to secure that the family property, as well as the daughter's offspring stayed within the community.
We notice that the prospective guardians are different from those in the *MHD*, and also that a woman may be appointed guardian. In *7* and *8*, however, the notion that a man may be a more desirable guardian is pursued:

pursišn 7:
mart ē kē duxt ē pat duxtarīh pat[1] zan ē dahēt, sardār kē?

passax^v^ 7:
ziyānak šōd hast sardārīh u zan rād bē ō šōd ī zan barēt. hakar ziyānak x^v^ēšsardār hē sardārīh pat ziyānak.

1. MS: *bē*.

IX

[illegible][1][2]

1\. [illegible][2a] [illegible][2a] [illegible]
[illegible][2][2b] [illegible]
[illegible][3]
[illegible][4] [illegible][5] [illegible]
[illegible]

[illegible][1]

2\. [illegible][6] [illegible]
[illegible][7] [illegible][2] [illegible]
[illegible][2b] [illegible][8] [illegible]
[illegible][9] [illegible][2] [illegible]
[illegible][2] [illegible][10] [illegible]
[illegible]

IX 1. *Written with red ink in* TD_2. 2. TD_2 *omits*. 2a. G [illegible]. 2b. G [illegible]. 3. G [illegible]. 4. G [illegible]. 5. G [illegible]. 6. TD_2 [illegible]. 7. TD_2 *adds* [illegible]. 8. *Thus* TD_2; G *torn*; *better om.* 9. G [illegible]. 10. TD_2 [illegible].

pursišn 8:
zan ē kē duxt ē pat duxtarīh frāc ō zan dahēt sardār pat kē?

passax^v 8:
cigōn man dānam: ziyānak duxt pat duxtarīh bē dātan nē pātixšāy.

Question 7:
If a man gives his daughter to a woman, who will be her guardian?

Answer 7:
The husband is guardian of the wife, and the woman (i.e. the daughter) will be handed over to the wife's husband. If the wife is her own guardian, she will assume guardianship.

Question 8:
If a woman gives her daughter as daughter to another woman, with whom will the guardianship rest?

Answer 8:
As I understand it: A woman is not entitled to give away her daughter.

If somebody gives away a daughter to a *pātixšāy*-wife her husband will, automatically, become the guardian of this girl. Only in the case of the wife being married by another contract, and if she is her own guardian, will the guardianship over the girl pass to her. It is evident from *question 8* and *answer 8* that there are limits to a woman's rights regarding guardianship; she cannot, like a male guardian, pass on the guardianship to somebody else unless in cases where she gives away her ward in marriage to a man who is also the guardian of her ward. We may conclude that even though circumstances had forced Zoroastrians to allow women to become guardians, the men had not lost their sense of male superiority, and they consequently placed quite severe restrictions on the authority that was allotted to women. In *9* the striking idea is broached that a woman may be made independent, may act as her own guardian, and may give herself away in a *pātixšāy*-marriage:

pursišn 9:
zan ē kē-š sardārīh pat mart ē, ān mart pātixšāy ka ān zan pat sardārīh bē dahēt aivap ka hac gētāh bē šavēt gōbēt kū-m tō pat tan ī x^{v}ēš sardār u pātixšāy kart hāh pātixšāy zan bavēt aivap nē?

passax^v 9:
cigōn man dānam: sardār ī gumārtak sardārīh ō kas dātan nē pātixšāy u ka kartak aivap būtak [u] sardārīh x^{v}ēš ō zanān pātixšāyīhā dātan u ka ān kē-š aviš dahēt bē mīrēt apāc ō būn šavēt, u ka-š pat tan ī x^{v}ēš sardār u pātixšāy kunēt pātixšāy zanīh xūp bavēt.

Question 9:
If we consider a woman, the guardianship over whom rests with a man; is this man entitled to pass on the guardianship over the woman to somebody else? or, if the man, dying, says, "I have made you your own guardian and thus independent"; can this woman then enter into a *pātixšāy*-marriage or not?

Answer 9:
As I understand it: An appointed guardian is not entitled to pass on the guardianship to another; if he is guardian by deed, or a natural guardian he may pass on the guardianship to a woman. If the woman to whom he has handed over the guardianship dies, it will go back to the original guardian. If

X.

1.

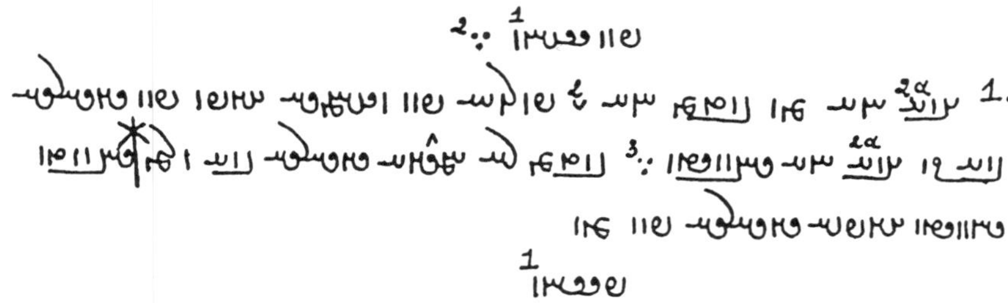

2.

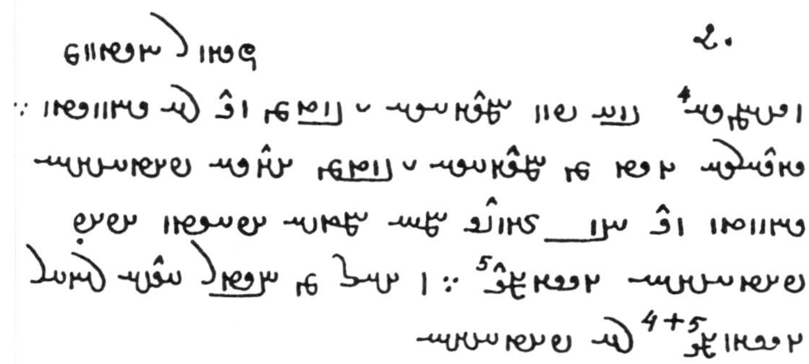

X

1. *Written with red ink in* TD_2. 2. TD_2 *omits*. 3. G *omits*.

2a. G 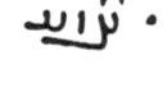.

4. TD_2 *adds* ∵ ; G *torn*. 5. *Thus* TD_2; *for*

he makes the woman her own guardian and independent, and she then takes a husband, her status as *pātixšāy*-wife is correct.

This seems to make all the preceding paragraphs superfluous. However, it is still the guardian alone who is entitled to make a woman independent: If not, the whole principle of guardianship would be nonsensical. Male control over the property of women is still very much in evidence. The reason why the circumstances of women attract so much notice should probably be sought in social conditions, which seem to have changed radically since the time of the *MHD*. One may easily imagine the Zoroastrian minority communities suffering from a scarcity of males, because the men had been lured away by tempting offers of prestigious posts in the dominating Islamic society. We know that many Iranians were employed by the Caliph in the period in question, and that these exerted considerable influence. Consequently, the female population in the Zoroastrian community became the repository of the Zoroastrian culture, as well as providing the community with new members. It is, therefore, not surprising that the law, despite its conservatism and its limitations, allowed the women greater control over their own, and their daughters' destinies than they had had earlier.

pursišn 10:
mart ē kē duxt ē purnāy pat zanīh aivap pat sardārīh bē ō mart ē dahēt, duxt nē hamdātistān sardārīh bē ōi dāt bavēt aivap-iš sardārīh pat kē?

passax^v 10:
cigōn man dānam: zanīh bē pat hamdātistānīh ī duxt tāi nē bavēt. sardārīh yuvat hac hamdātistānīh ī duxt ēnyā pātixšāy būtan tāi pit zivandak hamē kaš apāyēt apāc pātixšāy stātan u pas hac pitar kas apāc stātan nē pātixšāy.

Question 10:
A man gives his daughter, who is of age, to another man, either in marriage or into guardianship. If the daughter does not give her consent, will the guardianship still rest with this man or, if not, with whom shall it rest?

Answer 10:
As I understand it: Marriage can never take place without the daughter's consent, but guardianship is legitimate even without the daughter's consent. As long as he lives, the father is entitled to take back the guardianship (over his daughter) if necessary, but after the death of the father nobody is allowed to take it away from the appointed guardian.

Question 10 and *answer 10* correspond to the rule stated in the *MHD 36.12-16*, but without entering into the arguments put forward there: That the choice of husband is the daughter's own affair, whereas the disposing of her fortune is very much the affair of her guardian. This is characteristic of *Aturfarnbag* who, throughout his treatise, seems to be reluctant to go into sordid details about economic conditions, however much these must have been the underlying reason for many of the prescriptions.

pursišn 17:
zan ē ī yuvat hac ākāhīh ī pitar apāk mart pašn kunēt kū-m tan pat zanīh ō tō dāt. pas ka pitar ākāhīh bavēt u gōbēt kū-m[1] ēn mart apāc ēstēt, pātixšāy ka

1. B.T. Anklesaria (1969) has *kū hac*.

XVII

[illegible] ∴

1. [illegible]

[illegible] ∴

2. [illegible]

XVIII

[illegible] ∴

1. [illegible]

[illegible] ∴

2. [illegible]

XVII 1. *Written with red ink in* TD_2. 2. TD_2 *omits* 3. G [illegible]. 4. *Thus* TD_2; G *torn; for* [illegible] (?). 5. G *omits* 6. G *prefixes* [illegible] 7. TD_2 پادشاه *at the end of the line.*

XVIII 1. *Written with red ink in* TD_2. 2 TD_2 *omits*. 3. *Thus* TD_2; G *torn; better* [illegible]. 4. *Thus* TD_2; G *torn; better* [illegible] 5 **. G *torn; omitted in* G(?); *there is no space for these words* 6. TD_2 [illegible] 7. G [illegible] . . . 8. TD_2 [illegible] 9 G *torn*; TD_2 *adds* ∴ 10. *Better omit*

pat framān ī pitar apāc ēstēt u zan ī mart ē ī ditīkar bavēt ān mart ān zan pātixšāy aivap nē?

passax^{v} 17:
cigōn man dānam: ka-š sardārīh pat pitar bē ka pat hamdātistānīh ī pitar gōbēt adak-iš apāc ēstātan pātixšāy. cē ka nē pat hamdātistānīh ī pitar gōbēt pašn ī pat zanīh nē bavēt.

Question 17:
If a woman makes the following agreement with a man, without her father's knowledge: "I have given myself to you as wife", and the father becomes aware of it afterwards and says, "You must leave this man", is it then lawful if, at her father's command, she leaves the man to become the wife of somebody else? Will this woman become the *pātixšāy*-wife of the second man, or not?

Answer 17:
As I understand it: If the father is his daughter's guardian, and she gives her promise without her father's consent she is authorised to leave the man, since the marriage vow is not valid if given without the father's consent.

Question 17 and *answer 17* deal with a daughter who has married without her father's consent. According to the *AFS,* such a marriage must be declared invalid, and there can be no question of the woman being a *x^{v}asrāyūn*-wife. In this the *AFS* differs from the *MHD* which states that the daughter may continue in her self-chosen marriage, but that in doing so she will not inherit her father's fortune, and he will not have any control over her income. As usual, *Aturfarnbag* does not allude to the economic arrangements in the case, but he stresses the father's power over his daughter. We may conclude that either it was fairly unusual for women to have their own income, or that he wanted to suppress the economic aspects of the case in order to accentuate the spiritual issues involved. In fact, he repudiates the validity of a marriage that has been contracted by a daughter without her father's consent. In this *Aturfarnbag* differs from the *MHD* according to which this type of marriage was valid. This must also mean that the term *x^{v}asrāyūn,* mentioned in *question 2*, would not signify a marriage in which a daughter chose a husband for herself, but rather a type of marriage which did not fully conform to the terms of a *pātixšāy*-marriage.

pursišn 18:
zan ē ka-š šōd bē mīrēt hac ān šōd frazand x^{v}āstak nēst u zan x^{v}āstak-iš hast. ān zan pas hac ān bē mīrēt, frazand nēst, ān x^{v}āstak brāt x^{v}ēš aivap ān ī šōd rād hac ān x^{v}āstak stūr apāyēt gumārtan?

passax^{v} 18:
cigōn man dānam: andar dēn ētōn paitāk: kē zan rād cigōn sardār ō šōd dāt u-š x^{v}āstak ī frāc ōi dāt zan x^{v}āstak frāc hac ān šōd x^{v}ēš cigōn mart vitīrān bavēt tāi zan zivandak u uzēnak ī x^{v}ēš hac ān x^{v}āstak frēcvān kartan cigōn zan bē mīrēt x^{v}āstak pat stūrīh pat nabānazdišt ī šōd rasēt, ō brāt ī zan tis-ic nē rasēt, nē pat x^{v}ēšīh u nē pat stūrīh.

Question 18:
If a wife, at her husband's death has neither children nor wealth by this man, but has her own fortune, and subsequently dies without issue, will this woman's fortune then go to her brother absolutely, or must a *stūr* be appointed for her husband on the basis of this fortune?

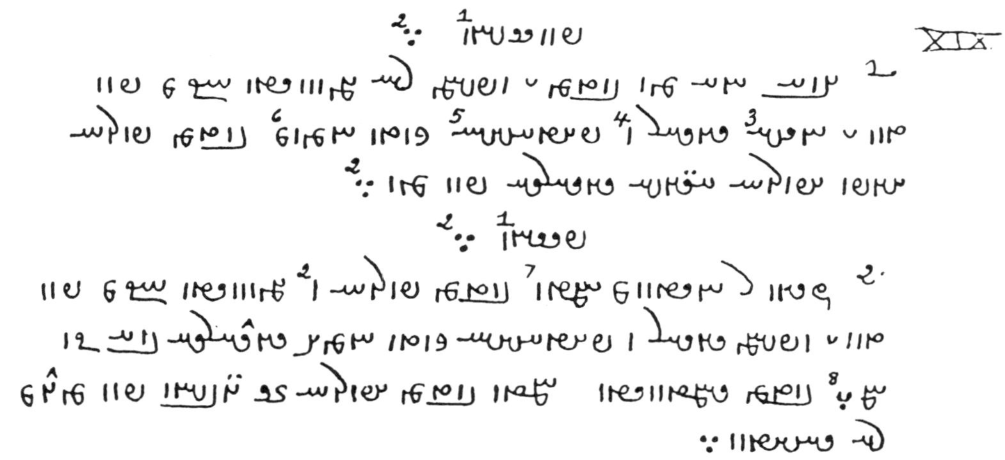

XIX

1. Written with red ink in TD_2. 2. TD_2 omits. 3. G [illegible] Thus TD_2; better [illegible]. 4. TD_2 [illegible]. 5. G [illegible]. 6. G [illegible]; TD_2 [illegible]. 7. TD_2 omits; G [illegible]. 8. G torn; TD_2 adds .:; better om.

Answer 18:

As I understand it: In the canonical texts the following is revealed: If a person, being a woman's guardian, has given her to a husband, he will, automatically, have transferred her fortune to the husband; consequently the woman's fortune belongs to her husband. When the husband dies the wife will live on the fortune for as long as she lives whereafter, at her demise, the fortune will go to her husband's closest relative in *stūrīh*. Nothing will go to the wife's brother, neither as his to dispose of, nor in *stūrīh*.

In *18,* the woman in question definitely has money of her own, but it is being held in a kind of trust on behalf of her deceased husband for the purpose of providing him with a *stūr* who can beget legitimate heirs for him. As the husband was her guardian, her fortune is his to enjoy even after death.

pursišn 19:

mart ē kē duxt ī x^{v}ēš rād gōbēt kū-m pat tan ī x^{v}ēš sardār u pātixšāy kart hom[1] duxt purnāy aivap apurnāy adak-iš sardārīh pat kē?

passax^{v} 19:

cigōn man dānam: ka duxt purnāy u gōbēt kū-m pat tan ī x^{v}ēš sardār u pātixšāy kart hē sardārīh bē ō im duxt rasēt. ka duxt apurnāy, ān gōbišn pat tis nē dāštan.

Question 19:

If a man says to his daughter, whether she be of age or not: "I have made you your own guardian and thus independent", with whom does the guardianship over her rest?

Answer 19:

As I understand it: If the daughter is of age and he says, "I have made you your own guardian and independent", then the guardianship over her will rest with the daughter. If she is not of age, such a declaration is not valid.

19 states unequivocally that a woman who is of age may act as her own guardian, which, one may suppose, would not prevent her from entering into a marriage of the *pātixšāy*-type, or a *x^{v}asrāyūn*-marriage, according to the definition in the *AFS*. Why then all the fuss about procuring guardians of the preceding paragraphs? It could be an attempt to strengthen the authority of the father. He alone can make his daughter her own guardian, and if he dies without having done so, the community will have to step in and provide her with a new guardian. Anyhow, it is evident, that, by now, guardianship as an institution has been considerably revised.

Rivāyat ī Ēmēt ī Ašavahištān (REA)

The text to be examined next is the *REA*. This text dates from the first half of the 10th century, and is thus later than the *AFS*. Like this, it is in the form of questions and answers, and covers many social and religious subjects. This was the period that saw the beginning of the mass-emigration of Zoroastrians to India, a sign that it was becoming increasingly hard for them to practise their religion in Iran, and

---

1. B.T. Anklesaria (1969) emendit to *hē*.

[illegible]

2 [illegible]

3 [illegible]

4 [illegible]

5 [illegible]

6 [illegible]

7 [illegible]

5. For [illegible]. 6. Better omit. 7. Better [illegible]. 8. For [illegible]. 9. Better [illegible]. 10. For [illegible]; see p. 14, l. 2. 11. ** Repeated by mistake. 12. For [illegible].

13. Better [illegible]. 14. For [illegible]. 15. For [illegible].

the *REA* reflects the struggle to hold on to the old practices and traditions under very difficult conditions.
The paragraphs that deal with the question of sardārīh will be presented in the same way as those in the *AFS*.

REA 5.2-20, 24-27:

2. hakar-iš tis andar nēst ān rād yuvattar dūtak-sardārīh 3 aivēnak bavēt. kartak, būtak, gumārtak.

3. ān ī kartak ān bavēt katakx^{v}atāy andar x^{v}ēš zīvandagīh sardārīh ī dūtak ī hūdātistān aviš kunēt. u-š dūtaksardārīh kartakīhā.

4. aivap mart ē ōšiyār ī 15 sālak pat sardārīh ī šāyēt pat pusarīh patīrēt hakar-iš pat pašn ī x^{v}ēš gīrēt.

5. u ān ī būtak ān ī ka katakx^{v}atāy hac āvām bē šavēt, adak-iš pus ē tanīzāt ī ōšiyār 15 sālak hast. im pus dūtaksardārīh būtakīhā.

6. ān ī gumārtak ān ī frāc hac vitīrišnīh ī katakx^{v}atāy pat dūtaksardārīh sacāktar, u-š āvām sardārān gumārēnd. u-š dātistān gumārtakīhā.

7. dūtaksardārīh pat ān zamān bavēt ka mart ī ē vēhdēn hac gētāh bē šavēt. zan u frazand apurnāyīk u ātaxš ī Varhrān pat dūtak, ka-c ēvak hac ēn 3 hast, adak-ic ō apāyēt. u-š brāt ī hambāy u pus ī purnāy u dūtaksardār u stūr ī kartak u pus ī patiriftak nēst, adak-iš kas ē, 1 ī sacāktar pat dūtaksardārīh bē gumārišn.

8. ōi pat dūtaksardārih sacāktar kē ō ōi ī viturtak nazdīk patvandtar.

9. hamē ōi ī nabānazdištar pat dūtaksardārīh ōi ī viturtak patkārtan x^{v}āstan frēcvānīk.

10. ka[1] rat aivap magupat aivap dastavar mat ēstēt, adak-iš patkārišnīh pat x^{v}āhišn stānišnīh dūtaksardārīh ō ēvak hacišān kunišn. gumārtan ī pat dūtaksardārīh hac-iš x^{v}āhišn stānišn.

11. hakar rat, magupat, dastavar ēvak-ic nē mat ēstēt ātaxš ī Varhrān pat šahr nazdīkīh hast, ēn patkārišn ō ātaxš matār ī ān ātaxš kunišn.

12. hakar-ic ān nēst u mart ī āsrōn hāvišt pēšak hast, kē dēn ākāhīhā tohm ē hast ō ōi patkārišn.

13. hakar ān-ic nē mat ēstēt, ō mart ē ī vēhdēn ī andar šahr u giyāk mas u cašmaktar u husravtar u pat ruvān dōstēh u šnāxtārīh paitāktar ō ōi patkārišn.

14. ka cigōn mat ēstēt u patkārišn kartan u gumārtan dūtaksardārīh pat ān ī mat ēstēt cigōn vēh šāyēt ōstovarān pat gumārtan nāmak stānēnd, adak-iš mātakvartar x^{v}ēškārīh ē, kū rāyēnītārīh ī kār ī dūtak pat dūtak sūtōmandīhātar u vēhdēn dātistānihātar kartan u rāyēnītan. u tūvān sāmānīhā kār ī dūtak ētōn rāyēnītan cigōn ka katakxatāy zīvandak bavēt. adak-iš kār ī zan u apurnāyīk ī andar dūtak ōi ōgōn rāyēnišn cigōn ān ī x^{v}at frāctar.

15. u ka ham/im dūtaksardārīh dēn u nikāh[2] u xūp rāyēnēt, adak-iš hac x^{v}āstak andar im dūtak hast pat mizd ī dūtaksardārīh sēnak masāy u bazāy

---

1. Ms: *'M*. Corrected to *ka* (*'MT*).

2. N. Safa-Isfehani (1980) p. 33 corrects this expression to *dēnīkīhā* which gives more sense.

8 [illegible]
[illegible] 9 [illegible]
[illegible]
[illegible]

10 [illegible]
[illegible]
[illegible]
[illegible]

11 [illegible]
[illegible]
[illegible]
12 [illegible]
[illegible]
[illegible] 13 [illegible]
[illegible]
[illegible]
[illegible] 14 [illegible]
[illegible]
[illegible]
[illegible]
[illegible]
[illegible]
[illegible]
[illegible]
[illegible]
[illegible]

16. [illegible]; for [illegible]. 17. Better [illegible]. 18. For [illegible] = [illegible]. 19. [illegible] is added and struck off after this word. 20. For [illegible]. 21. For [illegible]. 22. For [illegible]. 23. For [illegible]

masāy u vastargīn vahāk rād har rōcak šapān ē 3 panj ēvak drahm ē ī purr xᵛēšēt.

16. u-š kirpak-ic, ī hac xūp rāyētārīh frazandān ī andar dūtak, parvarišnīh ī āzār/ācār ō bavēt.

17. u-š im dūtaksardārīh tāi ān hangām ī patiš ka katakxᵛatāy ī rād pus ē ī ōšyār ī ō purnāyīh rasēt.

18. ka-š pus ō purnāyīh mat im dūtaksardār hac dūtaksardārīh gohrīk u dūtaksardār ān pus bavēt. ētōn-ic ka dūtaksardār xānak, u ēn-ic kū im cigōn katakxᵛatāy hac frāc ravēt.

19. ōi kē pat dūtaksardārišn sacāktar ka pat im giyāk mat ēstēt u-š pat sardārīh ī dūtak patkārtan tūvān adak-iš zamānīk pat dūtaksardārīh ī bē patkārišn.

20. ka-š patkārtan tūvān nē patkārēt gumārt patiš nē stānēt, adak-iš zamānīk tanāpuhl ē vinās u ziyān-ic andar dūtak bavēt, adak-iš ō būn.

24. hakar pas hac bē vitarišnīh ī katakxᵛatāy pēš kū kas ī sacāk pat dūtaksardārīh gumārt, u gumārt stānēt dūtak katakbānūk gātār ē frāc gīrēt, pātixšāy.

25. ka dūtaksardār nē gumārt, dūtak katakbānūk gātār bē frāc gīrēt u dūtaksardārīh pat gātār bē hilišn.

26. dūtak katakbānūk-ic gātār griftan pat ākāhīhā u dānišn ī āvām sardārān hast, ka ō gīrēt.

27. dūtaksardārīh kartak ān-ic ī gumārtak, ka dūtaksardārīh nē xūp rāyēnēt, u pat xᵛāstak 3 stēr andar dūtak hamē nīkērišnīkīhā. ziyān kunēt, adak-iš dūtaksardārīh āzār ō bavēt.

2. If there are no peculiar circumstances, there are three types of family guardianship: Designated guardianship, natural, and appointed guardianship.

3. "Designated guardianship" is the guardianship which has been passed on by the master of the house, in his own lifetime, according to the good law, to another person.

4. Only a son of the family, of sound mind, over fifteen years of age, can assume the family guardianship, if he will consent to it.

5. "Natural guardianship" is the guardianship assumed, at the death of the master of the house, by a son of his blood who is of sound mind, and over fifteen years of age. This son then holds the natural guardianship.

6. "Appointed guardianship" is the guardianship to which, at the death of the master of the house, the most suitable person is appointed. The leaders of the day entrust the guardianship to him, and he will then hold it by law.

7. It is necessary to appoint a guardian for the family when a Zoroastrian male dies and leaves a wife, children who are under age, and a *Varhrān* fire in his house. If only one of these three exists it is necessary. If the man does not have either a brother who is his business partner, a son who is of age, a family guardian, a designated *stūr*, or an adopted son, the guardianship over the family must be entrusted to the person who is the most suitable.

8. The most suitable person is he who is most closely related to the deceased.

[illegible] 15
[illegible]
[illegible]
[illegible]
[illegible] 16 [illegible]

[illegible]
[illegible]

[illegible] 17
[illegible]
[illegible] 18 [illegible]
[illegible]
[illegible]
[illegible]
[illegible]

[illegible] 19
[illegible]
[illegible]
[illegible] 20 [illegible]
[illegible]
[illegible]
[illegible]

24.** For [illegible] (?). 25. For [illegible]. 26. Thus in the MS.

27. For [illegible]. 28. For [illegible]. 29. For [illegible] (?).
30. For [illegible]. 31. Better [illegible]. 32. For [illegible] (?). 33. Better [illegible].

34. Better [illegible].

9. It is compulsory for the person who is most closely related to the deceased to claim guardianship over the family.

10. If a *rat*, or a *magupat,* or a *dastavar,* has arrived the claim of guardianship over the family shall be laid before one of these who must then entrust the guardianship (to the right person).

11. If no *rat, magupat,* or *dastavar* has arrived, but a *Varhrān* fire is in the district, then the claim must be laid, by the fire, before a person who visits the fire regularly.

12. If he has not arrived, the claim must be laid before the disciple of a priest who is of a religiously knowing family.

13. If such a person be not present either, the claim must be laid before a faithful Zoroastrian in the district, an elderly, well-known, well-reputed man who has shown veneration for the soul, and wisdom.

14. When this person has arrived and the claim has been laid before him, and the appointment been made in his presence, the appointment to the guardianship over the family must be written down by reliable persons. Hereafter the most important task of the guardian will be the managing of the family estate in the most profitable way, and wholly in accordance with the laws of the good religion. The guardian must administer his task to the best of his ability, as when the master of the household lived. The managing of the affairs of the wife and children under age of the family should be his foremost duty.

15. If he manages the affairs of the family carefully, and according to the laws of religion, he will be paid an adequate salary[1] out of the family property, and he will receive clothing at a value of 3/5 drachm per day, which amount is his personal property absolutely.

16. It is his duty to undertake the nourishing and bringing up of the children of the family. This duty is counted as meritorious vis-a-vis the religion.

17. He shall retain the guardianship until a son of the master of the house comes of age. The son must be of sound mind.

18. When a son has come of age, the family will be placed under his guardianship which means that the son will be guardian of the family. When he has become the family guardian he shall go on the same way as the master of the house (used to do).

19. When the most suitable person to take over the guardianship of the family has arrived, and is able to claim the guardianship, he must do so.

20. If he is able to claim it, but does not do so, or if he does not assume guardianship when he has been appointed to it, then he has committed a *tanāpuhl* sin[2]. Injuries sustained by the family will be detracted from his meritorious deeds.

---

1. On *sēnak masāy u bazāy masāy* see M. Macuch (1993) p. 211-4.

2. Sin originally punished by flogging, later by a high fine.

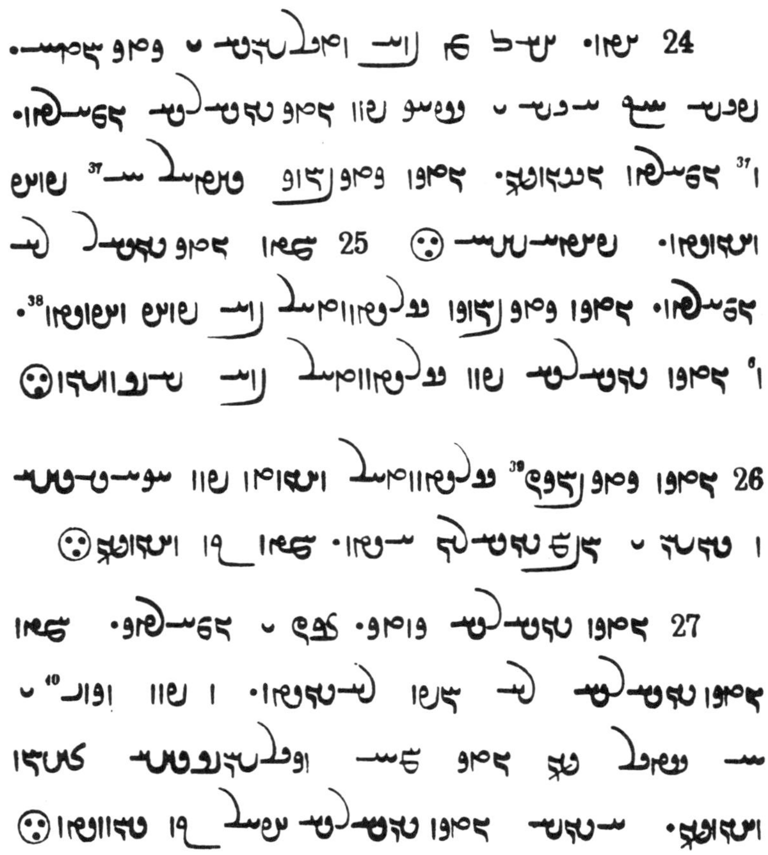

37. MS. adds ∴. 38. For [illegible].

39. Better [illegible]. 40. For [illegible] (?).

24. If the mistress of the house takes a lover after the death of her husband, and before a suitable person has been appointed guardian, and has taken on the guardianship, she is in her right to do so.

25. If no family guardian has been appointed, and the mistress of the house takes a lover, guardianship over the family shall be entrusted to him.

26. For the mistress to take a lover is perfectly in accordance with the religious rules and doctrines of the present leaders.

27. If the designated, or appointed guardian of a family does not manage the affairs of the family well, and demonstrably causes a loss of three *stēr* for the family, it will be detrimental to his guardianship.

The *REA* begins its discussion of guardianship with an enumeration of the different types of guardian. The first one treated is the guardian who has been designated by the late master of the house in his will. The second type is the so-called natural guardian (*būtak* meaning: the existing person), i.e. a son who is of age, which again must signify a *pātixšāy*-son. The third type mentioned is the so-called appointed guardian who has been appointed by the religious authorities in cases where the deceased had not appointed a guardian in his will, and where there was no grown-up son to take over the responsibility. Thus, all contingencies have been provided for, so that the family can be sure of having somebody to look after their affairs.

However, the priority between the first and the second type of guardian is not evident. We would, presumably, be inclined to think that the eldest, grown-up son must be the natural choice for a guardian, and that in cases where there was a son it must be unnecessary for a man to appoint another guardian in his will. This is by no means evident according to Zoroastrian law. A Zoroastrian male came of age when he was fifteen years old, and however clever and formally grown-up, a boy of fifteen would very rarely be sufficiently experienced to be able to take care of a family, and manage its economic affairs. For this reason, or because the son was in some other way regarded as unfit to become guardian, a man might want to leave his wife and younger children in the care of another. It thus seems likely that the question of priority between the two types of guardian is deliberately left vague, whereas there is no doubt that an appointed guardian will only be appointed in such cases where there is no son and no guardian appointed by will. If the master of a house-hold with a grown-up son chose a guardian for his family before he died, this guardian will have no say over the part of the family fortune which by right belongs to the son.

Down to the last particular, the text contains exact instructions as to whom one may appoint as guardian. This should probably be seen as a safeguard for the family against the danger of landing in the care of somebody who was on the point of defecting from the Zoroastrian faith. This would mean catastrophe, not only for the family, but also for the whole community since the property of the family would then no longer stay within the Zoroastrian sphere.

In *5.7* is given careful instruction as to when a guardian will be necessary. In the *AFS,* the widow and young children are mentioned, whereas in the *REA* the *Varhrān* fire seems to be equally important. This must be taken to signify that the house in which the fire is placed is as important as the family. This may be a more subtle way of pointing to the importance of property staying within the Zoroastrian sphere of influence.

In this late legal text, we meet the brother who is a business partner among those who should be considered first as suitable guardians. The notion of business part-

nership between brothers, which we saw discussed frequently in the *MHD*, does not otherwise seem to hold a prominent place in the *REA*. The reason for this should probably be found in the fact that the main pre-occupation of the *REA* seems to be the spiritual issues, whereas the *MHD* seems more concerned with economical problems. Nevertheless, we may conclude from this paragraph that a business partnership between brothers was still regarded as a particularly close relationship within the family.
In the *REA,* the closest attention is being paid to the actual procedure rather than to the persons involved in cases where a guardian must be appointed. We do not get the exact wording of the contract, but the text gives a complete list of acceptable religious authorities who might legitimise the appointment of the guardian (*5.10-14*). From this we may infer that priests were comparatively rare specimens in certain Zoroastrian communities. The provision that a priest or a person who is well versed in the holy scriptures be present at the appointment of a guardian also shows the desperate anxiety of the religious authorities to keep a firm hand even on lay affairs. If legal problems in the families were to be handled by laymen, different practices would inevitably grow up which again might lead to the adoption of common Muslim practices. On the other hand, the very form of the *REA* reveals the fact that a knowledge of the old scriptures could no longer be taken for granted; it may be seen as a compendium in which are listed the most important rules of conduct which should be followed by the faithful.
In *5.14-16* incl., the responsibilities and advantages of guardianship are examined. A guardian must be prepared to take on the management of the family's affairs as well as of the education and welfare of the children. If he follows the directions set down in the law, he cannot be criticized unless he does not exert himself as much as he is able to; this obviously implies that mistakes are pardonable. Being a guardian is considered as a kind of job and it is paid accordingly, not only in terms of money but also, and more importantly, in points added to the person's store of meritorious deeds which will benefit him in afterlife. It is also here that he will lose if he refuses to accept the job (*20*) i.e. a purely religious punishment. A *tanāpuhl* sin may, however be atoned by payment. There seems to be a hint here that the, sometimes, heavy task of guardianship was not sufficiently recompensed by the salary, and that other inducement was needed; hence the punishment for not accepting.
24-26 treat a problem that was also dealt with in the MHD, namely that of the widow who chooses a man for cohabitation, and thereby acquiring influence on her own and her children's future lives.
27 demonstrates that a family was protected by law against exploitation by dishonest or incapable guardians.

Unlike the *AFS*, the *REA* does not take into consideration the possibility that no close relation exists. The conclusion that the mistress of the house would act as guardian in such a case seems a natural one, but the possibility is not mentioned here. Another solution would be to appoint a *stūr* who could act as guardian at the same time.

REA 8.1-5

pursišn 1:
mart ē kē gōbēt, kū. stūr man mart mā gumārt. adak-iš vinās ō būn bavēt aivap nē. hakar-iš bavēt, cand bavēt.

[illegible]

1 [illegible]

[illegible]

[illegible]

[illegible]

2 [illegible]

[illegible]

[illegible]

[illegible]

[illegible] 3 [illegible]

[illegible] 4 [illegible]

[illegible]

[illegible]

5 [illegible]

[illegible]

[illegible]

[illegible]

1. Written with red ink. 2. For [illegible] (?). 3. [illegible] seems to be missing. 4. Better omit. 5. For [illegible].

6. Better [illegible]. 7. Better [illegible]. 8. For [illegible]. 9. Better [illegible].

*passax*ᵛ *2:*
mart ka ān ī cigōn apparnipišt gōbēt, hamgōnak (gōbišn)[1] rād, adak-iš vināš ē ō būn nē bavēt. bē-š ān-ic kirpak ī pat ...rīh[2] ī stūr kunišnīh u gumārišnīh u nāmgānīh ī pat gētāh aviš nē rasēt.

3. cē mart, ka-š frazand ī tanizāt nēst, hac kas pat pusarānīh (sic!) patīrēt.

4. u stūr u nāmgānīh ī pat gētāh hišt, vazurg sū[u]t ī tan u ruvān.

5. ē rād, andar vēh dēn, kār ī pus ī patīriptak u stūr ōgōn saxt guft ēstēt, ōgōn kū, ka xᵛat kas nē paitākēnēt, adak-iš stūr ē bē gumārišn.

Question 1:
A man says: "I do not wish a *stūr* to be appointed for me"; is this a sin which will affect his total of meritorious deeds or not? If it does affect it, to what extent?

Answer 2:
If a man says the above, he will not have committed a sin which will detract from his total of meritorious deeds, neither will he, however, be credited with the virtue of providing and appointing a *stūr* for adoption, and there will be no continuation of his lineage, or commemoration of his name in the material world[3].

3. A man adopts someone because he has no offspring of his own blood.

4. To leave a *stūr* and thus secure the continuation of one's own lineage, is of great benefit to body and soul.

5. This is the reason why the matter of adopted sons and *stūrs* is strongly emphasized in the good religion, and why if a man does not procure one for himself a *stūr* should be appointed for him.

The text does not distinguish between a *stūr* and an adopted son, but seems to imply that they are one and the same, the function of both, of course, being that of securing the continuation of a man's lineage. Dhabhar's translation of *stūrīh* as "adopted sonship" therefore seems perfectly acceptable although he explains the term *stūr* as "the person who has accepted the responsibility of an adopted son for one passed away". We may conclude that the sharp distinction which was made in Sasanian times has become blurred, and that the only difference which seems to have lingered on is that an adopted son can only be adopted while testator is still alive, while a *stūr* may be appointed both before and after his death.

The problem of what happened to the property of a renegade is taken up in:

1. Inserted by B.T. Anklesaria (1962).
2. B.T. Anklesaria (1962) completes to *pusarīh*.
3. B.N. Dhabhar in *Essays on Iranian Subjects*, Bombay 1955, p. 118 ff., translates *stūr* as adopted son.

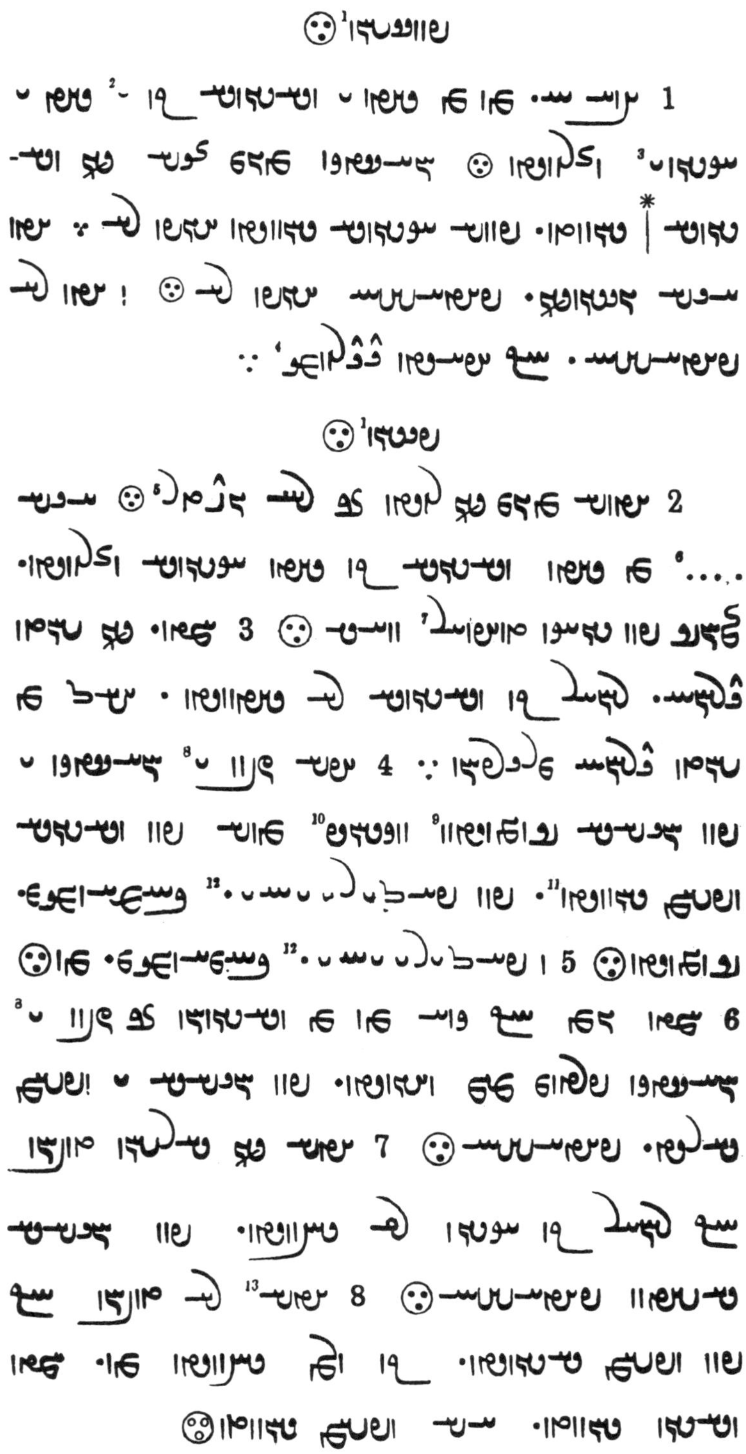

1. Written in the MS. with red ink. 2. Better omit. 3. For [illegible]. 4. For [illegible].

5. For [illegible]. 6. [illegible] omitted. 7. MS. has [illegible]. 8. For [illegible]. 9. For [illegible]. 10. For [illegible]. 11. Better [illegible]. 12. Better [illegible].

13. [illegible] written and struck off after this in the MS.

REA 25.1-8

pursišn 1:
mart ē kē hac dāt ī vēhdēnīh ō ī dāt ī akdēnīh[1] šavēt. x^{v}āstak ciš ī-š andar vēhdēnīh būt, pat-iš akdēnīh bavēt aivap nē. hakar kas stānēt, pātixšāy aivap nē. u hakar nē pātixšāy, kū apāyēt burtan.

passax^{v} 2:
hakar-iš ciš andar nēst ān rād yuvattar. kas[2] hac dāt vēhdēnīh ō dāt akdēnīh šavēt, zamānīk pat giyāk tanāpuhl vinās.

3. ka, andar sāl drahnāy, apāc ō vēhdēnīh nē āyēt, pas hac sāl drahnāy margarzān.

4. u-š hīr ī x^{v}āstak ī pat x^{v}ēšīh ēstēt u vindišn-ic kē-š pat vēhdēnīh x^{v}ēš bavēt, pat "paoiryāi dāmanam"[3] ēstēt.

5. u "paoiryāi dāmanam", kē.

6. ka ēn kū har kē hac vēhdēnān ān hīr ī x^{v}āstak fratom apar gīrēt, pat x^{v}ēšīh ī x^{v}ēš dārēt, pātixšāy.

7. hakar-iš andar dārišn tuvān kū apāc ō akdēn nē dahēt, pat x^{v}ēšīh dāštan pātixšāy.

8. hakar-iš nē tuvān kū pat x^{v}ēš dārēt, ō ōi dahēt kē, ka vēhdēn būt, aš x^{v}ēš būt.

Question 1:
If a man leaves the laws of the good religion for those of the infidels, will the property which was his when he was a believer remain his when he becomes an infidel or not? Is anyone entitled to take it away from him? If not, where does this property belong?

Answer 2:
If there is nothing in the case which requires a different procedure, someone who leaves the laws pertaining to the good religion for those of the infidels will instantly have committed a *tanāpuhl* sin.

3. If, within a year, he has not returned to the good religion, he will be regarded as a *margarzān*[4] sinner.

4. The returns of the property which he possessed, and the income which was his when he was a believer will belong to the "first of the creatures".

5. "First of the creatures", what does this mean?

6. It means that anyone among the believers who first seizes this fortune, and keeps it as his own, will be entitled to it.

7. If he can hold on to it, and is not persuaded to give it back to the renegade, he will be entitled to keep it as his own.

---

1. Emendi MS *akdēn ī* to *akdēnīh.*
2. B.T. Anklesaria (1962) emendit to *ē kē.*
3. Avestan expression.
4. Sin deserving death.

8. If he is not able to keep it in his possession, he shall give it back to the person to whom it belonged when the said person was a believer.

Question 25 and the answer to it provide us with a certain insight in the problems around Zoroastrian apostasy. The answer deals with the religious consequences first. The renegade will be stigmatised as a sinner, but only when there are no chances of his returning to his old faith will he become a sinner who deserves death. The economic considerations evidently come second to the spiritual issues. It is, naturally, of vital importance to keep people within the Zoroastrian community with their property and wealth, since the larger its possessions, the more secure the community. Thus, when defection was a *fait accompli* the property of the renegade was confiscated to the extent that the property was declared ownerless, thereby giving any Zoroastrian the right to seize it and defend it as his own. This must mean that the "private" property of a Zoroastrian was, in fact, considered the property of the community; accordingly, we must imagine that certain tracts of land, or certain parts of towns, were occupied by Zoroastrians who had formed a society with their own civil laws and traditions. We cannot know for sure whether its members were taxed individually by the Muslim authorities, or whether they paid jointly, but considering the practice elsewhere, it seems most likely that the taxes were collected in a bulk by the state collectors. A point in favour of the latter view is the fact that there is no mention in the *REA* of any meddling in the economic affairs of a new member of the Muslim society by the authorities. Apparently, there was no interference in the economical affairs of the Zoroastrian community by the Muslim authorities as long as the state-taxes were paid. Otherwise, it would not have been possible to regard the property of a renegade as ownerless, and free for any Zoroastrian to seize as his own. The renegade seems to have been regarded as subject to Zoroastrian laws still, and therefore not in a position to apply for help to the surrounding Muslim society to prevent his property from being seized[1].

There was, however, still the possibility that the renegade might fight back and recapture his property. In this clause we see reflected the whole precarious situation of the Zoroastrians making shift in an alien society, and their well-founded fear of the diminishing of their religious community. It is of the most vital importance to them to keep their group as intact as possible.

1. A.K. Lambton: *Theory and Practice in Medieval Persian Government*, London 1980, ch. VII p.5, note 1.

CAKARĪH

Cakarīh, like *ayōkēnīh,* is an institution designed to provide a man without issue with an heir, an essential feature in Zoroastrian family law.

Cakarīh is the abstract noun for this special type of marriage, and *cakar* is the corresponding adjective which may be applied to *zan* (wife), *mart* (husband), and *frazand* (children), both *pus* (son) and *duxt* (daughter). The people involved in this marriage as well as the children issuing from it are all called *cakar* only in relation to the *cakarīh* since they may well, at the same time, be *pātixšāy* in a different relationship. One might say that the *pātixšāy*-marriage is the precondition of the *cakar*-marriage as the lack of an heir in a *pātixšāy*-marriage would oblige the wife to conclude a *cakar*-marriage in order to procure the missing heir. Thus, the child of the *pātixšāy*-wife by her *cakar*-husband is the lawful heir of her *pātixšāy*-husband.

Over the years, scholars have discussed the etymology of the term *cakar*. Bartholomae was of the opinion that *cakar* must be a reduplication of the root *kar*. As he does not state, specifically, which of the bases of *kar*, it seems reasonable to suppose that he meant *kar*= "to do" which is the most common base[1]. This does not seem very probable, however, as no appropriate meaning can be deduced from this reading. A. Perikhanian, nevertheless, adopts the suggestion, and further interprets its meaning as "servant", referring to NP *cākar*, Ossetic *cayar*[2]. G. Klingenschmitt repudiates this reading on the grounds that MP *cakar* could not possibly have developed into *cākar*[3]; he does not offer any alternative solution, however. Ossetic *cayar* with a short vowel is no help since the vowels in Ossetic, generally, tend to become shortened, e.g. Ossetic *bazar* for NP *bāzār*, Ossetic *becal* for NP *bīcār*, Ossetic *patcax* for NP *pādšāh.*

At the suggestion of Sir Harold Bailey in a personal letter, I have looked into another possible base for *kar*, Indo-European *k^{u}*el*, "to turn, to attend to". This is the base for Sanskrit *cárati* and Avestan *caraiti*, "to be engaged in", Greek *πέλομαι* in *'αμφίπολος*, "maidservant", Lat. *anculus,* fem. *ancilla*, "servant". The meaning of this base "attend to" would fit both *cakar* with normal reduplication as well as to *cākar* with intensive reduplication which means that both derive from a common base: *k^{u}*el.*

MHD

Presupposing this denotation of *cakar*, the question of the function of the *cakar*-wife arises. According to the *MHD* her function is to provide her *pātixšāy*-husband with an heir by marrying as *cakar*, but only by analysing this term in its context will it be possible to understand the full implication of the institution since a specific definition is not to be found in the *MHD.*

---

1. C. Bartholomae (1918) p. 7, 32.
2. A. Perikhanian: "On some Pahlavi Legal Terms". *Henning Memorial Volume*, London 1970, p. 357.
3. G. Klingenschmitt: "Neue Avesta-Fragmente". *MSS* 29 (1971), p. 124.

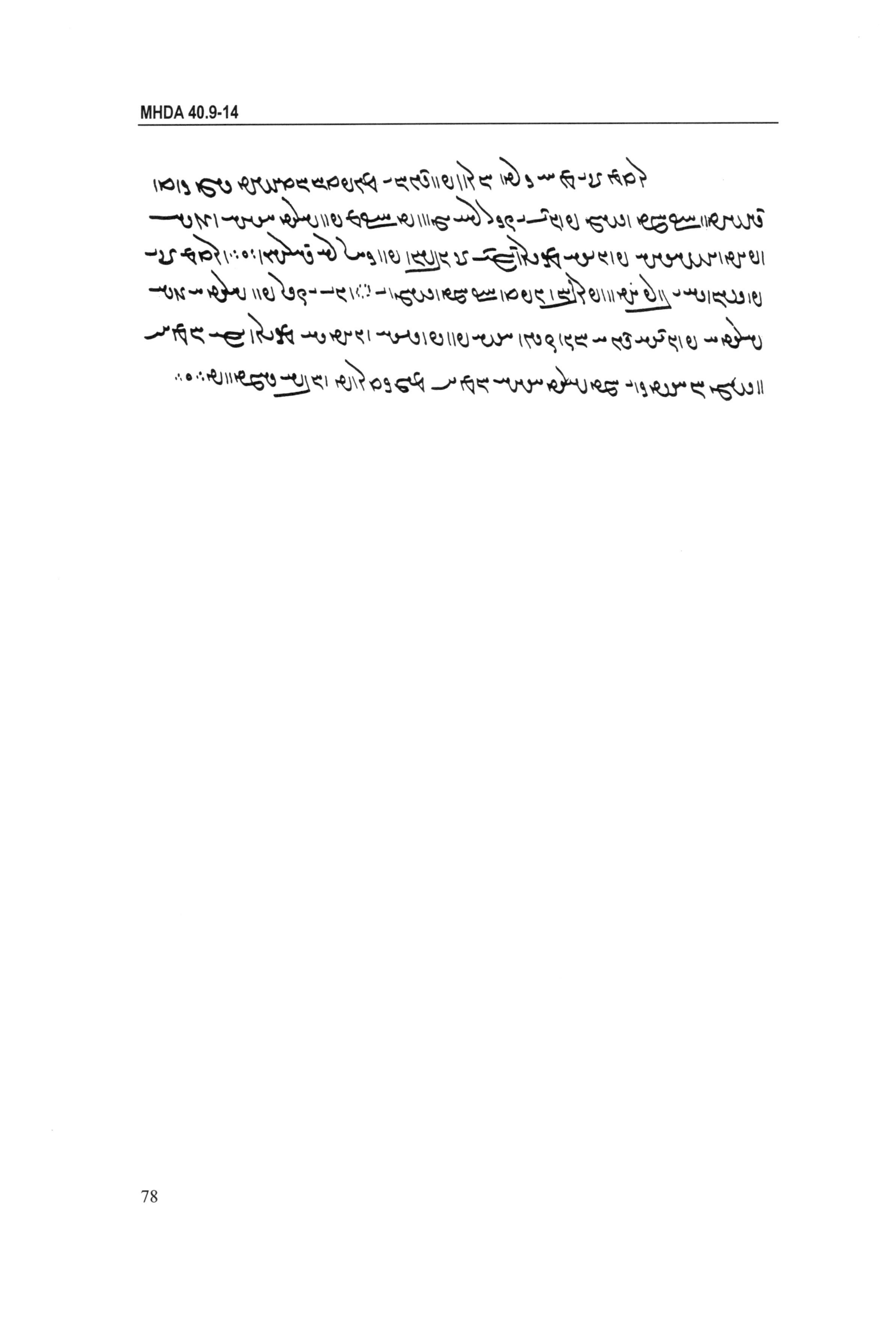

[illegible]

The following paragraphs from the *MHD* deal with the relations between *pātixšāy, sardārīh,* and *cakar:*

MHDA 40.9-14

apāk ān ī hac ē(v)kart x^{v}aran pat dīvān ī magupatān Artaxšer X^{v}arrah kart u dāšt kū ka zan frazand ī cakar rād gōbēt kūm pat pātixšāyīhā zanīh u pātixšāyīhā frazandī patigrift ān gōbišn pat kār nē dārišn. u apāk ān ī Pusānvēh ī Būrzātūr Farnbagān guft kū ka zan u (f)razand ī cakar pat pātixšāy zanīh pātixšāy frazandī dātistān ōgōn cigōn kas pat pusīh u duxtīh patigrift hē u zan x^{v}āstak-ī ka pātixšāyīhā hē apar manēt u aviš rasēt.

Together with that which was made and held by the united assembly[1] in *Dīvān ī Magupatān* from *Artaxšēr-X^{v}arrah*[2]: "If someone says about his *cakar*-wife or -child: 'I have taken you as *pātixšāy*-wife or -child', that declaration should not be considered valid". Also according to the opinion of *Pusānvēh ī Būrzātūr Farnbagān*[3]: "If someone takes his *cakar*-wife and -child as *pātixšāy*-wife and -child it should be judged the same as when somebody adopts a son and daughter, and if the wife becomes *pātixšāy* she will inherit property, and it will go to her[4]."

The first paragraph distinguishes clearly between *cakar* and *pātixšāy,* and since we know the rights and purposes of the *pātixšāy*-union, we must conclude that a *cakar*-union is something different. The purpose of this type of union must be of a kind that precludes its conversion into *pātixšāy*. On the other hand, however, there seems to have been an inclination on the part of *cakar*-husbands to convert their *cakar*-status into a *pātixšāy*-one judging from the analogy with adoption drawn by *Pusānvēh ī Būrzātūr Farnbagān* in his apparent attempt to legalise such a conversion. Whether he argues for an actual adoption of the wife and child as daughter and son as a way of carrying through a conversion without violating the rules, is difficult to ascertain. Anyhow, the consequences of adoption or conversion would be the same: The son would become the heir of his *cakar*-father, and the wife would inherit her share, precisely the point that the law sets out to prohibit. It seems then that parts one and two of this paragraph are in truth concerned with inheritance regulation[5].

One point becomes spectacularly evident: The *cakar*-contract is open to several interpretations. This presumably reflects an uncertainty as to the use of that type of contract.

The *MHD 70.3-12* may give us a key to an interpretation of this interesting comparison with adoption:

---

1. *ē(v)kart x^{v}aran* "united assembly". See A. Pagliaro: "IX *χ^{v}aran* 'riunione, assemblea, festa', arm. *χoran*", *Rivista degli Studi Orientali XXVI*, 1951, p. 47-51.
2. One of the five districts in the province of Pārs.
3. A jurist.
4. B. Hjerrild Carlsen: "The *cakar* Marriage Contract and the *cakar* Children's Status in the *Mātiyān ī hazār Dātistān* and *Rivāyat ī Ēmēt ī Ašavahištān*", *MIS*, Leuven 1984, p. 107: I have revised my former translation of the last sentence.
5. M. Macuch (1976) p. 377 finds no contradiction between the declarations.

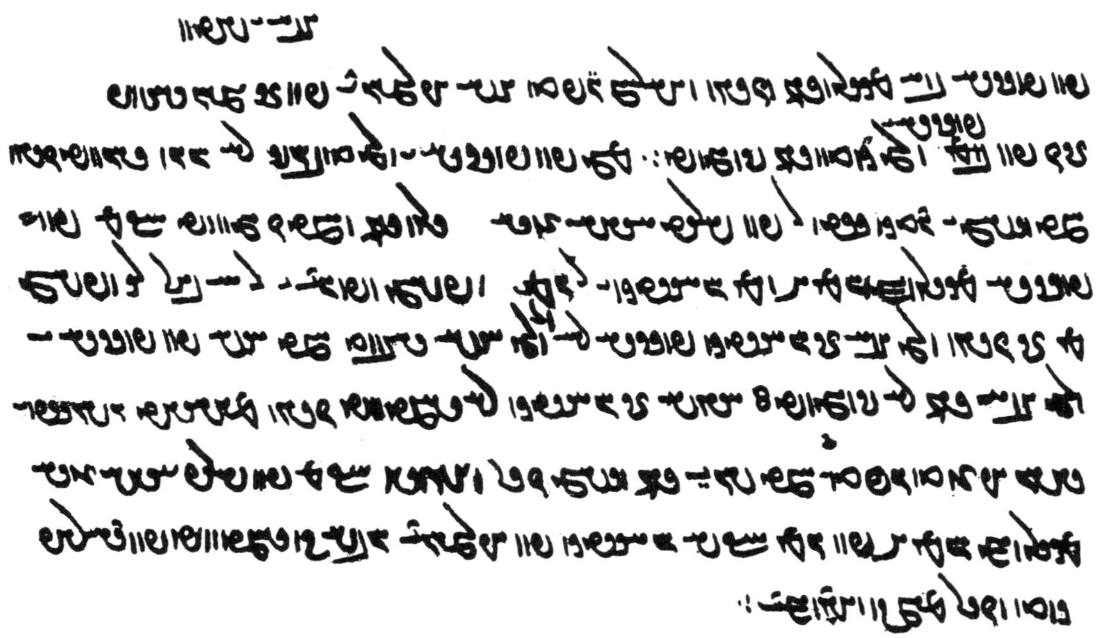

MHD 70.3-12

mart ī šahr pat pusīh bē patigīrēt u cigōn Vahrām guft ā-š aparmānd pat ān zamān bavēt ān-ic pat pusīh ī ōi kartan andar ēstēt, cē pat pusīh ī ōi tuvānīk nē ōgōn bavēt cigōn ka zan ī dūtak stūr pat pātixšāyīhā zanīh patigīrēt u ka-c gōbēt kū-m pat pusīh patigrift hē u hac x^vāstak ī man yūmē x^vēš[1] u frazand ī man ē bahr tō x^vēš hac ān cigōn ōi mart ān x^vāstak pusīh rād ō ōi kas dāt ka kas pat pusīh ī ōi mart andar nē ēstēt adak-iš ān x^vāstak nē rasēt. cigōn Māhdāt Gušnasp ī Gyānāpzōt guft ka šōd andar zan cakar kunēt kū-m pat pātixšāyīhā zanīh patigrift hē pat ēn kū-š x^vāstak pat aparmānd aviš ō rasēt pat Dārāvkirt vicīr apar ō kunēnd.

A man adopts a fellow-citizen, and, as stated by *Vahrām*, the inheritance will be his when he begins to act as son to that man, because he is able to undertake (the task of) being son of him; it is not so when he takes a wife who is family *stūr*, in a *pātixšāy*-marriage, also, if he says: "I have adopted you as my son, and part of my property will be yours on an equal footing with my wife and my child". In this way the man has bestowed his property because he has adopted that person. If the person does not become a son to the man, then the property shall not go to him. As *Māhdāt Gušnasp ī Gyānāpzōt*[2] has stated, on the occasion when a man declares to his *cakar*-wife: "I have taken you in a *pātixšāy*-marriage" a decision shall be made in *Dārāvkirt*[3] as to whether his property shall be inherited by her.

The interpretation of this somewhat intricate passage must be that an adopted person will become heir to part of the father's property provided he actually does become his adopted son, and thus acquires a position as if he were *pātixšāy*-son. Here is an example of an adoption that is desired despite the fact that the man had both wife and child, and consequently no great need of an extra insurance against dying without heirs. But the mortality rate was high, and it may have been usual to safeguard oneself by creating several possibilities of securing the continuation of one's lineage by adoption or by instituting *stūrīhs*. Moreover, the richer the man, the greater were his possibilities. In this case there is a stipulation, however, to the effect that the fellow citizen will be guaranteed part of the man's inheritance, if he actually does become his adopted son, i.e. they enter into a contract to be fulfilled at a later date. If the adopted son, contrary to expectation, suddenly finds himself obliged to return to his own family, in the case of the death of other sons in his family, for instance, he will have to renounce the adoption. Seen in this light the sentence about the *pātixšāy*-marriage with the *zan ī dūtak stūr,* makes perfect sense. A *pātixšāy*-wife who is completely bound to her husband's need of heirs is a far better insurance against childlessness.

The above passage then deals with problems of inheritance, just as did *MHDA 40.9-14*. We may conclude from the fact that a conversion from *cakar* to *pātixšāy* implied the right to inherit that a *cakar*-wife and -children did not have any right of inheritance. Furthermore, this right could not be bestowed by testator alone, but must be sanctioned by a higher authority. Since a man might adopt somebody without a court decision, the complication does not seem to lie in the transferring

1. A. Perikhanian (1973) p. 210 emendit to *zan* which I follow.

2. A jurist.

3. A town in Pars.

MHD 3.10-11

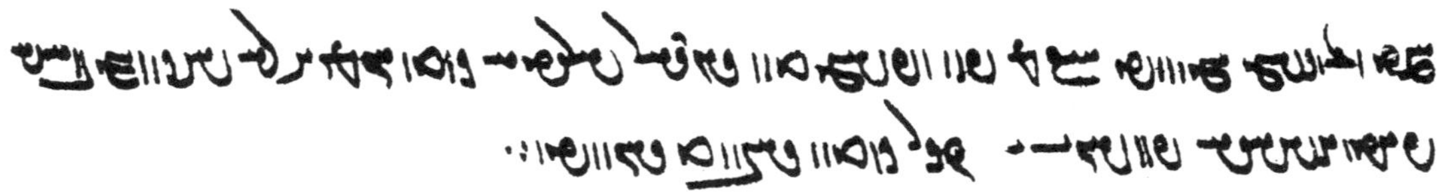

MHD 3.15 – 4.1

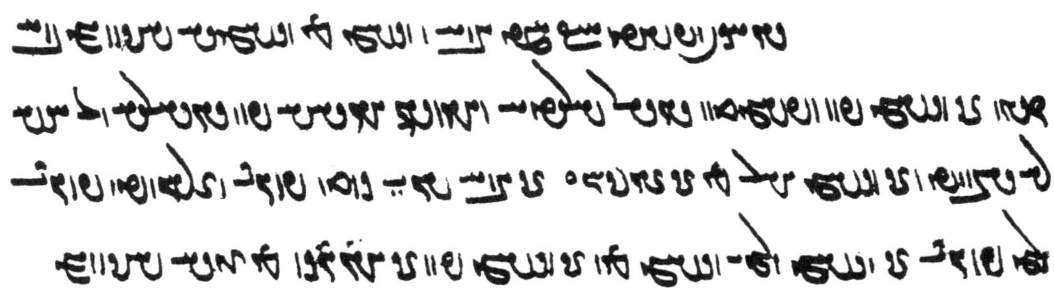

of rights, but rather in the duties attached to these rights, which in the case of *cakar*-wives and -children might clash with other duties. Therefore, every single case had to be considered separately and weighed in this light. However, the first paragraph hints at a modified point of view, probably from a desire to simplify the rules.
Thus, the question of *pātixšāy*-wife versus *cakar* is intricately bound up with the problem of guardianship. A comparison of *MHD 3.10-11.* and *MHD 3.15 - 4.1* will illustrate this:

MHD 3.10-11:

ka ō zan gōbēt kū-m xᵛēš tan sardār pātixšāy kart hē nē hilet bē-š pātixšāyīh pat šōd ī cakar kartan dāt bavēt.

If he (the husband) says to his wife: "You have been made guardian of your own person by me", he does not divorce her, but she has been given the right to take a *cakar*-husband.

MHD 3.15 – 4.1

giyāk 1 nipišt kū ka mart [u] zan hac zanīh hilēt bē cigōn ān zan pat xᵛēš tan sardār pātixšāy kunēt ēnyā-š pat sardārīh ō kas nē dahēt u zan pas hac ān zindakān ān mart šōd kart frazand zāyēt frazand ōi frazand ān zan ōi ī zan kē ān zan pat ān aivēnak hac zanīh hilēt.

It is written in one place: "If a man releases his wife from marriage and except for making that wife authorized guardian over her own person he does not otherwise give her in guardianship to anybody, and if the said woman later, the former husband being still alive, takes a new husband and bears children, these children will belong to the former husband who released the woman in the way stated above"[1].

The two passages taken together illustrate unequivocally the interaction of the *sardārīh*-, the *pātixšāy*-, and the *cakar*-relation. We may conclude that two possibilities exist for a *pātixšāy*-husband who wants to cease cohabitation with his wife: One is to transfer the guardianship to another man and divorce her; the other is to send her away giving her the right to be her own guardian i.e. letting her be in charge of her own money. To the husband this meant giving up the control of her fortune and the right to have sexual relations with her in order to achieve the desired result: Legal heirs produced by her in a *cakar*-marriage. This law is obviously open to misinterpretation. In the crudest case, a man who has grown tired of the wife whose fortune he has spent has a legal right to send her away to fend for herself while he retains the right to the children she might bear. There are indications in the *REA* that such cases of abuse did indeed occur. These will be treated later in the chapter on *cakar* in the *REA*.
To sum up: A *pātixšāy*-marriage constitutes a bond, which is stronger than that of *sardārīh*. Guardianship is concerned with economic relationship, whereas the *pātixšāyīh* signifies the intention of producing heirs to a man. Thus, the guardianship may be dissolved while retaining the *pātixšāy*-relation with all its implications, i.e. (as seen in *3.15 - 4.1*) any child born of the wife at any time will be the

1. M. Macuch (1993) interprets this differently; she is of the opinion that guardianship constitutes the right to the children.

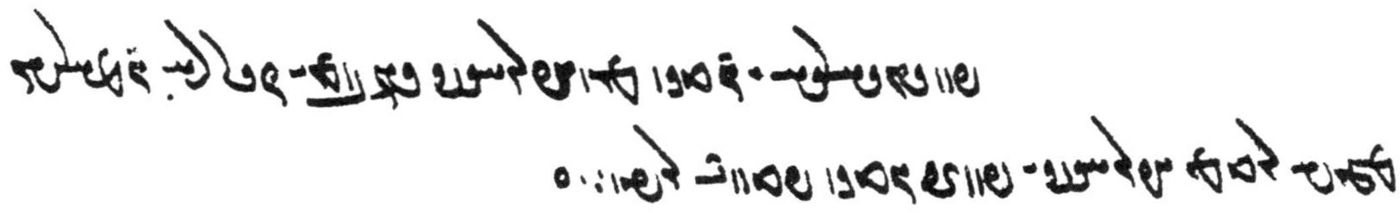

legal heir of her *pātixšāy*-husband. Only by transferring the guardianship, i.e. the administration of her fortune, over the wife to another man whose *pātixšāy*-wife she could then become, could the former *pātixšāy*-relation be dissolved. The *cakar*-marriage existed in cases where the guardianship had been dissolved, but had not been transferred to another man, and the *pātixšāy*-relation continued[1]. The point of these transactions was that children born in a *cakar*-marriage were indisputably the children of the *cakar*-wife's *pātixšāy*-husband. The conversion of a *cakar*-wife to *pātixšāy* is illegal, according to *MHDA 40.9-14*, because such a conversion would go against the whole idea of the *cakar*-union which was meant as a kind of emergency measure in cases where the *pātixšāy*-wife failed in her duty to provide her husband with an heir, but if she was expected to produce heirs by the aid of another man, one must have realized that the barrenness was the man's fault whether due to age or infirmity. The paragraphs that express the jurists' efforts to modify this rule must be seen as indications that difficulties arose when these rules were to be carried out in "real life". One may easily imagine the frustration and dismay experienced by a *cakar*-husband and -wife living together with their children. The man would have to secure heirs for himself by contracting a *pātixšāy*-marriage with another woman, which would mean the relegation of the *cakar*-wife to an inferior position in the house, as well as straining the economy of the whole household. The obvious thing for them to do would be to try to change the marital status of the *cakar*-wife. Since divorce was a legal possibility, this could be done, but only with the consent of the *pātixšāy*-husband, since only he could apply for a divorce. The *MHDA 40.9-14* seems to be concerned about a case in which a *cakar*-husband acted without having obtained the consent of the *pātixšāy*-husband. There may have been two reasons for this: Either the husband would not comply, or that he was dead. The first legal opinion advanced is that the conversion would not be legal, under any circumstance, the second that it is legal. The *MHD 70.3-12* puts the decision before the court. It seems safe to conclude from this debate that the issue must have been of some importance. The reason for this is, probably, that the *pātixšāy*-union that produced the necessary succession was at the time regarded as the stabilizing factor, just as the nucleus family is in modern society. Therefore, society was inclined to curb any attempt to put forward more liberal views on these matters.

As we have seen, a *cakar*-wife, having been released from her husband's guardianship, could become her own guardian. There are, however, other questions to consider in relation to *cakar* and *sardārīh.* From the passages in the *MHD* that deal with these questions, we may also glean useful information as to the general nature of the *cakar*-union.

MHD 27.14-15

pat sardārīh ī dūtak kē apurnāyīk andar pus ī cakar nē gumārišn cē-š apāk apurnāyīk ī pat ān dūtak patvand nēst.

A *cakar*-son cannot be appointed guardian over the family which includes a son who is under age, because he is not related to this infant.

This paragraph elucidates beyond any doubt the relationship of a *cakar*-son to his biological father: He is not related to him and his *pātixšāy*-sons. Legally, he is the son of his mother's *pātixšāy*-husband to whom he owes allegiance and duty. An-

1. B. Hjerrild (1988) p .66.

MHDA 14.9-10

MHDA 35.11-14

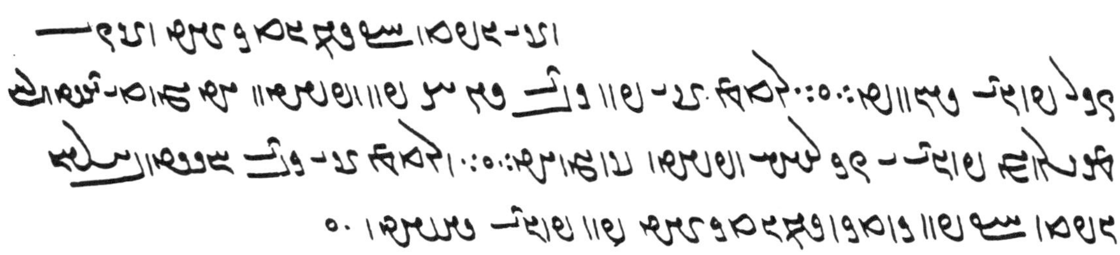

other interesting point in this paragraph is its implication that a guardian must be related to the family. This must surely have been issued at a time when one did not foresee any difficulty in procuring a relation as *sardār*, in contrast to a later age as described in the chapter on *sardārīh*. The same view is given in:

MHDA 14.9-10

pat stūrīh u dūtak-sardārīh pus u duxt ī cakardāt ī ōi kē stūr u dūtak-sardār apāyēt gumārtan nē gumārt.

A *cakar*-born son and daughter of a man who needs to appoint a *stūr* and family guardian cannot be appointed to *stūrīh* and family guardianship.

Here we see the limits to the usefulness of a *cakar*-child towards his *cakar*-father when it comes to the *stūrīh*. The point of view given in this paragraph must be a very strict, conservative one since a *stūr* would not be the direct successor, and anybody might, theoretically at least, be appointed; why then not *cakar*-children? Again, the explanation must be that the union is so tightly bound up with the procuring of heirs that one heir cannot be spared to the *stūrīh*. This strict view reflects the ancient, holy duty to continue the patriarchal line which lies at the root of this type of marriage, whereas the more lenient view, expressed elsewhere, must reflect the more pragmatic and practical view of the day. There does not seem to have been an easy solution to this conflict. The following paragraph is an example of the more pragmatic and "modern" view:

MHDA 35.11-14

- u ān ī guft kū andar dūtak zāt u ān-ic ī cakar frazand bavēt. apāk ān ī pat vas giyāk pat nipišt āvašt ī dastavarān patigrift frazand ī cakarīhā nipišt ēstāt. u apāk ān ī vas ōstavārān guft kū pat kartak andar dūtak zāt pat frazand dāšt.

And it has been stated: "All those born in the family, including the *cakar*-born, are children of the family." Together with the sentence set down in documents from many places under the seal of the *dastavars*: "He adopted a *cakar*-child." Also the sentence uttered by many men of learning: "A child born in the family was held to be of the family according to legal practice[1]."

We are here presented with a more lenient view of the legal relationship between *cakar*-children and their *cakar*-father[2]. The adoption of *cakar*-children is seen as a legal act, but the inclusion of a *cakar*-child in the family must be legalized, formally, by adoption despite the fact that *cakar*-children were regarded as part of the family in which they grew up. It is evident that opinions as to the legal status of *cakar*-children differ markedly. This must be put down to the fact that there are several different layers in the compilation of the *MHD*. Earlier rulings were not necessarily cut out when new considerations were taken in, and one might easily imagine cases in which the earlier and more strict view would be the one to adhere to, as in the case, for instance, in which a *cakar*-child were the sole heir to his mother's *pātixšāy*-husband. If, in such a case, the child were adopted into his *cakar*-father's family the whole idea behind the institution would be overset.

---

1. F. Shirazi-Mahmoudian (1975) p. 107 interprets this differently; M. Macuch (1976) p. 354 translates *pat kartak* as "in der Regel".

2. B. Hjerrild Carlsen (1984) p. 106.

MHD 48.3-7

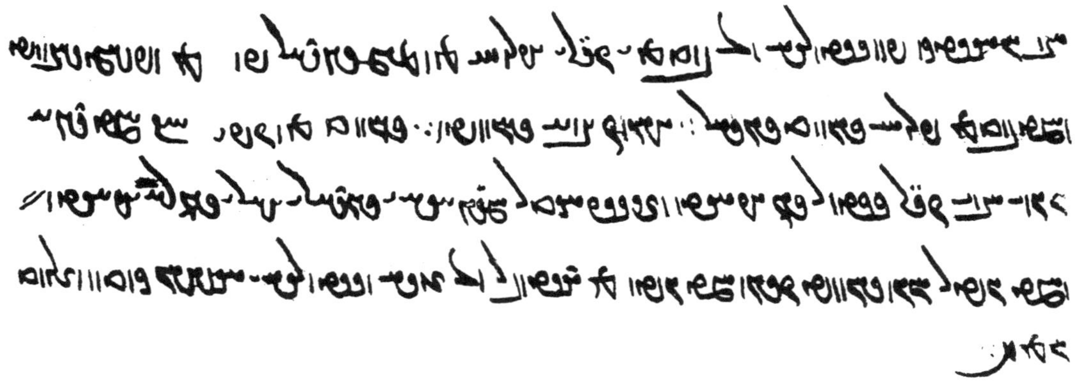

MHD 42.11-14

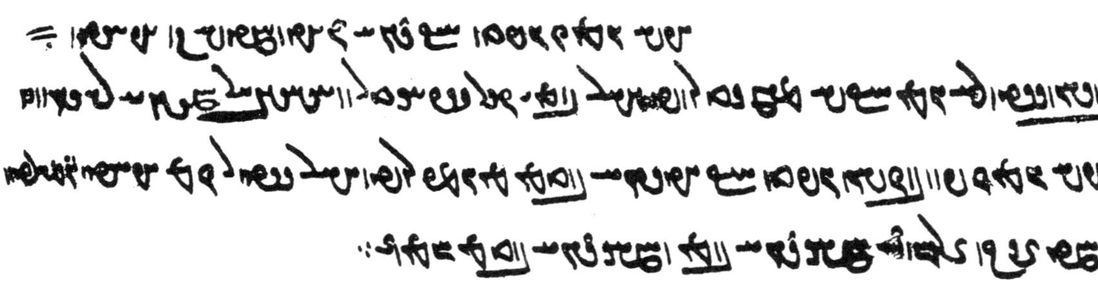

There is evidence in the *MHD* that a *cakar*-father could establish a closer bond with his daughter, as in the following case where he is guardian to the daughter:

MHD 48.3-7

pit xᵛāstak pat stūrīh ō duxt ī cagar (sic) ī apurnāy kē apar-sardār frāc hac xᵛēš dahēt u ka duxt purnāy būt sardār. an-ic mart bavēt. būt kē guft kū ka dātistān ōgōn ī pit ī cagar stūr andar apāyēt u ān sacāktar hamdātistānīh ī sardār ī pas andar nē apāyēt u ka yuttar ōgōn bavēt cigōn ka yuvat hac dastavar ō zanīh u stūrīh ī kas-ān kartan šūt hē.

About a case in which a father leaves his property in *stūrīh* to his minor *cakar*-daughter to whom he is guardian, and when coming of age she is given another guardian, the following has been stated: "If the legal decision has it that the *cakar*-father needs a *stūr* and the daughter is the most suitable, then the consent of her later guardian is not needed. If it is different, it will be as if she had married without authorization, and had become *stūr* of some other person".

In this case, the *pātixšāy*-father evidently transferred the guardianship of his daughter to her *cakar*-father. This may have been because he himself would be sure of having heirs, or, alternatively, that he found it difficult to perform his duties as guardian as the daughter was not living in his house. The *cakar*-father had provided for his daughter by instituting the *stūrīh* for her. The new guardian may have been given her because the *cakar*-father had grown old or ill, or she may have been married in a *pātixšāy*-marriage that would automatically make her husband her guardian.
Whatever the reason, the guardian's consent was not needed if the *cakar*-father happened to be in need of a *stūr*. When he has left her his property, and she is fit to undertake the duty there will be no impediments to her taking on the *stūrīh* and the property entering into a marriage in which she would produce the desired heir, according to, at least, one jurist's opinion. The meaning of the last sentence, however, is doubtful. In my reading of the sentence, *ka yuttar* ("if it is different") is taken as a parallel to *ka dātistān* ("if the legal decision is so") which I interpret thus: When there is no legal decision that the *cakar*-father needs a *stūr*, the daughter's taking on of the *stūrīh* and entering into marriage is useless, since it is not legal: The *stūrīh* is not hers.
It is evident from this paragraph that the authorities must approve and confirm a *cakar*-child's incorporation in the *stūrīh*-institution. The paragraph also tells us something about the position of the *cakar*-daughter. A *pātixšāy*-daughter would not have to submit to legal decisions about her right to take *stūrīh* or *ayōkēnīh* for her father, so once more we are presented with the fact that the relationship between *cakar*-fathers and -children is open to interpretations of various kinds.

MHD 42.11-14

u-š ēn-ic guft kū dātistān duxt ka-š ō apāyēt xᵛāst u nē ēn kū-š apar manēt pas pus ī cakar sacāktar u Vayayār hamdātistān nē būt u-š ēn-ic pat Bōzišn guft kū hakar dātistān duxt tis-ic nēst pas stūr cim apāyēt gumārtan ka ān ō zāyēnd hamāk dātistān pus u hamāk dātistān duxt hēnd.

And he (*Rāt-Ohrmazd*) has also said this: "If a lawful daughter ought to claim it (*stūrīh*), and this (shall) not (be) that she inherits it, then a *cakar*-son is more

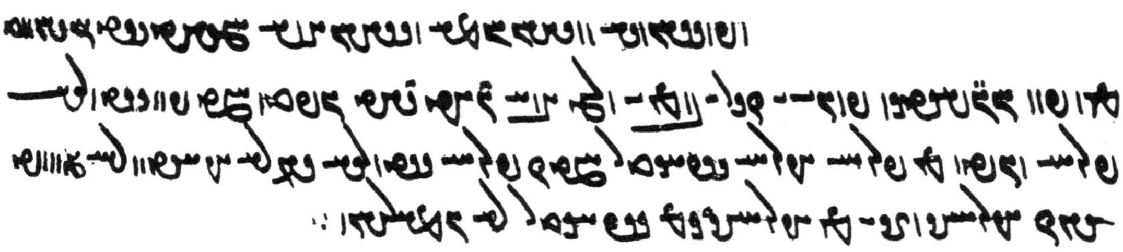

suitable", but *Vayayār* did not agree with this, and also said this following *Bōzišn*[1]: "Also if there is nothing for the lawful daughter, then there is good reason to appoint her as *stūr*, because those who are born to him are all lawful sons and lawful daughters."[2]

Here we have yet more evidence of the conflicting views on *cakar*-offspring. *Rāt-Ohrmazd* stresses the importance of the *cakar*-son, because if the daughter is not approved as *stūr* or for some reason is not suitable, the *cakar*-son will be a better choice. *Vayayār* is opposed to the idea of using the *cakar*-son because, he argues, if there is a daughter of the *pātixšāy* kind, there is no need to look elsewhere. The daughter is the obvious choice as, in accordance with all other laws, she will be either *ayōkēn* or *stūr* to her father depending on the way the guardianship has been arranged.

The choice of possible successors must have been extremely difficult in the case when no *pātixšāy*-son existed, and we must assume that practice varied, and that every candidate was subjected to careful scrutiny. Sasanian law seems both pragmatic and practical in that different legal interpretations co-existed with a view to finding the best possible solution in each individual case.

As a further illustration of the difficulties surrounding the choice of successor, let us turn to:

MHD 41.5-8

u Pusānvēh u Vēh-Ohrmazd u Siyāvaxš hamdātistān būt kē[3] pat hangōšītak frazand ī cakar ī pus ī ōi mart duxt dāt guft ka pat stūrīh purnāy apurnāy sacāktar ka-c purnāy stūrīh andar nē apāyītan rād gōbēt adak-ic apurnāyīk u ān ī hac apurnāyīk kam sacāktar nē gumārišn.

Pusānvēh, Vēh-Ohrmazd, and *Siyāvaxš* all agree that the *cakar*-child of this man's son and the daughter's child are equally suitable as *stūrs,* but the one who is of age shall be appointed, and if not he, the most suitable child who is not of age; if he who is of age says about the *stūrīh* that he does not need it, then he who is not of age shall be appointed and not a person who is less suitable than him.

Here are two interesting points; the first one is the fact that the choice of *stūr* is most important, so possible candidates must be examined thoroughly. It is, in fact, so vital to find the right person that it is deemed better to choose a person who is not of age rather than a less suitable grown-up. What features constitute suitability? Well, this is indeed an open question, but I suggest that suitability rests on two basic features, viz. family bonds and mental and physical health. The candidates mentioned here are both of the same blood as the person who needs a *stūr,* which indicates that blood relations are more suitable than are those who are not related by blood. It is, of course, essential that a *stūr* should be healthy and in possession of all his faculties since he is going to administer part of the family fortune and produce an heir.

1. All three jurists. *Bōzišn* mentioned in *MHD 40.3, 49.10, 76.8.*
2. Cf. M. Macuch (1993) p. 340; F. Schirasi-Mahmoudian (1975) p. 56.
3. M. Macuch (1993) p. 315 divides the sentences differently, but there is no punctuation here in the Ms. Therefore I take *kē* as referring to the three jurists mentioned.

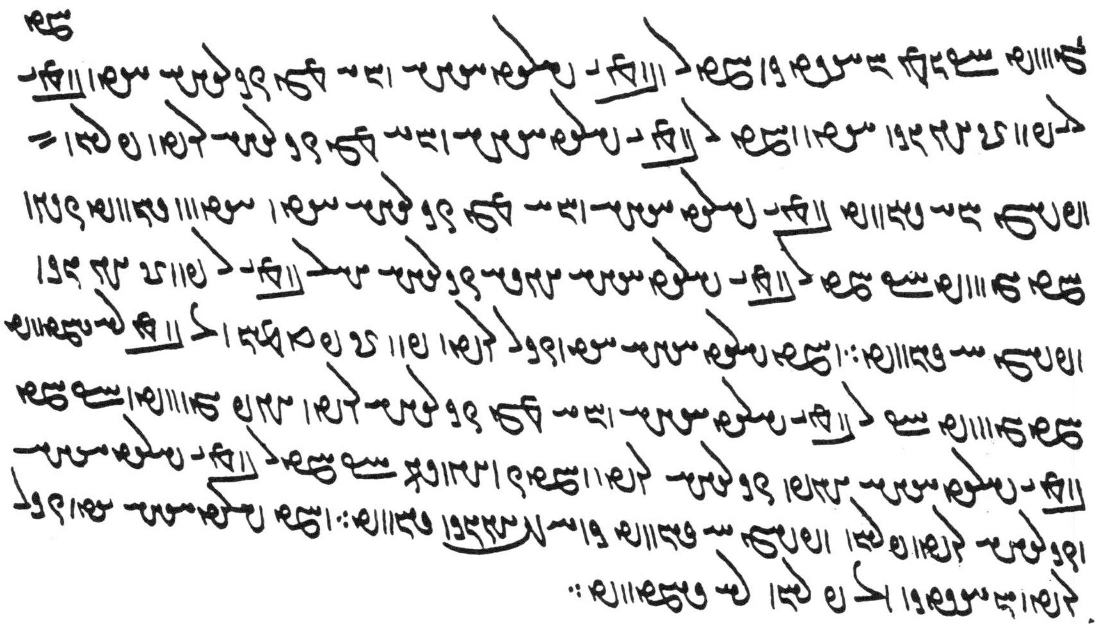

The second point of interest is the fact that the offspring of the *pātixšāy-* daughter and the *cakar*-child of the *pātixšāy*-son are regarded as equally eligible as *stūr* of their grandfather.

There are several references to children of *pātixšāy*-daughters elsewhere as, for instance, in the chapter on *ayōkēnīh* in which an obligation towards the maternal grandfather seems to be established, but the case of the *cakar*-child of the *pātixšāy*-son is somewhat different inasmuch as the *cakar*-child has no legitimate family ties with the grandfather. Undertaking of the *stūrīh* would mean that the *cakar*-child would beget sons who would be successors to the *stūrīh*-property of his grandfather. The successor would thus be great-grandchild of the man he succeeded; yet another example of the fact that *cakar*-children were felt to belong to their biological father's family.

MHDA 23.17 – 24.9

ka gōbēt kū ēn x^{v}āstak ka man u pus ī pātixšāyīhā u ē cē cakarīhā hast pus ī man ī pat ān aivēnak hast u ka man pus ī pātixšāyīhā u ē cē cakarīhā nēst Farrax^v x^{v}ēš ē bavēt pus ī pātixšāyīhā u ē cē cakarīhā hast ētōn bavēt cigōn ka gōbēt kū ka man pus ī pātixšāyīhā ēnyā cakarīhā pas pus ī man pat ān aivēnak hast x^{v}ēš ē bavēt. u ka pātixšāyīhā hast u cakar nēst pat ān patmān ō pus nē rasēt ka gōbēt kū man pus ī pātixšāyīhā u ē cē cakarīhā nēst aivap gōbēt kū ka pus ī pātixšāyīhā aivap cakarīhā nēst u ka-c kunēt kū ka man pus ī pātixšāyīhā u cakarīhā nēst Farrax^v x^{v}ēš (ē)[1] bavēt har 2 aivēnak bavēt. u ka pātixšāyīhā hast u cakar nēst x^{v}āstak ō Farrax^v nē rasēt.

When a man says: "If I have a *pātixšāy*-son as well as a *cakar*-son, this property (shall be given) to my sons who are such, and if I do not have a *pātixšāy*-son as well as a *cakar*-son, the property shall then go as personal property to *Farrax^v*." If there are both a *pātixšāy*-son and a *cakar*-son, it will be the same as if he said: "If I have a *pātixšāy*-son and also a *cakar*-son, then the property shall be theirs when my sons are thus". But if he has a *pātixšāy*-son, but no *cakar*-son, then the property will not go to this son because of the contract (*24.6*). If he says: "If I do not have a *pātixšāy*-son and neither a *cakar*-son", or if he says: "If I do not have a *pātixšāy*-son nor a *cakar*-son", and he also declares: "If I do not have a *pātixšāy*-son and not a *cakar*-son it will be *Farrax^v*'s property". Both forms mean the same. If there is a *pātixšāy*-son and not a *cakar*-son, then the property will not go to *Farrax^v*.

The context of this passage is concerned with the various formulas employed in contracts and deeds. It is used as an example to show how careful the phrasing of a deed must be in order to ensure that the intention of the testator is carried out. The first part of the paragraph shows a phrasing that will mean that the property goes to *Farrax^v*, a fictitious name often used in examples, if only one of the two types of sons exists. The next part is phrased differently, so that *Farrax^v* will get the property if only a *cakar*-son exists, but not if there is a *pātixšāy*-son, too. The various interpretations of the deed turn on the different use of conjunctions.

Although the passage is used as an illustration of the importance of the wording of legal deeds, it, nevertheless, yields certain information, as the example would certainly be in accordance with actual rules. It seems, however, a bit far-fetched that property should go to the sons only provided there were two kinds of these, and

---

1. Inserted by M. Macuch (1976) p. 90.

MHD 28.5-9

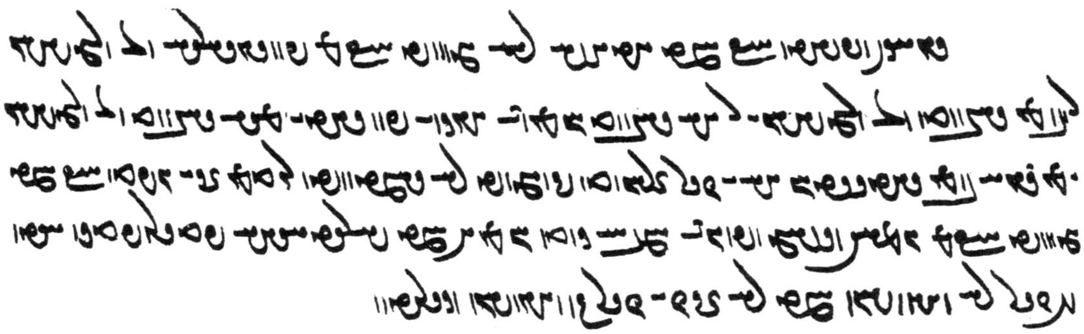

MHDA 4.13-14

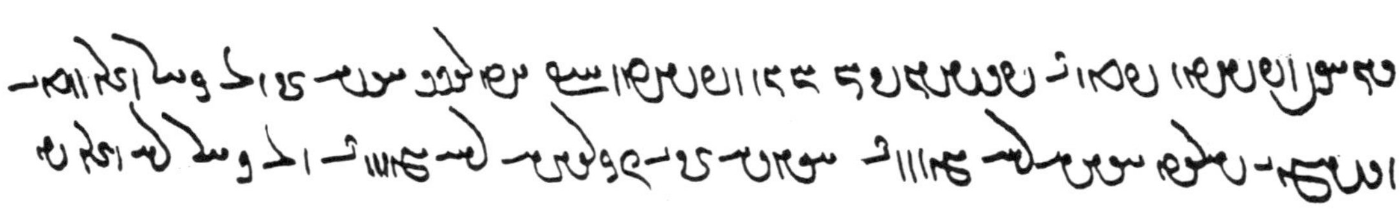

otherwise go to a third person. My suggestion is that the first part of the ruling (until *24.6*) is there to show how such a contract should not be done, how it would not carry out testator's wishes, whereas the correct phrasing follows after *24.6*, namely that testator wishes that his property should come to his *pātixšāy*-son, if there is one, independent of the existence of a *cakar*-son. However, if he has a *cakar*-son as well, the latter will share the property with the former. Only if no *pātixšāy*-son exists will the property go to *Farrax*[v], even if there is a *cakar*-son.
The very fact that such a fictitious case is being presented throws a certain light on the relationship between *pātixšāy*- and *cakar*-children. As we have seen, a *cakar*-son is rated lower than a *pātixšāy*-son, but is nevertheless regarded as a member of his *cakar*-father's family. Even though he is not entitled to a portion by law, his father may nevertheless decide to let him inherit the property in common with his *pātixšāy*-brother; the two of them will then hold the property as partners, in *hambāyīh*. A *cakar*-father might thus provide for his son; a necessary provision in cases where the son's *pātixšāy*-father did not leave him very much.
The status of *cakar*-children in their native family is further elucidated in:

MHD 28.5-9

giyāk 1 nipišt kū ka ātaxš rād gōbēt kū-m pat sardārīh ō ōi-šān man pus dāt ō ōi-šān ī man brāt dāt hēnd ēvak-ī pat dāt mas dāt ō ōi-šān ī hac dātistān pus dātistān brāt ī cakar zāt ēstēt nē rasēt apāk anī guft kū ka gōbēt kū-m yumē zan u frazand hambāy kart hē ka pātixšāyīhā patigriftak hast 2 cakar nē kunišn ka nē ān-ic ī cakar ō kunišn nikērītan.

In one place it is written: "If a person declares concerning a fire[1]: 'I have given it in guardianship to the eldest child of my sons and brothers', then it will not go to the *cakar*-born of the lawful sons and lawful brothers"; together (with this) another has said: "You are made partner by me together with wife and children", if there are two sons, a *pātixšāy* and an adopted son, a *cakar*-son ought not to be made (partner); if there are not the *cakar*-son may also be considered as partner.

The *cakar*-son could not be made guardian of the family fire (hearth), since he did not belong to this family. In this matter of the guardianship of the family fire, the holiest symbol of the continuity of the father's family line, opinions are unanimous. This task could only be entrusted to somebody with no other obligation, and who could be expected to stay within the family. Here we are dealing with the spiritual welfare of the family in contrast to the more worldly aspects of the life of the family in which a *cakar*-son might be considered as a possible partner, although an adopted son would have preference.
The difference between *pātixšāy* and *cakar* in the matter of disobedience is revealed in

MHDA 4.13-14

giyāk 1 nipišt patva(n)d pēšēnīkān ōgōn nipišt kū atarsakāyīh ān ō kār šut ī zan ī pātixšāyīhā rād gōbēnd adak-iš ān ī cakarīhā rād gōbēnd ō kār nē šavēt.

1. J.P. de Menasce (1964) p. 12.

MHDA 7.17 – 8.2

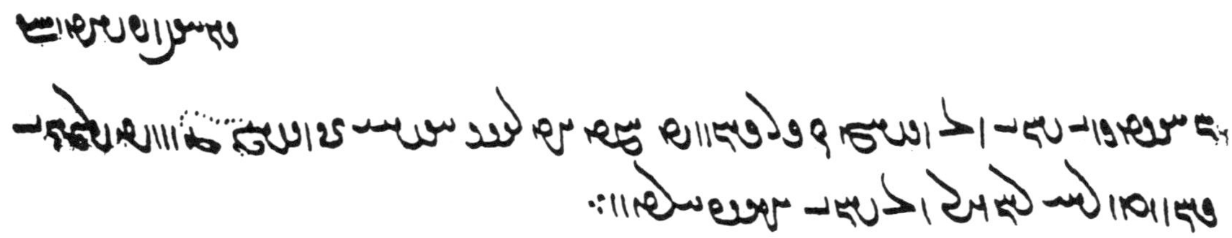

MHD 32.1-4

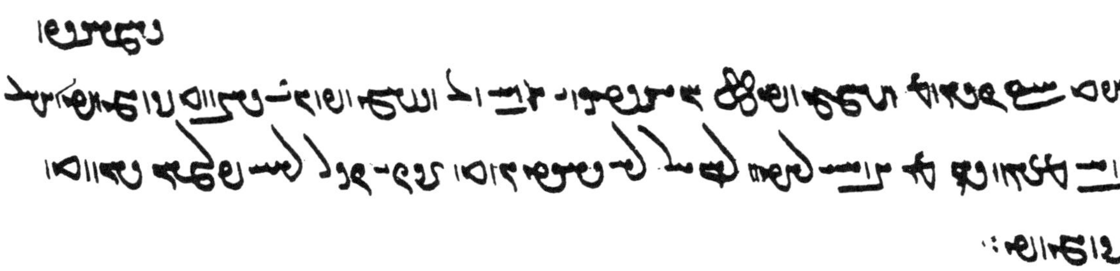

It is written: "The precedent (jurists) wrote about disobedience in relationships: The term disobedience may be used in connection with a *pātixšāy*-wife, but in connection with a *cakar*-wife the term cannot be used[1]."

The obedience in question is that which is owed to the lord of the house who is also guardian of the family, and which we find specified in detail in *MHDA 5.6-8*: It is the duty of a *pātixšāy*-wife to do the good works her husband asks her to do, and to refrain from doing that which he forbids her to do, and never to deny him her bed. *Pātixšāy*-sons are considered disobedient if they say they will not be sons of their father, and not fulfil their duty towards him.

It is interesting to note that the rule is said to have been written by the ancients, thus indicating that by the time of the compilation of the *MHD* such notions of disobedience were considered old-fashioned. The meaning, however, is quite clear; since the only obligation of the *cakar*-wife is towards her *pātixšāy*-husband, he must be the one to whom she owes obedience, except in the sexual relationship. In this, she owes obedience to her *cakar*-husband. *Cakar*-children are not mentioned here presumably because disobedience of children is only seen in relation to their *pātixšāy*-fathers.

It is no wonder that the texts show conflicting views regarding the notion of obedience of *cakar*-wives. They lived, after all, in their *cakar*-husband's family and were part of his household, and could thus create havoc in the family if they were allowed to do as they pleased. This may be the reason behind the different viewpoint, expressed in:

MHDA 7.17 - 8.2

giyāk 1 nipišt kū x^{v}āstak ī šōd ō zan ī cakar dahēt ka atarsakāyīh ī ān zan gōbēt framān ī būt rād apāc ō šōd apispārtan.

In one place it is written: "The property which the husband gives to his *cakar*-wife must be handed back to the husband in case he declares the wife disobedient in accordance with the accepted settlement."

Here the notion of disobedience is applied to the *cakar*-wife, and the text reveals the fact that the *cakar*-wife was accepted as an integrated member of the family. The *cakar*-husband would never hand over property to a person who was not felt to belong to his household. The *cakar*-wife then is securely rooted in the family, but at the expense of her independence: She had to bow to her husband's wishes and commands. The gift was given her on condition she behave according to a certain set of rules.

Even if wives behaved well, it was possible for a husband to retract a promise of a gift:

MHD 32.1-4

Jāmāsp guft kū cigōn-am āšnavēt x^{v}āstak ī mart ō zan u frazand dāt ēstēt u pas bē frōšēt hac mart ī rāt apāc nē āvurt ān-ic ī cakar rād framān būt ēstēt.

Jāmāsp[2] said: "I have heard it said that: A man's property which he has (previously) given to his wife and children, but later sells does not have to be

---

1. See M. Macuch (1976) p. 165, 191.

2. A jurist.

MHD 32.16 – 33.1

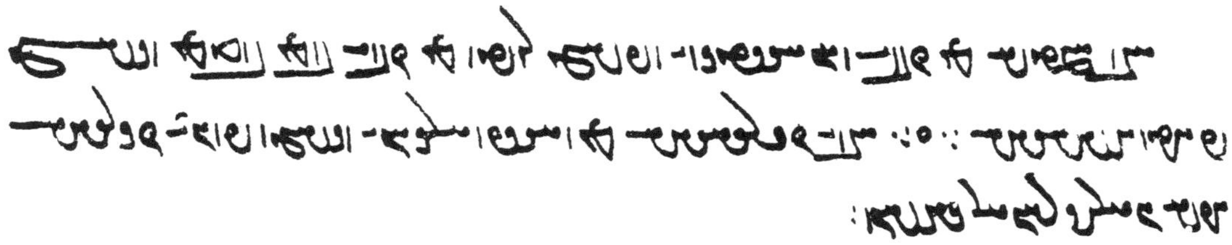

MHD 32.15

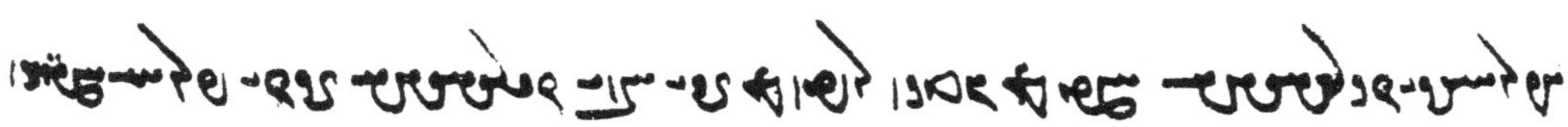

replaced by him; this applies also to a gift made over to a *cakar*-wife and -children."

This ruling must have been made in order to protect the head of a family, in case he needed money badly. The individual members of the household possessed their own fortunes, but the head of the family, as guardian, was responsible for the administration of the property, and the upkeep of the family, so it was possible to retract a gift if necessary.
That the protection of the head of a family might be carried further can be seen from the following passage:

MHD 32.16 – 33.1

pit ka-š hac hīr[ī] u x^{v}āstak ī x^{v}ēš nēst hac hīr ī pus duxt zan pātixšāyīhā. pit ī cakarī[hī]hā hac vāspuhrakān ī zan u frazand cakarīhā u-š gōhrīk apāc dahišn.

If a father has no wealth and property of his own, (he shall be supported) out of the wealth of his *pātixšāy*-son, -daughter, or -wife. A *cakar*-father shall be given part of the inheritance of his *cakar*-wife and -children, and a remuneration ought to be given back by him.

Thus, it is settled in the law that family members are mutually responsible for the upkeep of the family. In the case where a man's *pātixšāy*-wife and -children are to provide for him, he will not be asked to pay anything back. Since they were each other's heirs, they are financially bound together despite their separate fortunes. But in case his *cakar*-wife or -children are obliged to provide for him out of the wife's *pātixšāy*-husband's estate he must be ready to pay the money back. The reason for this clause is that no financial bonds exist between *cakar*-wife and -husband; he is not her guardian, and they do not inherit each other, so the money she gives him must be considered as a loan.
In the chapter on the nourishment and maintenance of the body, *MHD 32.15*, we find a brief reference to *cakar*-children:

MHD 32.15

apurnāyīk ī cakarī[hī]hā ka hac dūtak nēst hac ān ī pit cakarī[hī]hā ān-ic ī purnāy hamgōnak.

If there is no payment from his family for the upkeep of a *cakar*-child under age, then his *cakar*-father must pay for him; the same applies for a child who has reached his majority.

So, *cakar*-children must be clothed and fed by their *cakar*-father if their *pātixšāy*-father is unable to support them. This explains why *cakar*-fathers are sometimes eager to convert these children into *pātixšāy*. If a man has fathered children as heirs to another man who turns out not to be able to pay for the raising of the children, let alone leave them anything after his death, it is understandable that the *cakar*-father who by law is obliged to provide for them would want them to become his *pātixšāy*-children in order to acquire some compensation for his endeavours.

There is evidence that the *cakar*-marriage may be put to a different use:

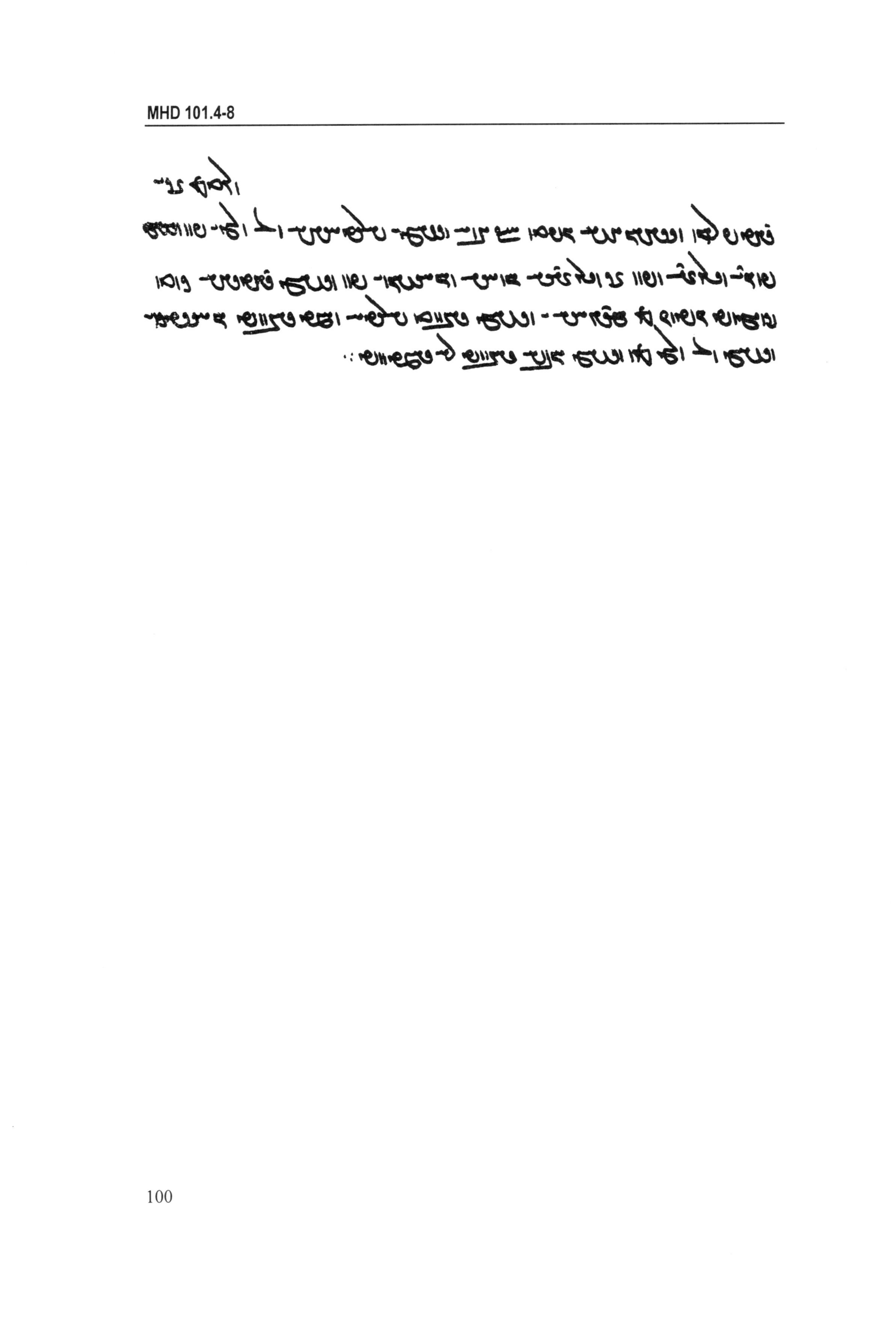

[illegible]

[illegible]

[illegible]

[illegible]

[illegible]

MHD 101.4-8

u apāk ān ī Dātfarroxᵛ u Siyāvaxš guft kū mart zan ī pātixšāyīhā ō ōi ī pat[1] frazand niruzd u pat ān niruzdīh avinās u xᵛahišn ī pat zan dātīhā kart ēstēt yūt hac hamdātistānīh ī zan dāt pātixšāy u ka dahēt xᵛāstak ī zan ō ōi kē zan aviš dahēt nē raset[2].

The following was said by *Dātfarroxᵛ* and *Siyāvaxš*: "A man is authorised to give away his *pātixšāy*-wife without her consent to one who is in trouble because of his children, and is not himself to blame for the need (situation), if he has declared his wish in the correct manner to his wife; and if he gives her away, her property will not go to him to whom he gives away his wife."

Here is a case in which the wife is given away not to attend to her *pātixšāy*-husband's need of heirs, but to attend to the needs of another man. As any potential children of this new union would belong to the *pātixšāy*-husband, the reason cannot be that the man needs an heir, but rather that he needs a woman to govern his household and care for his children. The stipulation about her property indicates that the union in question must be a *cakar*-union. The new husband has no right over her possessions, but the text does not mention the question of *sardārīh*. From other paragraphs dealing with this problem we know that a *pātixšāy*-husband would dissolve his guardianship over his wife when she was about to enter into a *cakar*-marriage, and she would become her own guardian and as such take over the management of her own affairs. This may be the implication of the last clause in the paragraph.

It is noteworthy that a husband can give away his wife without her consent to another man with the only stipulation that it should be done in a formally correct manner. Superficially, this looks like an expression of charity towards the poor man who is in bad need of a woman in his household, and who, for some reason, has not been able to ally himself in a *pātixšāy*-marriage. He gets a manager of his household without having to pay for it, and one, furthermore, who has no claim on the family fortune. She is obliged to leave a home in which she held a respected position as *pātixšāy*-wife, and will now be more or less at the mercy of her new cohabiter. He will have no authority over her financially, but she will have nowhere else to go if the situation should become intolerable. The husband who gave her away may have done so because he found her no longer attractive, and did not want her in his house any more as a possible source of trouble if he was about to contract a new marriage. It rather seems as if this rule offered the opportunity for a man to get rid of an unwanted wife as long as he could find a home for her somewhere. Seen from the point of view of the wife it looks very much like a poor exchange; she would be in a much less secure position.

AFS

In the *AFS* the only discussion of the *cakar*-union comes in connection with questions of economy and spiritual benefits. We find no definition of the term, and we

---

1. In the Ms *NYSH* (*zan*) is deleted with a stroke. M. Macuch (1993) p. 614 retains the word.

2. C. Bartholomae (1918) p. 29, 36.

LXXI

[illegible] [1] ⁖ [2]

1. [illegible]

[illegible] [1] ⁖ [2]

2. [illegible]

LXXI 1. Written with red ink in TD_2. 2. TD_2 omits. 3. TD_2 [illegible]; G [illegible]. 4. TD_2 [illegible]. 5. G adds [illegible]. 6 Thus TD_2; for [illegible] (?); G torn. 7. Thus TD_2; for [illegible] (?); G torn. 8. G omits. 9. Thus TD_2; better [illegible]. 10. Thus TD_2; for [illegible]. 11. TD_2 [illegible]. 12. TD_2 adds ⁖. 13. For [illegible].

may therefore assume that other laws existed and that the rules applicable to the union were sought there.
One passage is concerned with inheritance:

AFS 71.1-2

pursišn 1:
mart-ē kē-š pus[1] ē purnāy būt u-š xᵛāstakīhā būt frāc ravēt[2] [tan][3] pit pus-ē ī cakarīhā būt u-š pat stūrīh patīriftak dāšt[an] u pas pat ān ēcand frāc ravēt ēn kū xᵛāstak ī pitar ō dūtak ī ān pus kē pēš hac pitar raft šavēt aivap nē u hakar šavēt cand šavēt.

passaxᵛ 2:
xᵛāstak ī pitar u nēm apar ān-ē dahišnēh ī dūtak ī pus apazūtan u nēm ō ān ī pus ī patīriftak [u] dātan.

Question 1:
There was a man who had a son who had reached his majority, and he also had some property; but the son died. His father had a *cakar*-son whom he had adopted as *stūr*. Later the father dies. The question then is this: Does the property of the father go to the family of the son who died before the father or not? And if it does, then how much of it?

Answer 2:
Half of the father's property shall be added to that of the son's family, and half shall be given to the adopted son.

The purpose of the paragraph is to make clear the question of the sharing of inheritance, and the point made here is that even if the son predeceases his father he is still his heir. His share of the inheritance will be added to the share his family has already had. Another interesting point is that in the *AFS* there seems to be no doubt about the *cakar*-father's right to adopt his *cakar*-son; the fact that he is adopted in *stūrīh* is yet another proof that adoption and *stūrīh* were regarded as more or less the same in the minority Zoroastrian societies. It is evident from the above passage that the adopted son had the same hereditary right as the *pātixšāy*-son, since they had equal shares, i.e. he did not just become a *stūr* with the former limited advantages of this status, but he acquired the full *pātixšāy*-status.

The next paragraph in the *AFS* about *cakar* is concerned with the rights of the *cakar*-wife:

AFS 73.1-2

pursišn 1:
zan-ē ī cakar kē-š pus-ē ī purnāy hast ka yūt hac dastavarīh u ākāsīh ī pusar šōd kunēt šāyēt aivap nē?

---

1. B.T. Anklesaria (1969) emendit to *pus*. *BRTH* must be *BRH*, as will be seen from the words following.
2. B.T. Anklesaria (1969) emendit to *raft*.
3. B.T. Anklesaria (1969) omits *tan*.

LXXIII

[illegible]

[illegible] 1
[illegible]
[illegible]

[illegible] 2.
[illegible]
[illegible]
[illegible]
[illegible]

[illegible]
[illegible]
[illegible]
[illegible]
[illegible]

LXXIII 1. *Written with red ink in* TD_2. 2. TD_2 *omits*. 3. G [illegible]. 4. *Added in* TD_2 *above* [illegible]. 5. *Thus* TD_2; G [illegible]. . 6. TD_2 [illegible]. 7. G [illegible]...... . 8. G ...[illegible]. 9. G [illegible].... . 10. G [illegible]. 11 TD_2 [illegible].

12. G [illegible]. 13. G [illegible]. 14. G [illegible]. 15. *Thus both*. 16. G [illegible]; TD_2 [illegible]. 17. G [illegible]. 18 TD_2 [illegible]

passax[v] *2:*
pat cāštak ī Pēšaksīr ētōn cāšt kū Aparag guft hē. cakar ka yūt hac dastavarīh ī dūtak sardār šōd kunēt aš cagarīhā zanīh xūp bavēt. yā ahmāi vīsat[1]. Dātfarrox[v] Vehšāpōhr guft hē nē xūp bavēt bē-šān nē šāyēt ē rād vicīrīnītan cigōn Aparag pat xūpīh vicīrīnēt adak ōi-šān pat nē xūpīh apastāk gukāhīh nē āvurt. cigōn ka ān nē xūpīh ān-šān guft bahr statan ī ān cim rād hāh adak-iš andar gātār griftan ī ētōn kū bahr ī dūtak nē barēt vinās dōšišnēh ē hangārīh nēst.

Question 1:
There is a *cakar*-wife who has a son who is of age; if, without the permission and knowledge of her son she takes a husband, is she allowed to do this or not?

Answer 2:
In the Teaching of *Pēšakšīr*[2] it is set down that *Aparag*[3] said: "If a *cakar* (-wife) takes a husband without the authority of the family guardian, then a *cakar*-marriage will be (considered) proper, 'she who sees for herself'[4]. To this *Dātfarrox*[v5] and *Vaxšāpōhr*[6] answered: "It is not proper"; since *Aparag* declares the marriage proper, they cannot maintain this point of view as they did not produce evidence from the *Avesta*. The reason why they said it was not proper might be that it meant taking away part of the estate. But a love relationship in which one chooses a partner in a way which does not imply a diminishing of the family fortune cannot be called sinful.

The question under discussion is whether a *cakar*-wife has the right to choose a husband for herself[7]. We may safely assume that the *cakar*-marriage in question is a second marriage for the woman, and that she was bound to her *pātixšāy*-husband. The latter must be dead, and her *cakar*-marriage must have been dissolved, either by the death of the husband, or because the contract had expired. She was thus free of any marital bonds, and could look around for a new husband, so she chose for herself a husband/lover, a *gātār*; this type of marriage is perfectly legal, as corroborated by the first statement in the paragraph here. The *MHD* and the *AFS* differ in that this self-chosen marriage in the *AFS* falls under the category of *cakar*, whereas in the *MHD* it calls for a special kind of contract, as shown in the chapter on *sardārīh*. The fact that the alternative view of *Dātfarrox*[v] and *Vaxšāpōhr* is presented to the reader with an explanation is highly revealing.
Nowhere in the holy law texts is it set down that a *cakar*-wife might not enter a marriage without the family guardian's authorisation, when she had produced the heir for her *pātixšāy*-husband. The simple explanation of this fact is that on entering into a *cakar*-marriage a woman became her own guardian; the jurists behind

---

1. Avestan expression.
2. A jurist who was head of a school of law. He is mentioned in *MHD 42.17, 50.17, 61.9*, and in *MHDA 11.10, 26.11*.
3. A jurist who founded a law school. He is often mentioned in the *MHD*.
4. The Avestan quotation by *Aparag* corroborates the validity of the marriage. See also G. Klingenschmitt (1971) p. 114.
5. A jurist known from *MHDA 4.15* as the author of the *Pursišn ī Dātfarrox*[v].
6. Mentioned in *MHDA 35.15* as *mōgān-handarzbed*, cf. M. Macuch (1993) p. 14.
7. Cf. B.T. Anklesaria (1969) p. 42 about *cakar*.

LXXVI

[illegible][1] ∴[2]

1. [illegible][3] [illegible]
[illegible]
[illegible] ∴[4]
[illegible][1] ∴[2]

2. [illegible][5] [illegible][3]
[illegible]
[illegible] ∴[2]

LXXVI 1. Written with red ink in TD_2. 2. TD_2 omits. 3. Thus TD_2; G torn. 4. TD_2 omits; G torn. 5. Thus TD_2, for [illegible]; G torn.

the *AFS* therefore have had problems finding a valid explanation. The very idea behind the alterations of these later law texts seems to have been to secure the integrity of the family estates and prevent their being divided, and thereby more vulnerable. One hoped that the family guardian could be relied upon to choose steadfast Zoroastrians as husbands for their wards. On the other hand, it is firmly stated that the contracting of a marriage of the above type would leave the wife's share of the estate locked up; it could not be released, so this problem, at least, would seem to have been solved according to the law. It was obviously felt to be dangerous that a woman could so easily contract a new marriage union for herself; there was a widespread feeling that the control of a family ought to be in one hand that could be relied upon to choose trustworthy husbands for the women of the family.
The rules embodied in the *AFS* are especially concerned with conduct in religious matters, and spiritual rewards, as can be seen from the following paragraphs:

AFS 76.1-2

pursišn 1:
ēn kū frazand cakarīhā kār u kirpak ī kunēt cē ān ī ō pit ī pātixšāyīhā cē ān ō pit ī cakarīhā rasēt pat tan pasēn ō kū šavēt.

passax^v 2:
hakar-iš yūt hac tōmēh pit ī zāyāk ciš andar nēst cahār ēvak hakar x^{v}arišn dārišn hac pit ī zāyāk hac cahār 3 bahr pit ī zāyāk x^{v}ēš bavēt.

Question 1:
The question is the following: When a *cakar*-child performs good deeds and pious duties, which of these will then benefit the *pātixšāy*-father, and which the *cakar*-father? In the future body[1], to whom will they (the good deeds) go?

Answer 2:
If, apart from the fatherhood, the biological father has nothing to do with the child, one fourth will be his; if the biological father provides food and clothing, three parts out of four will belong to the biological father.

This seems sophistic reasoning reminiscent of medieval theological speculations in Europe. But for the Zoroastrian it was of vital importance to store good deeds to ensure an afterlife in paradise, hence the old struggle about the *cakar*-sons. Both fathers had an interest in them, but in the period in which the *MHD* was created all the problems concerning *cakar*-sons were of a worldly kind, basically centred on the question of inheritance. True, the intention behind the *cakar*-institution was to provide a man without sons with an heir in accordance with the Zoroastrian ideal of continuing one's lineage until the resurrection, but we never find theological speculations of the sort we are confronted with here. The present text seems to convey an urgency to ensure for oneself as many good deeds as possible, and it also, apparently, warrants the transferring of these from one person to another. Fulfilment was hoped for in the life hereafter, whereas the actual life on earth had become a struggle for the faith, and for the rights of the Zoroastrian community against the secular power of the state in which they felt themselves to be an outcast minority. Small wonder that they seem to have focused on the life to come.
So being a father, be it biological or legitimate, has an estimated value of one fourth of the son's good deeds. The person who feeds and provides for him during

---

1. *tan(ī)pasēn*. Cf. M. Boyce (1975) I p. 236 note 32.

L XXVIII

[illegible]

1. [illegible]

2. [illegible]

L XXVIII 1. Written with red ink in TD_2. 2. TD_2 omits. 3. G [illegible]. 4. G (torn) [illegible] . . 5. Thus both; for [illegible] = [illegible]. 6. Thus TD_2, for [illegible]; G torn. 7. G (torn) [illegible]. 8. G [illegible]. 9. TD_2 omits; G torn. 10 G [illegible]. 11. TD_2 [illegible]; G (torn) [illegible] . . . .

his upbringing then acquires another two fourths. So, the conclusion must be that the *cakar*-father and the *pātixšāy*-father are on a completely equal footing as to fatherhood. Taken together with the above passage on adoption it becomes evident that the position of the *cakar*-father in relation to his son is a much better one than the one purported by the *MHD*.
Religious questions also crop up in connection with the *cakar*-wife:

AFS 78.1-2

pursišn 1:
mart ē zan ē pat pātixšāyīhā zanīh bē patīrēt u-š apāk[1] nē xᵛafsēt u-š pas pat cagarīhā zanīh ō mart ē dāt ēn kū-š mēnōyīhā ān zan pātixšāyīhā bavēt aivap nē?

passaxᵛ 2:
ka pašt ī pat gōbišn ētōn bavēt aš zanīh būt apāk xuftan nē hamāl cē ka-c apāk nē xuft zan ī pātixšāyīhā bavēt.

Question 1:
A man takes a wife in *pātixšāy*-marriage and does not sleep with her, and later gives her to another man in a *cakar*-marriage. (The question now is) this: Will she be his *pātixšāy*-wife in the spiritual life or not?

Answer 2:
If the oral contract is thus, then her marriage came into being. It is not equal to sleeping with her, because even if he did not sleep with her, she is his *pātixšāy*-wife.

In this passage, we acquire information on two subjects, viz. *cakar* versus *pātixšāy*, and on the importance of the *pātixšāy*-marriage, which is here seen as a bond that transcends death. The marriage bond is forever, and the *pātixšāy*-couple will be together in the eternal, spiritual life. The bond is not broken by the husband's decision to give her to another man in a *cakar*-marriage. The *cakar*-husband will solely enjoy her company in this life. It is interesting to note that consummation of the marriage is not necessary as confirmation of the contract, all the more so in a society in which the greatest religious importance is attached to the procreation of life in general, and to children in particular. The reason might be that the *pātixšāy*-union was regarded as the centre of every family, which in turn constituted the Zoroastrian society, and as such was an institution so indispensable that nothing must be allowed to interfere with its validity.

REA

The *REA* has lengthy discussions of the *cakar*-institution, but without any apparent system or method; nor do we find any attempt at a definition of the phenomenon. It will therefore be necessary to analyse each statement carefully in order to obtain an overall view.
REA 1.5-6 forms part of an answer to *REA 1.1 ff.*, translated in the chapter on *ayōkēnīh* (see below, p. 161):

1. *apāc* emendi to *apāk*.

5 [illegible] [28] [illegible]
[illegible] [29]......

[illegible] [30] [illegible]
[illegible]

6 [illegible]
[illegible] [31] [illegible]
[illegible] [32] [illegible] [33]
[illegible]
[illegible] [34] [illegible]

28. Better [illegible]. 29. Better add [illegible].

30. Better [illegible]. 31. Better [illegible]. 32. For [illegible].
33. Better [illegible]. 34. For [illegible].

REA 1.5-6:

5. u hakar dānēt kū pat pātixšāyīhā zanīh dāštan nē dastavarīhā, u-š pat pātixšāyīhā dārēt, pat giyāk tanāpūhl vinās, u pat sāl drahnāy margarzān.

6. hamē ka bē dānēt kū-š pat pātixšāyīhā zanīh dāštan nē dastavarīhā, u-š pat zanīh apāyišnīk adak-iš zamānīk pat ayōkēnīh ī brāt u cakarīh zanīh zan kunišn. u-š pat ayōkēnīh ī brāt dārišn. hac vinās apparnipišt apēcār.

5. And if he knows that it is not legal to have her in a *pātixšāy*-marriage, and yet he keeps her in such a marriage, he will immediately have committed a *tanāpuhl* (sin), and after a year a *margarzān* (sin).

6. When he knows that it is not legal to have her in *pātixšāy*-marriage, but he needs her for marriage, she should then be made his wife in a *cakar*-marriage for as long as she is *ayōkēn* for her brother. In that case he will be free of the above-mentioned sin.

So, a man is not allowed to keep his wife in a *pātixšāy*-marriage, if she has an obligation towards her father or brother. The present case is further complicated by the fact that he had married her before the said obligation was known to him. In such a case, a change of marriage contract is required immediately or else he, not she, will have committed a grave sin. It is his duty to change the contract, as the man only has it in his power to do so.

It is a remarkable fact that she, as an *ayōkēn*, had to use the *cakar*-marriage contract, i.e. this type of contract in the *REA* is employed as a kind of general contract in cases where the *pātixšāy*-union is out of the question. The explanation lies near at hand. The purpose of both these types of union is to supply a man who is not the biological father with an heir, and in both types of union the husband is not guardian of his wife, and they have no claims on each other's property.

In the *MHD,* there is no mention of the *cakar*-contract being used for other types of union. We have no evidence as to the phrasing of marriage contracts[1], but I believe, as pointed out in the chapter on *sardārīh* that the contracts were made to fit each individual case, more or less, although they must, of course, have followed some general rules. Whether a woman was *ayōkēn* or *cakar,* the words of the contract were presumably more or less identical. The *REA* seems to take the consequences of this, and, as usual, strives to regulate and simplify the law.

Another noticeable difference between the *REA* and the *MHD* is that in the *MHD* we do not find the coupling of the *margarzān* and *tanāpuhl* sins with marriage- and general family legislation. The rules and laws in this field were formed to fit the traditions and needs of the Zoroastrian community, and were extremely flexible and practical. In the *REA*, on the contrary, sins and their punishment are brought forward with much vigour. This would seem to imply that it had become increasingly difficult to impress upon the members of the community the importance of upholding ancient customs without fairly strong inducement. This must have been particularly difficult in the performance of such duties as *ayōkēn* and *cakar*, which did not benefit the performer, but would work towards an eternal life for a man for whom the married couple may not always have cherished the warmest feelings. In other words, natural family bonds and the nation-wide traditions of

---

1. A late form of a contract is preserved (A.D. 1278). See D.N. MacKenzie: "The Model Marriage Contract in Pahlavi", *K.R. Cama Oriental Institute Golden Jubilee Volume*, Bombay 1969, p. 103-12.

[illegible][1]

[illegible] 1
[illegible]
[illegible]
[illegible][2]
[illegible][3]
[illegible] 2 [illegible]
[illegible]
[illegible] 3
[illegible]

[illegible][5]
[illegible][6]
[illegible] 4 [illegible]
[illegible]
[illegible][4]
[illegible]
[illegible]

1. Written with red ink. 2. For [illegible]. 3. For [illegible].
4. For [illegible]. 5. For [illegible]. 6. For [illegible].

the Sasanian Empire had weakened considerably. It had become necessary to adopt strong measures against those who violated tradition, to counteract the beginning dissolution of the families and thereby the whole community.

Question 7, which is presented as a case study, includes the answers to several questions. It will be necessary to present the greater part of the text in order to illuminate and understand the references to *cakar*.

REA 7.1-4, 6-8, 11-12:

pursišn 1:
mart ē kē-š zan ē ī pātixšāy bavēt. mart vitīrān bavēt. u pat handarznāmak gōbēt. kū. ēn zan hac zanīh u stūrīh man apēcār. hac ān xᵛāstak kē-š bē ō pātixšāy ī im mart burt būt, apāc[1] im zan dātan framāyēt[2].

2. im mart cigōn ān ī apparnipišt vinās ī ōh būn bavēt aivap nē?

3. u hakar zan pas hac bē vitīrišnīh ī mart gōbēt kū, man nē dānist kū pat handarznāmak cē nipišt ēstēt. hakar sardārīh apāc nē patīrēt u hac sardārīh ī im mart bē nē ēstēt. adak pātixšāy bavēt aivap nē?

4. u hakar mart pat handarznāmak bahr ī hac xᵛāstak ī xᵛēš pat ahlavdāt bē kas ē dahēt zan hakar cakar bavēt ciš-ic duš-patkārišnīh pat-iš kartan šāyēt aivap nē?

passaxᵛ 6:
u pat gōbišnīh mart zan hac zanīh ī im mart hilēt, nē bavēt. ka-š avināsīhā u akāmakīhā hac zanīh hilēt. ka-c ziyānak pat-iš xᵛansand. adak-iš vinās bavēt pādak tanāpuhl.

7. ka-c zivandak, aivap ka-c frāc hac šōd ziyānak pat hištārīh hamdātistān nē bavēt. adak-iš dātistān ēn kū pat pātixšāyīhā zanīh ī im mart ēstēt.

8. xᵛāstak ī andar dārišnīh ī ziyānak. bē hakar andar ....[3] pat zanīh an, pašn u astišn apar xᵛāstak ī kart ēstēt. ān rād yuttar. ēnyā-š pat dūtak ī šōd ī pātixšāyīhā dārišn.

11. u hakar zan ī cakar adak-iš frāc hac xᵛēš pat apēcārīh ī zan ī cakar hac-iš gōbišn ē nē hamē apāyēt. cē-š xᵛat hac-iš apēcārī(h).

12. bē hakar-šān pašn ē u astišn ē miyān hast adak-iš zan ī cakar ka šōd cakar hac āvām šut adak-iš sardārīh ī pat patkārišn ī ō xᵛāstak hac hišt ī šōd cakar nēst nē-c ō xᵛarišn u dārišn ī hac šōd hišt cakar.

Question 1:
A man who has a *pātixšāy*-wife is passing away, and in his will he says: "This woman is now free of any marriage bond and *stūrīh* towards me". As to the property she brought into the *pātixšāy*-marriage with this man, he orders that it be given back to his wife.

2. Has this man, accordingly, committed a sin that will affect his spiritual stock of good deeds, or not?

---

1. *apāk* emendi to *apāc*.
2. N. Safa-Isfehani (1980) p. 46 emendit to *frāmōšēd*.
3. Ms: *wspwtn'*.

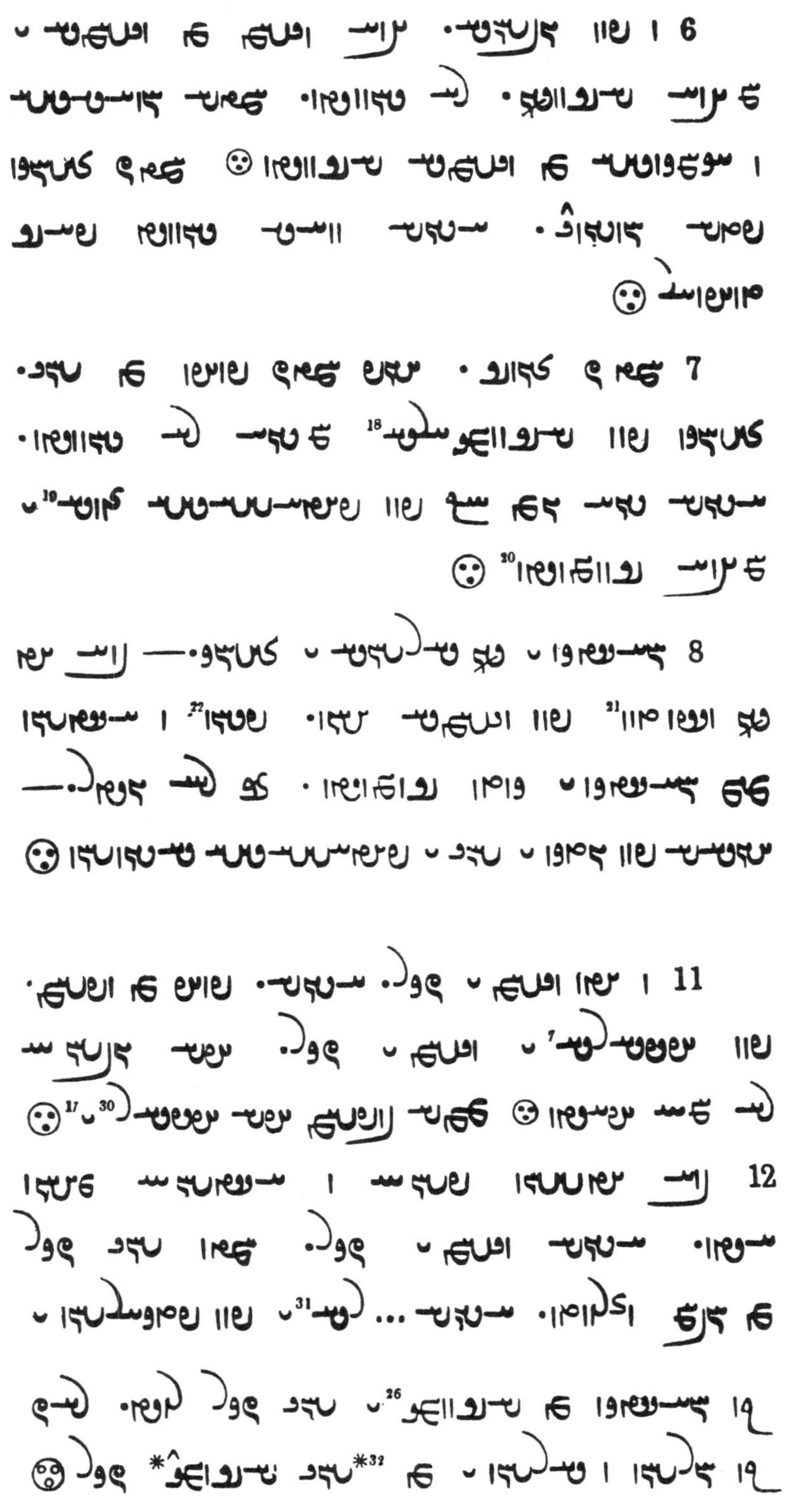

18. For [Pahlavi]. 19. Better [Pahlavi].

20. Better [Pahlavi]. 21. For [Pahlavi] (?). 22. For [Pahlavi].

30. For [Pahlavi]. 31. For [Pahlavi]. 32. ** Better [Pahlavi].

3. Further, if the wife, after the death of her husband, says: "I did not know the terms of the will"; if she does not renounce the guardianship, and does not reject guardianship from this man, will she then be *pātixšāy* or not?

4. And if the man in his will states that he wants to give some of his own property to someone as a rightful gift[1], and if it is to a *cakar*-wife, is it then proper to contest this or not[2]?

5. (The main point in this paragraph is that a divorce is not legal without the consent of the wife, except in cases where the wife has committed a grave sin, as, for example having intercourse with another man, or having it during menstruation, or practising sorcery.)

Answer 6:
When a man in a declaration releases his wife from marriage, this is not to be, (he is not allowed to) divorce her when she has not committed any sin and is not willing; if, moreover, the wife is contented to remain[3] with him, then his sin is on the level of *tanāpuhl*[4].

7. If the wife does not agree to a divorce, whether her husband be dead or alive, then the law declares her to be still in a *pātixšāy*-marriage with him.

8. The property in the *pātixšāy*-wife's possession should stay in the family of her *pātixšāy*-husband, if no other agreement has been reached in the marriage contract[5] with regard to the property.

11. In case the wife is a *cakar*-wife, then a declaration about her freedom is not necessary after the husband's demise, because her freedom (comes) of itself from this (the husband's death)[6].

12. Unless there has been a contract and agreement between them, the *cakar*-wife, in case of her *cakar*-husband's demise, has no authority to make a claim on the property left by her *cakar*-husband, not even food and clothing.

Question 7, with its answers, presents various general rules in a fictitious case study. We hear of a man who takes some extraordinary measures on his deathbed, causing some rather radical changes in the family. In fact, he divorces his wife *post mortem*. The reason for this drastic step is not made explicit. The only excuse for such odd behaviour would be that the man realized that his estate was not sufficiently large to bear being divided into the usual shares. A *pātixšāy*-wife's share

---

1. Cf. M. Macuch (1993) p. 261; M. Boyce: "The Pious Foundations of the Zoroastrians", *BSOAS* 31, 1968, p. 283; A.V. Williams: *The Pahlavi Rivāyat Accompanying the Dādestān ī Dēnīg*, vol. I, Copenhagen 1990, p. 279.

2. N. Safa-Isfehani (1980) p. 47 translates differently: "...and if the wife is a *cagar*, should be treated in an inferior manner."

3. M. Macuch (1993) p. 78 translates differently: "Auch wenn die Frau (später) damit einverstanden ist, (selbst) dann gilt sie (die Entlassung) als *tanāpuhl*-Vergehen."

4. N. Safa-Isfehani (1980) p. 49 translates differently: "For example, if a man divorces his wife despite her dissatisfaction and unwillingness, and the wife is happy with him, then his sin equals *tanapuhl*."

5. It is not possible to decide what verb was here intended, but the meaning must be something like "entering" or "contracting".

6. Sh. Shaked in *Bibliotheca Orientalis* XLV, No 1-2, 1988, has *apēcārīh*: "Exemption" (from being wife and proxy).

equalled that of a son, so if the estate is so small that such a share would not be sufficiently large to constitute a living, the head of the family might decide that his son/sons must have it all, while his wife would have to make do with the fortune she brought into the marriage. If this was large enough for her needs, he had probably decided wisely, at least from a financial point of view.

There are other interesting features about this case. In *7.2,* the question is raised whether such a procedure can be considered just with regard to the religion. Divorce, as such, is legal, but this particular kind of divorce was obviously brought about in order to deprive the *pātixšāy*-wife of her inheritance, and therefore spurious in the extreme. This is why it is considered a sin and would therefore figure on the deficit side in the final account when the man's good and bad deeds were being weighed up against one another. The wife would come to occupy an inferior social position, not only because she would be poorer, but also because the stipulation in her husband's will would seem to show a low regard for her.

It is thus highly understandable, that the wife should object to the stipulations of the will, as we see in *7.3*. She would have to claim ignorance of the terms of her husband's will, and to refuse to be released from his guardianship. In this way, she would continue to be his wife, although he was dead, and the guardianship would serve its main purpose as the legal, economic bond between husband and wife. Divorce was legal only in cases where the wife had committed a sin grave enough to justify such a procedure, or else by mutual agreement (*7.6*). If a husband sought divorce on any other pretext, or on no pretext at all, he would be judged a *tanāpuhl*-sinner. So, the wife in this case is justified in her contesting of the husband's will. One consequence of her continuing as his *pātixšāy*-wife would be that her fortune would stay part of the family property, and she would still be a member of the family sharing its economic conditions, unless a special clause had been written into the original marriage contract.

The answer to *7.4* comes in *7.11*, but *7.9* acts as a kind of prelude to this answer which is by no means a straightforward one; on the contrary, it is a frame around a whole set of rules about something entirely different. This is, in fact, the general tendency in the *REA*: Direct questions, often in the form of case stories, and answers which to a certain extent follow the case, diverging to cover as many legal questions as possible.

In *7.9* general rules about the treatment and upkeep of a wife and a widow are given. The *pātixšāy*-wife was, naturally, clothed and fed out of her husband's income in a manner which reflected the social position of the family; viz. a rich man could not let his wife be dressed in rags; the wife of a poor man, on the other hand, could not claim finery and jewels, unless the marriage contract stipulated a fixed sum for her personal use. Also, if the husband had decided that she should live in a better style than the rest of the family, she should be allowed to continue to live in this way, but if, on the contrary, he has left her less well off than the rest of the family, a larger sum of money must be made available for her. In case (*7.10*) he has made provision for somebody else in his will, and this provision makes it impossible for her to maintain her accustomed standard of living, the provision must be altered in her favour.

The sentence in the middle of *7.9*: "For the husband there is no way to divorce her otherwise" seems completely out of place, unless we interpret it in the following manner: The *pātixšāy*-wife must be secured her usual standard of living, and if she agrees to a *post mortem* divorce, a certain sum of money must be transferred to her, so that she can be dressed and fed as before out of her husband's property. If this is so, one can easily imagine cases where the wife would agree to a divorce.

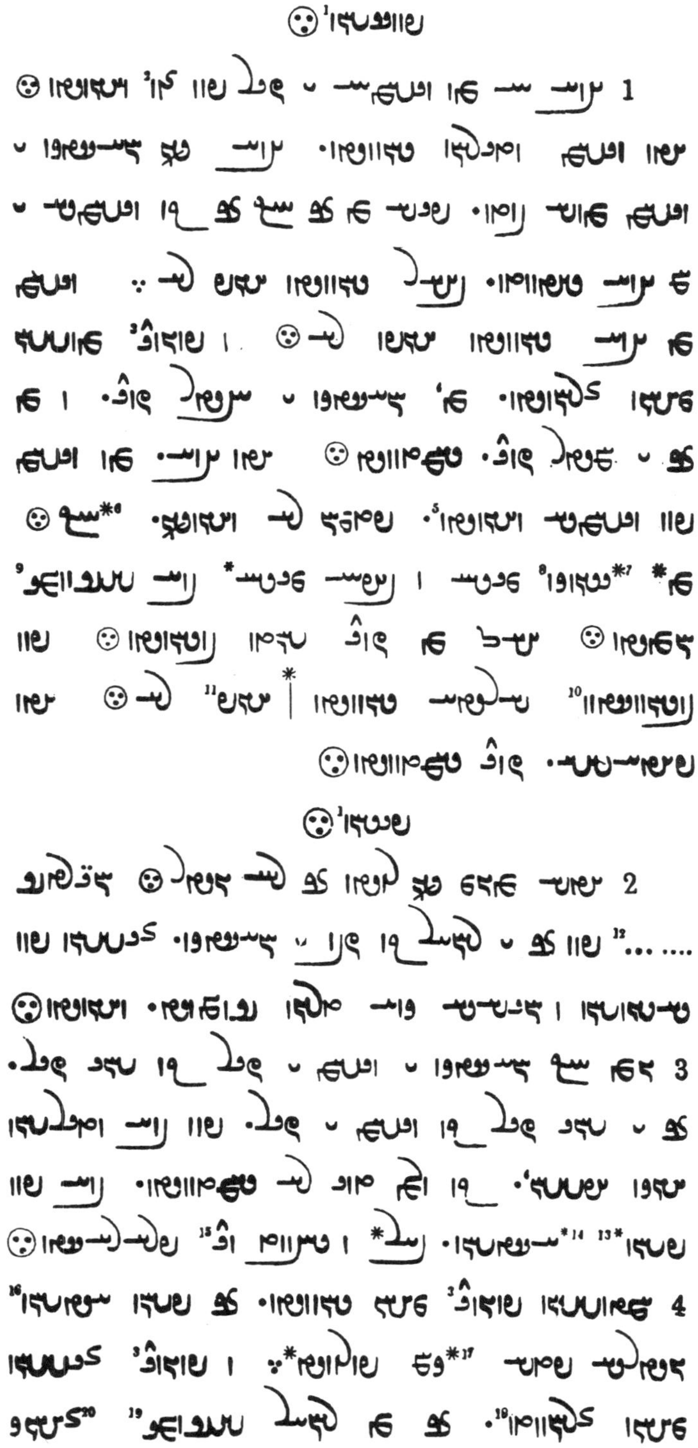

1. Written with red ink. 2. For [illegible].

3. For [illegible]. 4. MS. adds [illegible]. 5. MS. has [illegible]. 6** For [illegible]; see above p. 85, n. 8. 7** See above p. 17, n. 25; p. 78, ll. 6, 10–11. 8. Better [illegible]. 9. For [illegible]. 10. Better [illegible]. 11. MS. has [illegible]. 12. [illegible] omitted.

13. MS. has [illegible] with [illegible] inserted above [illegible] as an emendation. 14** MS. has [illegible] with [illegible] inserted above [illegible]. 15. MS. has [illegible]. 16. For [illegible]. 17** Thus in the MS.; for [illegible] (?) or [illegible] (?) or [illegible] (?). 18. Better [illegible]. 19. For [illegible]. 20. MS. prefixes [illegible].

She would then no longer be under the sway of her husband's family, and she would be free to contract a new *pātixšāy*-marriage[1]. This should not be too difficult, provided she was young enough, as she was economically well off.
This answer also includes part of the answer to *7.4*, namely that the claim of a *pātixšāy*-wife to her husband's property must take precedence over other charitable provisions he may have made in his will.
As to the *cakar*-wife, on the other hand, her different position is made clear. *7.11* is thus the answer to *7.4*: A *cakar*-wife cannot contest her husband's will, as she has no right of inheritance. She is provided with food and clothing during his lifetime, but at his death she loses these benefits, unless he has made a special stipulation to the contrary in his will.
In the main, *REA 7.11* confirms the rules set down in the *MHD*, except that here the fact that a *cakar*-wife is without means to do anything about her position is being further emphasized.
From the choice of phrases and the special emphasis of this passage, in contrast to the treatment of the same subject in the *MHD*, we learn quite a lot about the situation of a *cakar*-wife. She might, theoretically, occupy quite a good social position, but only if she was in the possession of a wealthy *pātixšāy*-husband. If not, the position of *cakar*-wife must have been less than desirable, for at least two reasons: More often than not, the *cakar*-wife would not be the only wife in the household. If the household included a *pātixšāy*-wife, the latter would take precedence over the *cakar*-wife who would occupy an inferior position. If the latter was a penniless widow her position would be further degraded, and she would live precariously at the mercy of her husband, and at the beck and call of the *pātixšāy*-wife. If she outlived her *cakar*-husband, her situation would be grim, indeed.
The question of inheritance between *cakar*-husband and -wife is not explicitly mentioned in the *MHD*, but in the passage (*101.4-8*) discussed above, we find it stated explicitly that the fortune of the *pātixšāy*-wife cannot be transferred to another man, so the *cakar*-husband could not usually benefit from his wife's wealth.
The next passage from the *REA* deals with problems in connection with rules of inheritance.

REA 23.1-25:

pursišn 1:
mart ē kē zan ē ī cakar pat zanīh[2] gīrēt. hakar zan vitīrān bavēt, mart andar xᵛāstak ī zan kē-š būt, pēš hac ān kū ān ō zanīh ī im mart āmat, bahr bavēt aivap nē. zan hac mart bavēt aivap nē. u frazand[3] kē-šān miyān zāyēt hac xᵛāstak ī pitar cand, u ān ī mātar cand rasēt. hakar mart kē zan pat zanīh gīrēt. patmān nē kunēt kū-m hac sēnok masāy u bāzāy masāy bē hišt hēt. pas hac cand sāl xᵛāhēt. pat xᵛāstan pātixšāy bavēt aivap nē hakar pātixšā cand rasēt.

passaxᵛ 2:
hakar ciš andar nēst ān rād yuvattar hangirtīk .... pat ān ī apāc ō hīr ī xᵛāstak i-šān pat dārišn u xᵛēšīh har dō ēstēt, gīrēt.

---

1. See B. Hjerrild (1988) p. 70-1.
2. Ms: *znn*.
3. Ms: *prdnnd*.

[illegible] 5 [illegible] [3] [illegible]

[illegible] [21] [illegible]

[illegible]

[illegible] 6 [illegible]

[illegible] [22] [illegible] [19] [illegible]

[illegible] 7 [illegible] [23] [illegible]

[illegible]

[illegible] 8 [illegible] [24] [illegible]

[illegible] [25] [illegible]

[illegible] [26] [illegible] 9 [illegible]

[illegible]

[illegible] [27] [illegible] [28] [illegible]

[illegible] 10 [illegible]

[illegible]

11 [illegible]

[illegible]

12 [illegible]

[illegible]

[illegible]

[illegible]

[illegible] [19] [illegible]

[illegible] [29] [illegible]

21. Better omit.

22. For [illegible]. 23. For [illegible]. 24. For [illegible]. 25. For [illegible].
26. For [illegible]. 27. For [illegible]. 28. Better [illegible].

29. For [illegible].

3. ēn kū xᵛāstak ī zan ī cakar ō šōd cakar, ān ī šōd cakar ō zan ī cakar pat bē vitīrišn ēvak hac-išān ō ōi dit nē rasēt bē pat pašn astišn bahr u dāt tāi frārāst.

4. ka-šān frazand miyān bavēt ān pašn astišn yuvattarīh pat-iš kam *pwlwn-yt*[1]. u frazand i-šān miyān zāt. ān hac apāc hišt ziyānak gīrēt.

5. ka ziyānak vitīrān hakar frazand ēvak u hamāk ō ān ēvak. hakar pus. pat xᵛēšīh u hakar duxt. pat ayōkēnīh ī mart ī pātixšāyīhā rasēt.

6. hakar vēš kū ēvak pus duxt hēnd. and-cand hišt mātar. miyān-šān pusīhā u duxtīhā baxšišn.

7. hakar pus ēvak-ic nēst. duxt dō hast. ēvak hac-išān ayōkēnī(h) pit ī pātixšāyīhā.

8. bē hakar ān ī mēh nē xᵛāhēt. pat ān ī kēh[2] frāc hilēt. andar hac-iš ān ī mēh pat-iš sacāktar.

9. u ayōkēnīh pat har kē hac-išān bē ēstēt. ayōkēnīh rād. hac sē bahr dō bahr bē stānēt. ān ī dit sē ēvak-ē.

10. hakar šōd nē kunēt. u u-š pit-ic cakar frāc ravēt u-š stūr apāyēt gumārtan.

11. ēn duxt ī cakar pat stūrīh pitar cakar sacāktar. pat-iš bē gumārišn.

12. hakar pēš kū-š pitar ī cakar bē vitīrēt. šōd kunēt. pātixšāy zan ī im šōd bavēt. pas pitar ī cakar bē frāc ravēt. u-š stūr apāyēt gumārtan. ān duxt ī šōd kartak nē rasēt. u hišt pitar ī cakar. adak-iš *hw'l'ysn*[3] pat-iš vēh.

13. ēn pat-iš nikērišn kū frazand hac zan ī cakar pat pusarīh u duxtarīh patīrift ēstēnd aivap nē. ēn-ic kū-š zan frazand pātixšāyīhā hast aivap nē.

14. cē hakar-iš frazand hac zan ī cakar. pus pat pusarīh u duxt pat duxtarīh. patīgrift ēstēnd. u-š zan u frazand pātixšāyīhā hast. baxšišn ī-š apar hīr ī xᵛāstak apar frazandān pātixšāyīhā. ān-ic patīgrift pusīhā u duxtīhā. pus zan-ic pātixšāyīhā apāk-išān hambahr cigōn pus-ī.

15. u hakar-iš frazand hac zan ī cakar pus pat pusarīh. duxt pat duxtarīh. nē patigrift ēstēt. u-š zan frazand pātixšāyīhā hast. hamāk ō zan u frazand pātixšāyīhā rasēt. ō ān ī cakar rād nē rasēt.

16. adak-iš zan frazand pātixšāyīhā nēst. ān ī hac zan ī cakar ...[4] pusarīh duxt pat duxtarīh. patīrift ēstēt. pusīhā duxtīhā ō frazand zan ī cakar rasēt.

17. hakar-iš frazand hac zan ī cakar pat pusarīh u duxtarīh nē patigrift ēstēt.adak-iš xᵛāstak hamāk pat stūrīh ēstēt ēvak-ē hac frazandān ī hac zan ī cakar pat-iš sacāktar. u ka hamāk hast hac[5] hēnd vicīn ī pat-iš fratom pat pus ī mēh pat stūrīh ī pit ī cakar bē gumārišn. u-š hamāk xᵛāstak ī pitar ī cakar pat rāh ī stūrīh bē aviš rasēt.

18. hakar ān ī mēh pat stūrīh nē šāyēt. an pus hast šāyēt. bē ō ān ī pas hac ān ī mehtar rasēt pat stūrīh gumārtakīhā.

---

1. Sic! incomprehensible.
2. B.T. Anklesaria (1962) has *kas* here.
3. Corrupted spelling.
4. B.T. Anklesaria (1962) inserts *BRH PWN = pus pat*.
5. *hast hac* is without any meaning here, *hast* probably misspelt for *ētōn*.

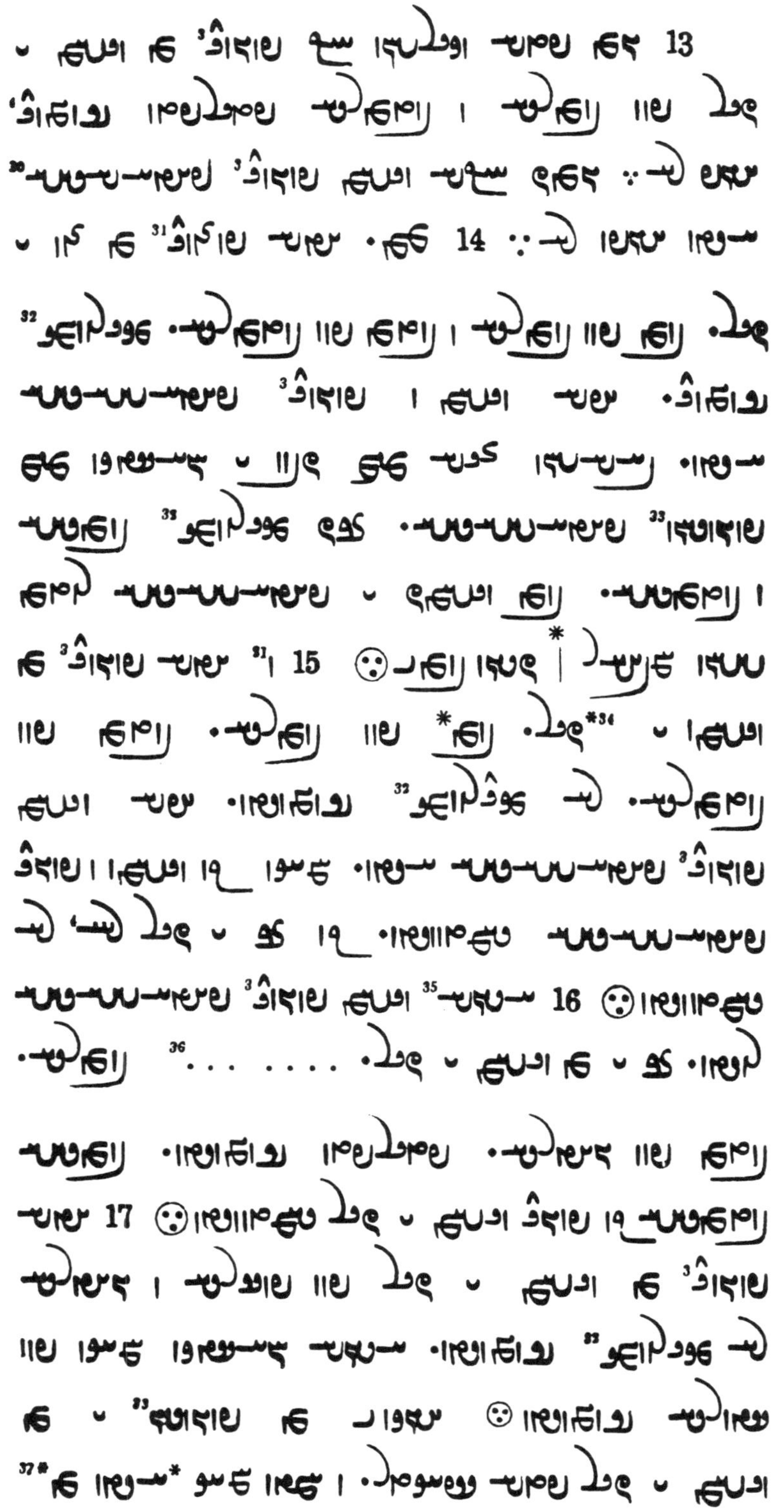

30. For [illegible]. 31. For [illegible].

32. For [illegible]. 33. For [illegible]. 34** Repeated in the MS. by mistake. 35. For [illegible]. 36. [illegible] omitted by mistake.

37**. For [illegible].

19. u hakar pus nēst. aivap ān ī hast pat stūrīh nē šāyēt. duxt ēcand hēnd. hac-išān ēvak ayōkēnīh u stūrīh ī pitar ī cakar. u pat-iš bē gumārišn.

20. u-š x^{v}āstak ī pitar ī cakar hamāk pat rāh-īh stūrīh ī pitar ī cakar bē aviš rasēt. stūr dūtak katakbānūk ī pitar ī cakar bavēt.

21. hakar hac zan cakar ēvāz ēvak duxt hast. adak sax^{v}an pat-iš dō aivēnak. ēvak ān ī ka-š mātar zīvandak. ēvak ān ī ka-š mātar nē zīvandak.

22. cē hakar-iš mātar zīndak. ān ēvak duxt adak-iš ayōkēnīh u stūrīh ī pitar ī cakar gumārtakīhā bē aviš rasēt. apāk hamāk x^{v}āstak ī pitar cakar.

23. u pas. ka-š mātar frāc ravēt. u-š an frazand pat yuvat hac ēn duxt-ē. kē pat ayōkēnīh stūrīh pit ī cakar gumārt ēstēt. nēst. x^{v}āstak im zan bē hilēt. pat stūrīh ī-š šōd pātixšāyīhā ēstēt. ō ōi ravēt kē andar dūtak ī ōi nazdīk patvandītar u sacāktar.

24. u hakar mātar ī im duxt nē zīvandak. im ēvak duxt ayōkēnīh pitar ī pātixšāyīhā bavēt. u-š x^{v}āstak ī mātar hamāk bē aviš rasēt. stūrīh ī pit ī cakar bē ō ōi rasēt kē-š andar dūtak nabānazdištar.

25. hakar-iš ēn duxt ī zan ī cakar pat duxtarīh patīrift ēstēt. u-š x^{v}āstak vēš kū x^{v}āstak ī stūrīh. kamīh ē andar nē āyēt.

Question 1:
A man takes a *cakar*-wife in marriage; if she dies, does the man succeed to a share of the fortune she possessed before her marriage with him, or not? And will the wife succeed to a share from the husband or not? And a child born to them, how great a share of the father's fortune would it be entitled to? And of the mother's, how much will go to the child? If the man who takes the woman in marriage does not make a contract which says: "You have left me sufficient for my needs"[1], and after some years he wishes to do so, is he entitled to make this demand or not? If he is, how much will go to him?

Answer 2:
If nothing else speaks against it, the answer may be summed up as follows: "Of what is left of their property, each may take what is necessary for his or her personal needs[2].

3. It is like this: The property of the *cakar*-wife will not go to the *cakar*-husband or vice versa at the death of one or the other of them, unless there has been an agreement[3] upon a share up to one cubit[4].

4. If they have children, this agreement will hardly be different[5], and with children born to them, the wife will get a share of what is left.

1. C. Bartholomae (1923) p. 23.
2. I have taken *dārišn u x^{v}ēšīh* as a hendiadys; N. Safa-Isfehani (1980) p. 162 translates: "They are entitled to take the capital of each other".
3. N. Safa-Isfehani (1980) p. 162: "on existing conventions".
4. This is a measure of length = 18 inches. Here, however, the reference must be to a well-known, to us unknown, amount of money.
5. The last words must be erroneously transmitted. B.T. Anklesaria (1962) p. 88 emendit to *kam šahōt*.

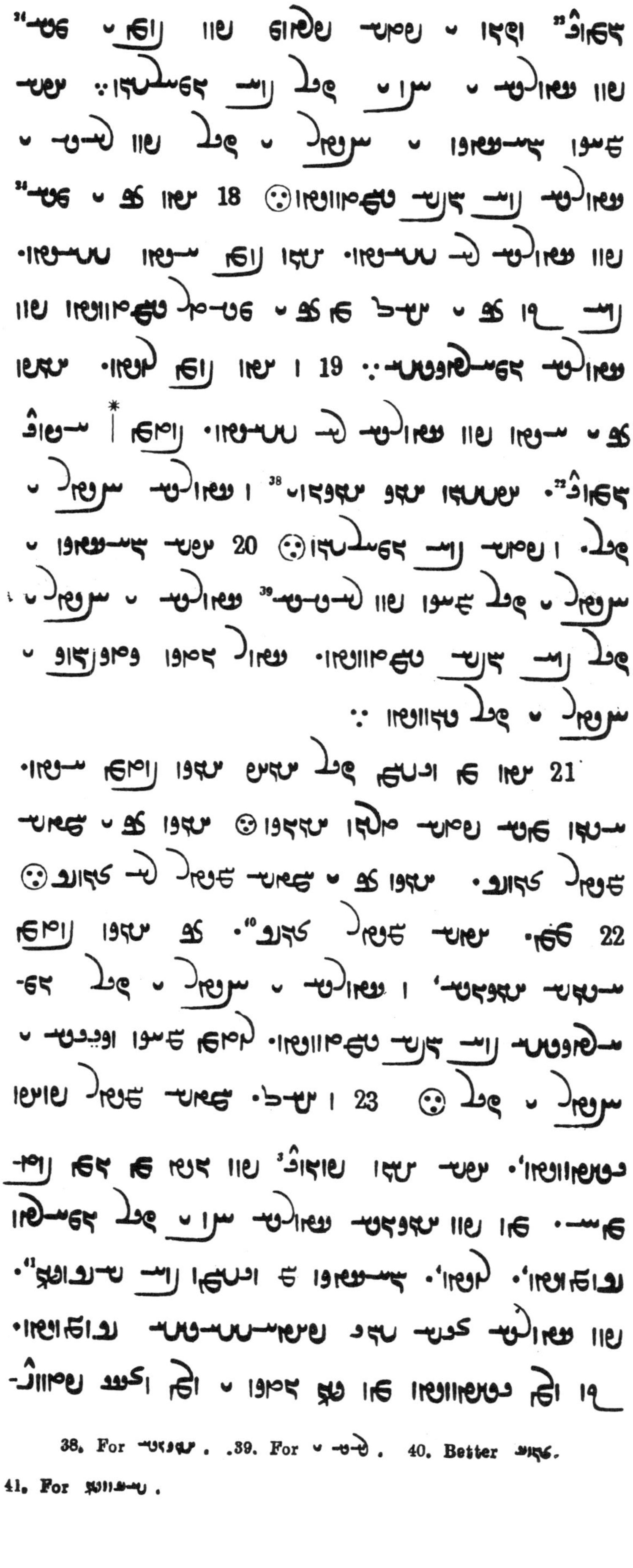

38. For [Pahlavi]. 39. For [Pahlavi]. 40. Better [Pahlavi].

41. For [Pahlavi].

5. When the wife dies, if there is one child, everything goes to that child. If it is a son, it will be his personal property, if a daughter it will be held in *ayōkēnīh* for her mother's *pātixšāy*-husband[1].

6. If there is more than one son or daughter, what is left by their mother shall be shared between them in accordance with the rules about sons' and daughters' shares[2].

7. If there is no son[3] but two daughters, one of these shall take *ayōkēnīh* for her *pātixšāy*-father.

8. But if the elder does not want (the *ayōkēnīh*), it shall pass on to the younger. The elder, however, is the most suitable for this.

9. And she who takes on the *ayōkēnīh* will, because of this, have two shares out of three, whereas the other one will have one share.

10. If this one does not marry, and her *cakar*-father also dies, a *stūr* ought to be appointed for him[4].

11. This *cakar*-daughter is then the most suitable as *stūr* to her *cakar*-father, and she ought to be appointed (*stūr*).

12. If this daughter marries before her *cakar*-father dies, she will be the *pātixšāy*-wife of her husband. When the *cakar*-father then dies, and must have a *stūr* appointed for him, the married daughter cannot be appointed *stūr*; so having left her *cakar*-father, the best thing for her will be *x^{v}asrāyūn*-marriage[5].

13. The following ought to be considered: Are the children of the *cakar*-wife adopted as sons and daughters or not? And also whether there is a *pātixšāy*-wife and children or not.

14. If he has adopted the children of his *cakar*-wife as his sons and daughters and he also has *pātixšāy*-wife and -children, then the adopted son or daughter are entitled to their share of the property on equal terms with the *pātixšāy*-children.

15. If he has not adopted the children of the *cakar*-wife as his sons and daughters, and there is a *pātixšāy*-wife and -children, everything will go to the latter and her children, and the *cakar*-wife and children will get nothing.

16. If he has no *pātixšāy*-wife and -children, but has adopted a *cakar*-son and -daughter of his *cakar*-wife, it (the property) will go to these children, according to the shares of sons and daughters.

17. If he has not adopted the children of his *cakar*-wife as sons and daughters, then all of his property will be in *stūrīh*. One of the *cakar*-wife's children will be the most suitable for this appointment. If all of them are

1. N. Safa-Isfehani (1980) p. 162 translates: "...to the man who accepts her *ayōkēnīh*".

2. A son would get the double of a daughter's share.

3. Ms: *pit*, but I follow B.T. Anklesaria's emendation (1962) to *pus*.

4. N. Safa-Isfehani (1980) p. 164 translates to "her" which is meaningless, as no *stūr* is appointed for women.

5. Cf. A. Perikhanian (1970) p. 349-57.

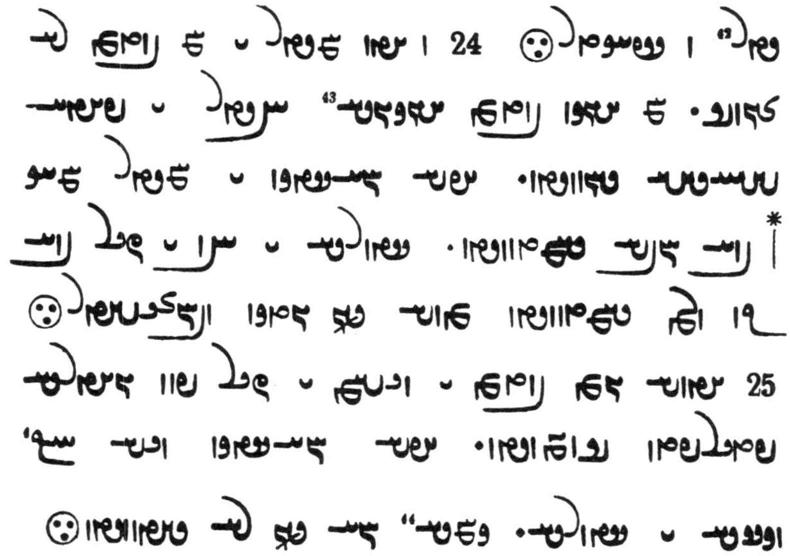

42. For [illegible]. 45. Better [illegible]. 44. For [illegible].

equally suitable then the eldest ought to be appointed to the *stūrīh* of his *cakar*-father, and the whole of his *cakar*-father's property will come to him by way of *stūrīh.*

18. If the elder son is not able to take over the *stūrīh*, then another son can do so in *stūrīh gumārtakīhā*[1].

19. And if there is no son, or if he cannot take the *stūrīh*, and there are some daughters, one of these should be appointed to *ayōkēnīh* and *stūrīh* of the *cakar*-father.

20. All of the *cakar*-father's property then goes to her by way of *stūrīh* for the *cakar*-father; she becomes her *cakar*-father's *stūr* and lady of the house and family.

21. If there is only one daughter of the *cakar*-wife, there are two possible procedures, one to be followed when the mother is alive, the other when she is not alive.

22. If her mother is alive, the *ayōkēnīh* and *stūrīh* for her *cakar*-father will come to her by appointment together with the whole of his property.

23. At the death of the mother,[2] if there are no other children, except the said daughter who was appointed *ayōkēn* and *stūr* for her *cakar*-father, the property of the *cakar*-wife will pass into *stūrīh* for her *pātixšāy*-husband. It will then go to the person in his family who is most closely related, and also the most suitable.

24. If the mother of the said daughter is not alive, then this only daughter shall become *ayōkēn*[3] for her *pātixšāy*-father, and all her mother's property shall come to her. The *stūrīh* of the *cakar*-father will then go to the person in the family who is most closely related.

25. If the daughter of the *cakar*-wife has been adopted as daughter, and the property is greater than that required for a *stūrīh*, a smaller share will not go to her[4].

The questions and answers referring to *cakar* continue in:

REA 31.1, 3-7:

pursišn 1:
mart-ē kē zan ē cagar pat zanīh gīrēt. nē dānēt. aš vinās bavēt aivap nē. u hakar-iš bavēt. cand bavēt.

passax[v] *3:*
hakar-iš im mart ēn zan ī cakar[y] pat cagarīhā zanīh zan[y] kunēt. xūp. vinās-ē nē bavēt. hakar yuttar. zan kartan kār-ē hast fraškartīk. pat cimtar apāyēt kartan. u dō aivēnak bavēt. ēvak pātixšāy u ēvak cakar.

---

1. Appointed.

2. N. Safa-Isfehani (1980) p. 170, translates to "father" without explanation. The Ms clearly has *mātar*.

3. Ms has *ayōkēnīh.*

4. Cf. M. Shaki: "Two Chapters of the Rivāyat ī Emēd ī Ašavahištān", *Oriental Studies*, Tblisi 1983, p.49-51.

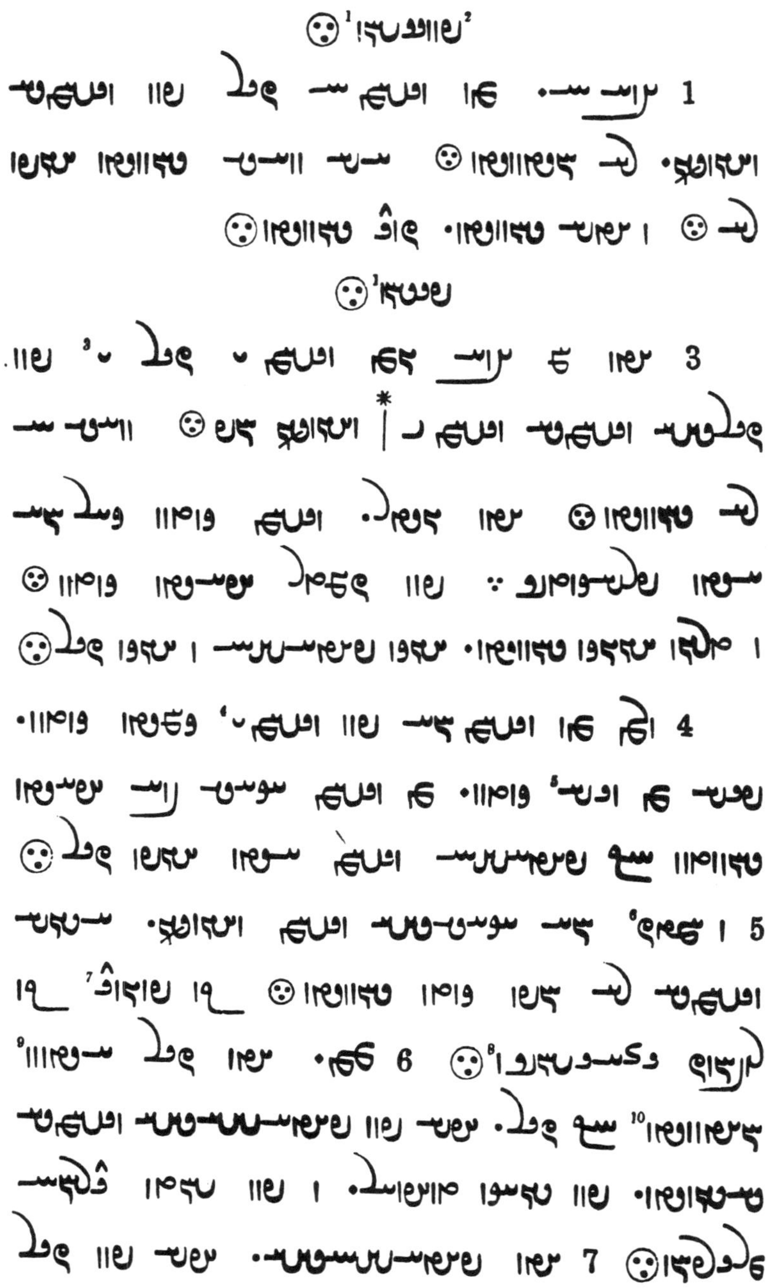

1. Written with red ink. 2. Repeated with black ink. 3. Better omit.

4. For [illegible]. 5. For [illegible]. 6. [illegible] seems to be struck off. 7. For [illegible]. 8. For [illegible]. 9. For [illegible]. 10. For [illegible].

4. ōi kē zan-ē pat zanīh kāmēt kartan. pēš hac zan[1] kartan. hac zan ākāh bē apāyēt būtan kū pātixšāy zan hast aivap cakar.

5. u ka-c ē ākāhīhā zan kunēt. adak-iš zanīh nē xūp kart bavēt. ō frazand ō ruvān-ic vizāyišnīk.

6. cē. hakar cakar hast u dānēt kū cakar. u-š pat pātixšāyīhā zanīh dārēt. pat giyāk tanāpuhl. u pat sāl drahnāy margarzān.

7. hakar pātixšāyīhā. u-š pat cakar zanīh gīrēt dārēt. ān zanīh u šōdīh nē xūp. višōpišnīk apāyišn.

Question 1:
If a man takes a *cakar*-wife who, unknown to him, has obligations elsewhere, will this man then have committed a sin? If he has, how great is the sin?

Answer 3:
If this man makes this *cakar*-wife his wife in a *cakar*-marriage, then everything is perfectly straight, and there is no question of sin. If, on the other hand, he wants to be united with a woman in a marriage bond which will endure till the regeneration of the world, then he must do it properly[2]. There are two ways: One is *pātixšāy* and the other is *cakar.*

4. He who wants to take a wife in marriage must find out whether she is already a *pātixšāy*- or a *cakar*-wife before he makes her his wife.

5. If she is, and he still makes her his *pātixšāy*-wife then the marriage is not properly established; it will be injurious to the children and also to the soul.

6. Because, if she is *cakar,* and he knows this and yet keeps her in a *pātixšāy*-marriage he will have committed a *tanāpuhl*-sin, and after a year a *margarzān*-sin.

7. If she is *pātixšāy* and he enters into a *cakar*-marriage with her, it will not be a proper marriage, according to the law, and it ought to be dissolved.

Question 23, with its answers, deals with inheritance problems in connection with *cakar* marriage contracts, explaining in detail the question put forward in *question 7*[3].

The discussion in *23.1* aims at elucidating the legal subtleties surrounding the problems of inheritance between *cakar*-wife, -husband, and -children.

A very interesting point emerges in the second half of the passage. It appears possible for the *cakar*-husband to insert certain claims in the marriage contract, viz. that he shall be left a part of the *cakar*-wife's property, sufficient for him to subsist on. The problem raised is whether such an addition to the contract could be made after the marriage had existed for several years. The reality behind such a clause must be, that the husband, being sufficiently well off at the time of marriage to forego pressing such a special clause, suddenly, after some time, finds himself in difficulties which call for financial support.

There is no mention of a similar possibility for a *cakar*-wife, but in the answer (*23.2*) which follows directly, it is stipulated that they may both take as much as is needed for survival out of each other's property. This seems to be inconsistent

1. Ms corrupt here.
2. *cimtar* of *cim*. *-tar* seems to be intensifying.
3. N. Safa-Isfehani (1980) p. 160 ff. translates differently.

with the statement made in *7.11*, so we must assume that the clause comes into use only in cases where the parties involved are totally deprived of the means of existence. These opposing views may reflect disagreement among the jurists, as we have seen in the *MHD*. A diverging opinion is, however, always presented as such in the *MHD*. The implementing of the clause would be a practical solution in case one of the *cakar*-spouses became poor, and as they were living together also a very natural one, although it is at variance with the whole idea of *cakarīh*. At the time of the *REA* it would have become remarkably stupid not to use the above-mentioned clause, since a person unable to support himself within the Zoroastrian community might by then be sorely tempted to seek employment in the surrounding Islamic society; a course which would most certainly result in loss of true believers.

Judging from the space allotted to the *cakar*-institution in the *REA* and the detailed discussions of it compared to that in the *MHD*, even allowing for the fact that the *MHD* is incomplete, it seems safe to assume that the *cakar*-marriage had become fairly common, or that the priests/jurists tried to promote this type of connection by playing down its most unpalatable traits. If the *cakar*-marriage had become fairly common, the rules of inheritance must have come to be seen as somewhat unfair. In a family in which an *ayōkēn*-daughter was married in *cakarīh* to a husband who did not already have a *pātixšāy*-wife the system must have seemed very unfair indeed, and a great strain.

The *cakar*-marriage, apart from being an accepted way for a woman to support herself, might certainly also provide a penniless man with the means he was looking for. *Ayōkēn*-daughters, or *cakar*-wives (widows) with substantial fortunes at their disposal must have been much coveted by these unfortunates, despite the fact that the offspring of such a union would not belong to the man. It seems reasonable, considering the built-in lack of security in this type of union, that the law should provide the man with the opportunity to seek financial support in the case of his wife's death. However, although the above-mentioned possibility existed, the law still adhered strictly to the original purpose of *cakarīh*. The law even states (*23.3*) a limit to the amount of money transferable to a *cakar*-spouse, at the same time firmly reiterating the provision that *cakar*-spouses are not entitled to inherit each other. In *23.4* this provision is somewhat mitigated by the statement that a wife might get something if there are children in the marriage. Logically, this ought not to place the wife in a better position with regard to inheritance, as the said children would automatically belong to her *pātixšāy*-husband. So, the fact that the clause has been included must mean that both the conception and the usage of the institution *cakarīh* had changed considerably over the years.

The ties between a *pātixšāy*-husband and his *pātixšāy*-wife who was living with her *cakar*-husband with whom she had children, must have been of a theoretical nature rather than real ones. So even though the laws of old were transmitted and observed, mitigating clauses were added so as to make the old institution of *cakarīh* palatable to people living under altered conditions of life, without actually abolishing the idea of *cakarīh*.

The wife's own property, her inheritance from her father and her *pātixšāy*-husband would go to her children. Her son, fathered by her *cakar*-husband would become the heir of her *pātixšāy*-husband, and thus her fortune would stay in the family of the latter by being inherited by her son. If she and her *cakar*-husband failed to produce a direct heir, their daughter must endeavour to produce one; i.e. she must marry in *ayōkēnīh* for her mother's *pātixšāy*-husband, i.e. her own legal father. Therefore, her mother's fortune would come to her conditionally: She might live off the proceeds, but the principal would go to her son who would be heir to her mother's *pātixšāy*-husband.

Theoretically, the inheritance could be transferred by generations of women until, finally, a son was born, reached his majority, and took over the property[1]. Already by the second generation the reason for these clauses must have seemed to be fading into the distance, at least, to the women who had to submit to these quaint rules in order to serve their male relatives' need to continue their line until the end of time.

23.7 operates with the possibility of two daughters one of whom will take on the *ayōkēnīh* of her mother's *pātixšāy*-husband. According to the rules, this ought to be the elder of the two, but she could refuse and in that case, the younger would take over. Here we have an indication of the scope of women's right to decide for themselves. The *ayōkēnīh* was attended by certain privileges in that the *ayōkēn*-daughter would inherit a son's portion. It must therefore have seemed most feasible that the girl with the smallest chances of making a good match should take on the *ayōkēnīh*.

23.10-12 must refer to the daughter who is not claimed as *ayōkēn* for her *pātixšāy*-father. She would certainly be the most proper person to undertake a *stūrīh* for her *cakar*-father, unless she had already married as a *pātixšāy*-wife before it became evident that the *cakar*-father would die without an heir; in that case, another *stūr* must be appointed. This rule is, of course, only applicable in cases where a *cakar*-father has no *pātixšāy*-children himself nor a *pātixšāy*-wife, or, at least, one who is young enough to provide him with an heir in a *cakar*-marriage.

The latter part of *23.12* is extremely obscure because of its phrasing. I take it to mean that the daughter, having found a husband for herself to whom she could be *pātixšāy*-wife, will be far better off than if she had become *stūr* for her *cakar*-father, despite the fact that she would then not have any share in property left by him. The statement, that *x^vasrāyūn*-marriage would be better for her might refer to the fact that her *pātixšāy*-father had died, and, in case a new guardian had not been found for her, she would have to find a husband herself, cf. the chapter on *Sardārīh*.

23.16 is concerned with the relations between *pātixšāy*- and *cakar*-children and the adoption of the latter. Before the distribution of an inheritance one would, necessarily, have to find out how many legal heirs there were, i.e. *pātixšāy*-wives and -children; this point is most expressly stated, once again. However, the adoption of a *cakar*-child converted the status of this child to that of *pātixšāy* with its consequent right to inherit. The nature of adoption is being emphasized so that nobody can remain in doubt of the position of an adopted child.

The text does not discuss whether the permission of the *pātixšāy*-father was needed prior to an adoption, or whether it is to be inferred from the clauses about the *ayōkēn*-daughter, that as long as one child remained for the *pātixšāy*-father, the rest of them might be adopted by the *cakar*-father, should he so wish.

It is made abundantly clear, however, that the relation between *cakar*-father and -children is the object of much speculation and regulation. The established law of old, inseparable from the orthodox religion could, of course, not be changed, but within the bounds of the law there was a certain liberty of interpretation. These changing interpretations reflect changes in the community. The *cakar*-father wanted his own children[2], the rules concerning this must have come to be felt as

1. Cf. A. Perikhanian (1983) p. 654.

2. See B. Hjerrild Carlsen (1984) p. 112.

constricting and confining, and the above speculations and adaptations may have been the first beginnings of the final abolishment of the institution of *cakar*.

If a man had no *pātixšāy*-offspring, and had not had any opportunity or sufficient foresight to adopt a *cakar*-child, one of his *cakar*-children must be appointed *stūr* for him. The eldest was once again seen as the most proper choice. It is a curious fact that although Zoroastrian law does not operate with primogeniture with regard to hereditary rights, all sons had an equal share, it still upholds the principle of choosing the eldest, whenever a choice has to be made.

The question of a daughter as the only available *stūr* is the subject of much debate. In *23.19-25,* several cases of this are under discussion and various solutions are brought forward. The *REA* takes a firm stand about the difference between adoption and *stūrīh*, whereas the *AFS* seems to mix them up. Here adoption of a person means placing this person on an equal footing with a *pātixšāy*-child, whereas the appointment of a person to *stūrīh* will mean some financial gain for this person, while the property itself will be inherited by the said person's offspring.

If a *cakar*-daughter was appointed *stūr,* she would have the administration of her father's property, and she would preside over his house and family; altogether an enviable position in relation to which even her husband must have held an inferior position. He would have had no authority over her, his only function being the fathering of her children. Reality may, of course, have been different in many cases, but according to the law, she was completely her own master.

It is evident from *23.22 ff.* that the *cakar*-father's need of an heir is given much more space and consideration here than was the case in the *MHD.* All the rules here are, nevertheless, based on a solid, down-to-earth weighing of the possibility of producing heirs to both the *pātixšāy*- and *cakar*-husband.

If a *cakar*-husband at his death left no other offspring than his *cakar*-daughter, she would undertake to secure his succession if her mother was alive. The mother would then be able to take a new *cakar*-husband and thus produce an heir to her *pātixšāy*-husband. If this should fail, the daughter would still not, at this point, be entitled to give up her *stūrīh* for her *cakar*-father in favour of her *pātixšāy*-father. The only means available for her to improve the situation somewhat would be for her to make her mother's fortune available for a *stūrīh* for her *pātixšāy*-husband. If, however, the mother was already dead, then, the *cakar*-daughter would, according to the rules, be obliged to fulfil the original purpose of her mother's *cakar*-marriage, and the *cakar*-father would loose both child and fortune, as both would automatically go to the heirs of the *pātixšāy*-father.

It is a most significant fact that in the *REA 31.1 ff.* we find a further elaboration of a question that has already been treated before. It seems as if it must have become necessary to stress the difference between *pātixšāy* and *cakar* in order to underline the importance of the distinction. The ensuing punishment in case the distinction was not upheld strengthens the impression that the priests were finding it increasingly difficult to keep the members of their community within the bonds of the traditional rules. In the light of this, the many alterations that we find in the *REA* compared to the *MHD* become even more understandable.

In the *REA,* the adoption of *cakar*-children is discussed in connection with inheritance. Thus, the idea of adoption must be generally accepted. This view is supported by a statement in *Šāyast nē-Šāyast*[1]:

1. F.M.P. Kotwal: "The supplementary Texts to the Šāyast nē-Šayast", *Det Kongelige Danske Videnskabernes Selskab, Historisk-filosofiske Meddelelser* 44,2, Copenhagen 1969, ch.xii. 14.

...u vas hēnd kē ēn mēnišn stūr nē gumārēnd kū-mān frazand ī cakar pat pusīh patīgrift hast.

...and there are many who do not appoint a *stūr* with this in mind: We have adopted a *cakar*-child as our son.

In contrast to the *REA,* the *Šāyast nē-Šāyast* does not consider *cakar*-daughters suitable for adoption.

The *MHD* omits the question of adoption of *cakar*-children altogether, except in one example under *MHDA 40.9-14* which is consistent with the general attitude of the *MHD*. The adoption of *cakar*-children is out of the question and thus not worth mentioning in the law. One should, of course, bear in mind that the *MHD* is not a complete law code.

As we have already shown, all *cakar*-children are considered fit to enter into *stūrīh* for their *cakar*-father, even the eldest son, whereas in the *MHD* we have conflicting views on the question of allegiance of *cakar*-children[1], although it seems to be generally accepted that a *cakar*-daughter might act as *stūr* of her *cakar*-father.

Finally, in the *MHD* we find the term *ayōkēnīh* employed exclusively in connection with *pātixšāy*-daughters, whereas in the *REA* the term is also used about contracts between *cakar*-father and -daughter.

The changes that we find in the *REA* seem, to a certain extent, to be based on views already existing at the time of the *MHD*, only expressed, however, as conflicting viewpoints.

1. MHD 42.11 ff.

AYŌKĒNĪH

To any serious and right-minded Zoroastrian, the procuring of heirs, and the continuation of the line of descent until the Resurrection, is an obligation. This resulted in the creation of increasingly complicated systems and rules of inheritance. One way for a son-less man to procure an heir for himself could be to oblige his daughter or his sister to marry after a special contract according to which the offspring of the marriage became the legal heirs to their mother's father or brother. A daughter or sister fulfilling this obligation was called an *ayōkēn* and the institution was termed *ayōkēnīh*[1].

The etymology of this term is doubtful. A. Perikhanian[2] explains the term as a lost Avestan *aēno-kaenā* = "expiator, redeemer". M. Shaki[3] suggests a corrupt Pahlavi form of the Avestan *yō hē pasčaēta*. G. Klingenschmitt[4] thinks that the term might be connected with Sanskrit *ayogū, ayugū* = "without a companion" (brother or sister), which is the Sanskrit term for an only daughter of a woman. H.P. Schmidt[5] also finds this construction attractive. Mazahéri[6] proposes yet another solution to the problem, namely *ēvkānīh/ēvaknīh* = "unique héritière de son père". In this, he is followed by J.P. de Menasce[7]. I myself am rather in favour of Klingenschmitt's solution, as the other suggestions seem to be based on somewhat unsound linguistic deductions. As for Shaki's *yō hē pasčaēta*, this is emphatically not synonymous with *ayōkēn*. We shall return to this later.

The institution of *ayōkēnīh* has equivalents among other Indo-European peoples. We know of it from Indian rules of inheritance, where an *ayōkēn* was called *putrika*, and from the Greek *'επίκληρος*. These laws are obviously centuries older than the Sasanian law, but the evidence they provide is interesting from the point of view of comparative legal history, and also because it points to a common Indo-European origin of the institution.

The existence of the institution is testimony to the fact that women could not succeed to the patrimony, originally. A daughter would not serve the sacred purpose of being heir to a man; the heir must be a man who would take upon him the cult of the ancestors. The existence of the epiclerate proves that the idea of the continuation of the blood-line in a direct line was strong; otherwise one of the agnatic circle would have done just as well, as we know from agnatic societies like the ancient Arabian.

The Greek word *'επίκληρος* is self-explanatory: *'επί* = with, *κλήρος* = patrimony, i.e. the daughter goes with the patrimony, and through her the heir proper, a son, succeeds to the inheritance. The daughter's son, *θυγατριδούς*, is from his birth con-

1. Cf. M. Macuch (1985) p. 190.
2. A. Perikhanian (1970) p. 352.
3. M. Shaki: "The Concept of Obligated Successorship in the *Mādiyān ī hazār Dādistān*", *Acta Iranica* 5, 1975, p. 227-8.
4. G. Klingenschmitt (1971) p. 168 note 10.
5. H.P. Schmidt: *Some Women's Rites and Rights in the Veda*, Poona 1987, p. 48.
6. A.A. Mazahéri: *La Famille Iranienne aux Temps Anté-Islamiques*, Paris 1938, p. 94.
7. J.P. de Menasce (1964) p .34.

sidered the son of his maternal grandfather. In *Isaios,* he is presented as participating with his grandfather in the family sacrifices, especially the sacrifice to *Zeus Ktesios*, the protector of the family property[1].
According to Indian law, the son-less father gives away his daughter in marriage on condition that the son she might bear will be his son who can undertake the celebration of the funeral rites in his honour[2].
According to both Indian and Greek law, the basis for this institution is an acknowledged obligation, but whereas in Indian law it rests on a contract issued by the father in each individual case, in Greek law it is part of the father's right to dispose of the patrimony in his will. In both, however, the issue is the same, namely to provide a male heir. The *'επίκληρος* and the *putrika* must be considered as intermediary successors, not themselves heirs, but inherited along with the property to carry on the father's blood to the successor[3].
There is no indication in either Roman or Germanic law of the existence of this institution. Roman law focuses upon adoption in cases where no male heir could be produced, and as for the Germanic peoples, one might perhaps ask whether the well-known Grimm fairy tale tag of the hero who inherits the princess and half the kingdom could have its origin in the same principle. The husband would get half the property as a reward for securing the succession, and the other half would be set aside for the prospective son.

MHD

The institution of *ayōkēnīh* was an extremely important feature of Sasanian laws of wills and succession. A whole chapter in the *MHD* is dedicated to the subject, but, unfortunately, there is no evidence in the Avestan texts. However, as these mostly deal with religious questions of another order, this is not surprising. The Sasanian law-texts, on the other hand, treat of religious ideas applied to ordinary social life.
According to Zoroastrian succession law, the line of succession must be direct. Only direct descendants of testator can inherit, so if there is no son, he must have one produced by other persons by a contract set up by the law. Only if this is done by way of *ayōkēnīh* is the bloodline carried on; if done by *stūrīh*, by adoption, or via his wife's *cakar*-marriage, his line will only be carried on symbolically. In this late form of Zoroastrianism this did not seem to matter greatly, as the important thing was to have one's name carried on in the prayers of the son. This very abstract approach to the problem of succession is well known also from Indian and Greek law, and we may thus assume that *ayōkēnīh* is the oldest way of substituting a missing heir, stemming from a time when the blood relationship was the primary issue. During the Sasanian period, where the keeping of the family property on family hands was of paramount importance next to religion, *ayōkēnīh* was only one possibility among many others to secure the succession. It may have been the one which was preferred judging from the fact that a girl could be obliged to become *ayōkēn* even though she was married as a *pātixšāy*-wife.

---

1. Isaios, On the Inheritance of Kiron, § 16.
2. Manu IX, 127 ff.
3. H.P. Schmidt (1987) p. 55 ff.; see also C.W. Westrup: *Mand og Kvinde*, København 1941, p. 128 ff.

The chapter in the *MHD* opens with the words *dar ī ayōkēn yō hē pasčaēta* (*21.4*). This phrase has been interpreted in different ways, and has lead to some confusion as to the relationship between the term *ayōkēn* and the term *yō hē pasčaēta*. A. Perikhanian[1] finds here a synonym for *stūrīh*. M. Shaki sees, as mentioned above, *yō hē pasčaēta* as synonymous with *ayōkēn* and denoting a special form of *stūrīh* i.e. *ayōkēnīh*. G. Klingenschmitt[2] suggests that *yō hē pasčaēta* could mean "den Sohn (bzw. in MHD 22.3, die Tochter) der Erbtochter", and in this he is followed by Schirasi-Mahmoudian[3].

The problem seems to be that none of these explanations will fit all the instances given in the text, which means that the inner logic of the law text will be upset. As a remedy, I propose to take as my starting point the paragraph in the text which is unquestionably unequivocal as to its meaning, and use this as a key to the understanding of the term[4].

MHD 22.8-9

yō hē pasčaēta apar [u] pus duxt ī pātixšāyīhā u zāhak manēt.

The *yō hē pasčaēta* rests with a *pātixšāy*-son, or -daughter, and[5] their progeny.

Yō hē pasčaēta is translated by Bartholomae[6] as "wer ihm alsdann" from the Avestan. This would mean successor, but as the Avestan here seems to be used as standard expression, we might take it as an equivalent of an abstract noun viz. succession. Shaki's translation, "obligated successorship" is apt, but it might rather be understood as the "right and obligation to succession".

This passage is the only one in which a *pātixšāy*-son is mentioned in connection with *yō hē pasčaēta* which is probably why its significance has been overlooked. It is, in fact, only natural that the *pātixšāy*-son should be mentioned only once since the existence of such a son would preclude any problems with regard to the succession or the inheritance, generally. If, on the other hand, no *pātixšāy*-son existed, the whole machinery of providing the man with an heir would be set in motion. One solution could be to employ his daughter as *ayōkēn* which would mean that she was obliged to carry on the *yō hē pasčaēta*, and as intermediary successor act as the link between her father and his heir, her son. It is not surprising that the complex legal question of succession in cases where no sons exist should occupy more space in a law text than the completely unproblematic "normal" succession from father to son. But the fact has given rise to the surmise that *yō hē pasčaēta* must be synonymous with either *ayōkēn* or *stūrīh*. The first arises from the chapter heading of *MHD 21.4*, to which I propose the following translation: "Chapter on

1. A. Perikhanian (1970) p. 353.
2. G. Klingenschmitt: "Die Erbtochter im zoroastrischen Recht nach dem *Mādiyān ē hazār Dādistān*". *MSS* 21, 1967, p. 68.
3. F. Shirazi-Mahmoudian (1975) p. 165.
4. I put this explanation of the term forward at the International Colloquium in Leuven in 1990, publ. 1993. See B. Hjerrild: "*Ayōkēn*: Woman between Father and Husband in the Sasanian Era". *Medioiranica*, Leuven 1993, p. 81-2; M. Macuch (1993) p. 180, is of the same opinion.
5. M. Shaki (1975) p. 235 reads *ī*, and translates "capable of begetting children", but Ms clearly has *u*.
6. C. Bartholomae (1923) p. 39.

MHD 47.7-12

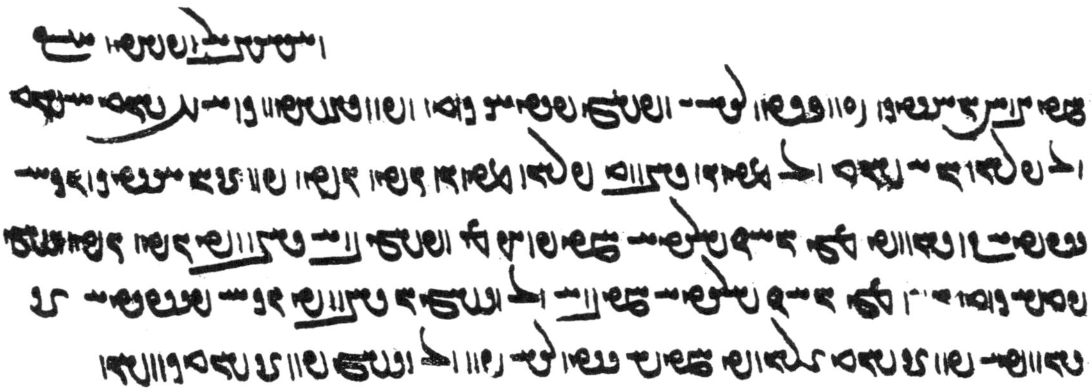

MHD 21.10-15

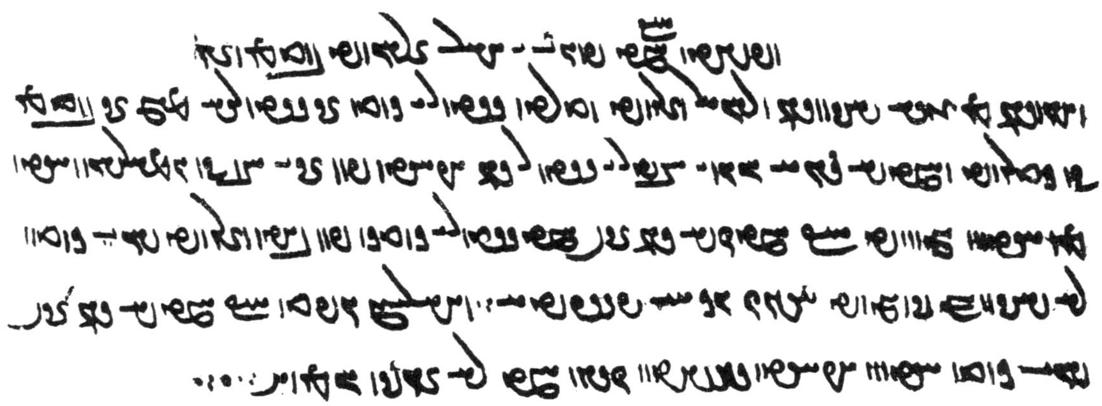

the *ayōkēn* (as) successor". This seems perfectly logical, as she is indeed the successor on condition that she has no brother.
As to the term being synonymous with *stūrīh*, we may look to:

MHD 47.7-12

Vāyayyār nipišt kū ka mart ē x^vāstak pat stūrīh ī x^vēš paitāk kart u pat dāštan har 2 sāl ē sāl ō Farrax^v ē sāl ō Mihrēn dāt Farrax^v u Mihrēn yut yut pat ān x^vāstak yō hē pasčaēta ōh bavēt cē ēt-ic pātixšāy. ka frāc har x^vēš bē dahēt yut yut zan(ān) pat-iš kart xūp, cē ēt-ic pātixšāy ka bē ō zanān dahēt. yō hē pasčaēta ān bavēt ī pat ān sāl zāyēt ka-š stūrīh pat ō zan pat ān sāl kunišn.

Vayayār[1] wrote: "If a man has designated part of his property for his own *stūrīh* and gives it to be held a year at a time by *Farrax^v* alternating with *Mihrēn*, then this property will come to the two men separately, as this is in accordance with the law. If, on his own account, he gives the property to the wives, it will also be in accordance with the law. The *yō hē pasčaēta* will be the person born of the woman who holds the *stūrīh* in that particular year."

The case described here is, obviously, a complex one, and illustrates the intricate measures a man could be forced to take in order to provide himself with an heir. This man, apparently, had only one *stūrīh*-fortune to operate with as otherwise he might have devised two *stūrīhs*. To set up a *stūrīh* one must have a fortune of at least 80 *stērs*[2], thus the device of the alternating years. *Farrax^v* and *Mihrēn*[3] must naturally marry to fulfil their obligation, and testator is free to transfer the *stūrīh* to the wives instead of the husbands. His chances of obtaining an heir are now much greater, as there are two couples involved in the process. The child born of the couple who holds the *stūrīh* that particular year will then be the successor to the *stūrīh*-fortune, i.e. the *yō hē pasčaēta*. In this case, then, the succession works by way of the *stūrīh*-institution, so that the inheritance is being administrated by *Farrax^v* and *Mihrēn* until the time when the heir proper is born to one of them, a son who will carry on the testator's name, and be the owner of the *stūrīh*-property. The next passage is also concerned with *yō hē pasčaēta*.

MHD 21.10-15

nipišt kū ka frazand ī pas zāyēt duxt u zindak pit šōd kunēt hac zanīh hilēt u apāc šavēt vitart stūr ī kart ān stūrīh apar ān duxt ōh manēt u ka-š dātistān ōgōn ī pitar ī stūr andar apāyēt pat ān ī pit ōh gumārišn u hast kē ētōn gōbēt kū ka-c-iš andar ān ī ka stūr ī kartak pat baxt šavēt šoy kartan nē hišt ēstēt adak-ic yō hē pasčaēta. Vahrām guft kū ka-š andar ān ī šōd kart ētōn apāyēt dāštan cigōn ka nē zindak hē.

The law states the following: If the last child born is a daughter, and she takes a husband while her father is still alive, and her husband releases her from the marriage and she returns (to her father), then the *stūrīh* will be taken over by the daughter (in case of) the demise of the instituted *stūr*, and if there has been a legal decision that a *stūr* is needed for the father she should be appointed as such for her father. The law also states that if she is married at

1. A jurist.

2. The required sum for setting up a *stūrīh* according to *MHD 45.2, 46.4, 82.13, 109.4*.

3. Signifying any man.

MHD 21.5-8

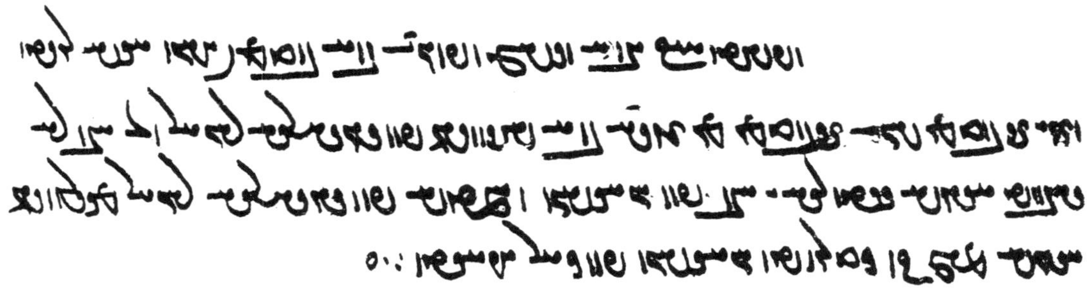

MHD 21.15 – 22.3

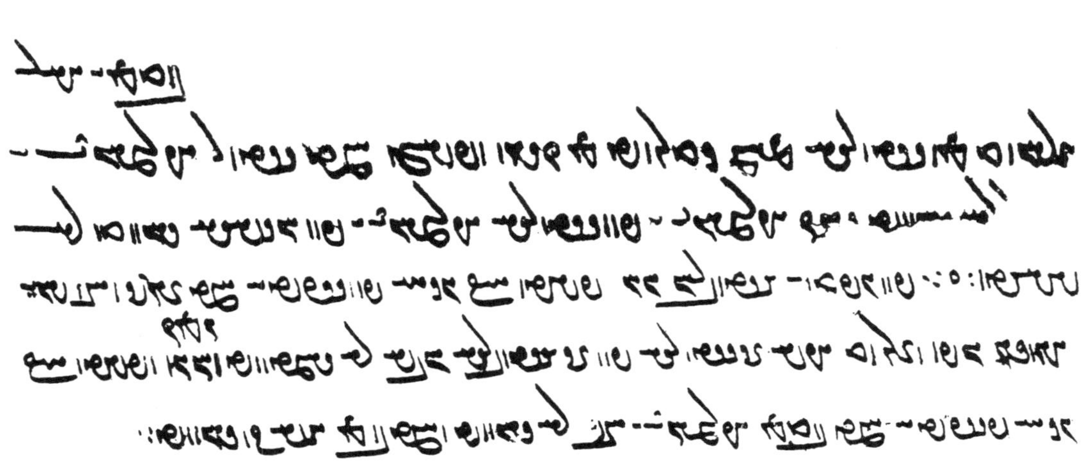

the time of the demise of the instituted *stūr*, and not divorced, she will become *yō hē pasčaēta*. *Vahrām*, on the other hand, maintains that while she is married she shall be considered as non-existent for the office of *stūrīh*.

As in the preceding case, the prospective *yō hē pasčaēta* here is a daughter who can only function as an intermediary successor. The question is: Can she become a successor if she is already married? Apparently, there is consensus that she can if she obtains a divorce. Only the jurist *Vahrām* is of a different opinion, which is faithfully recorded. He regards a married daughter as non-existent for this purpose. The possibility of the daughter's acting as *ayōkēn* is not considered here; instead, she will become *stūr*. The father, in this case, has already instituted a *stūr,* which may be the reason why this solution has been thought necessary. In this instance, at least, *21.10-15* differs from

MHD 21.5-8

nipišt kū mart zan u frazand bē duxt 1 ani kas nēst u ān ī ān duxt šōd ān duxt hac zanīh bē hilēt pat sardārīh apāc ō pit nē dahēt, adak-iš stūrīh ī pit pat x^{v}āhišn u ka-š pat sardārīh apāc patigīrēt, adak-iš apar ō manēt u x^{v}āhišn pat kār apāyēt.

It is written: In case a man has neither wife nor children except one daughter, and the husband of this daughter dissolves his marriage with her without giving her back to her father's guardianship, she may take over the *stūrīh* for her father if she demands it[1]; but if she is taken back to her father's guardianship she will inherit it[2] and must demand it.

It is evident from the above example that it is the question of guardianship that determines the daughter's way of taking over the *stūrīh* of her father. She would, without any question, succeed to it, if her father were guardian and consequently economically bound to her, but if he were not, she would have to apply for it, and a decision would have to be made as to whether she was suitable or not. Apparently, opinions among jurists differ on this point as seen from the following passages:

MHD 21.15 - 22.3

duxt ī pas zāt kē stūrīh apar manēt hac cigōn x^{v}ēš ka stūr aparmānd ī pitar[3] nē bavēt andar-ic aparmānd ī pat stūrīh aparmānd pat x^{v}ēšīh būt nē šāyēt.

pat guft ī dastavarān ōgōn nipišt kū yō hē pasčaēta ka zindak pit šōd kunēt xūp šut u-š ān stūrīh pat ān dastavarīh aviš nē rasēt.

ēn-ic ōgōn nipišt kū yō hē pasčaēta ka duxt aparmānd ī pit nē bavēt u ka pus a-š ōh bavēt.

1. M. Macuch (1993), p. 175: "...dann wird das *stūrīh* des Vaters durch Anforderung (eines *stūr* besetzt)."; See also Kommentar p. 181.

2. Cf. G. Klingenschmitt (1967) p. 63: "...da wird es (das Vermögen) ihr vererbt."

3. Ms is not clearly written in this place, and G. Klingenschmitt (1967) p. 60, emendit to *pitar*.

MHD 23.13-14

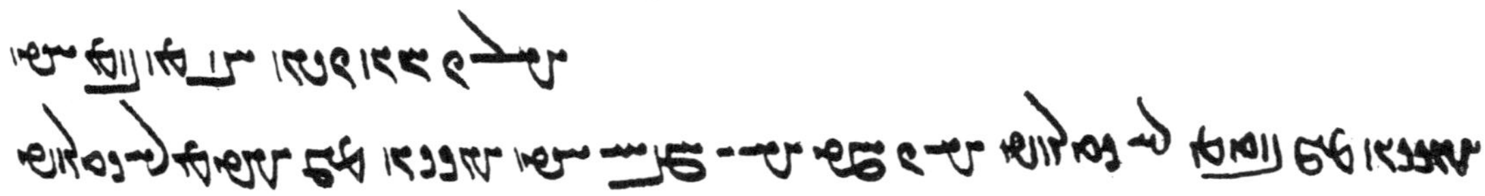

MHD 89.17 – 90.1

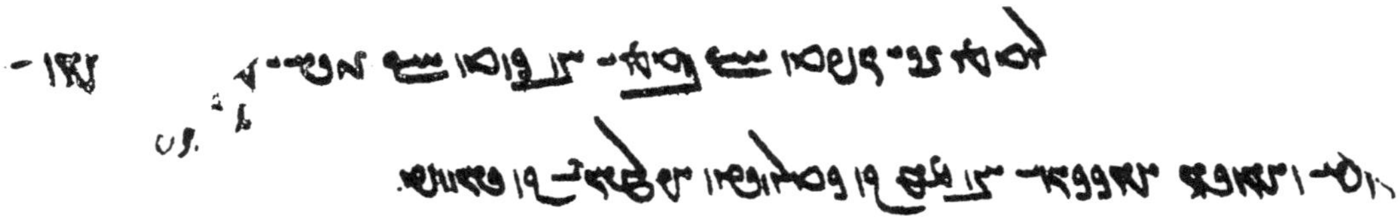

The last born daughter who succeeds to the *stūrīh* will not as a *stūr* have a right to the full inheritance[1] of her father as her own; inheritance in *stūrīh* can never become a personal possession.

According to the declaration of the authorities of law the following is written: "It is right, if the *yō hē pasčaēta* (the successor) marries and leaves while her father is still living, and the *stūrīh* will not be transferred to her according to this declaration". It is also stated that if the *yō hē pasčaēta* is a daughter the full inheritance from her father will not be hers, but if it is a son, it will be his.

So, according to some jurists, the fact that a daughter marries does not preclude her from taking on the *ayōkēnīh* or the *stūrīh* for her father, whereas others are of the opposite opinion. We must suppose people to have opted for the legal opinion which best fitted their own purpose since they could claim legal authority for both practises. What is interesting, however, is that the opposing opinions illustrate the fact that people held different views as to family relationship. Some, apparently, considered daughters as belonging to the family into which they were born, while others held that a daughter, as soon as she was married, would belong solely to her husband's family. The latter opinion is put forward as a counter-proposal, so we must assume that the former is the one that is most generally held.[2]
22.3 states briefly the principle of succession. A son will inherit as the real heir, but a daughter as *stūr* will only be an intermediary between her father and his true heir.
The same principle applies to cases of *ayōkēnīh*:

MHD 23.13-14

pas-ic ōgōn cigōn pit kē pus hast ayōkkēn apar duxt nē manēt; brāt-ic ka brāt ī hambāy hast ayōkkēn apar xᵛah nē manēt.

Finally it is thus, that a daughter cannot act as *ayōkēn* for a father who has a son; nor will a sister become *ayōkēn* for her brother if he has an associate partner brother.

The fact that an *ayōkēn* is not needed in cases where there is a son makes the nature of *ayōkēnīh* absolutely clear. The fact that a partner brother can take the place of a son is yet another proof of the importance of the idea of partnership. It looks as if the relationship between partner brothers comes very close to that between father and son.
The difference for a daughter between undertaking *stūrīh* and *ayōkēnīh* is illustrated in

MHD 89.17 - 90.1

apāk ān ī guft kū duxt ī pit kart kū zanīh ī Mihrēn kun, (zanīh) nē kunēt ayōkkēn ī pit apar ōh manēt u aparmānd ōh bavēt.

With the jurist who said: "(If) a daughter refuses to marry *Mihrēn* whom her father told her to marry, she will succeed to the *ayōkēnīh* of her father, and the full inheritance will go to her."

---

1. *aparmānd* is explained by M. Macuch (1993) p. 418-21 as the full inheritance as opposed to the inheritance divided into parts. I think her interpretation is correct.

2. B. Hjerrild (1993) p. 85.

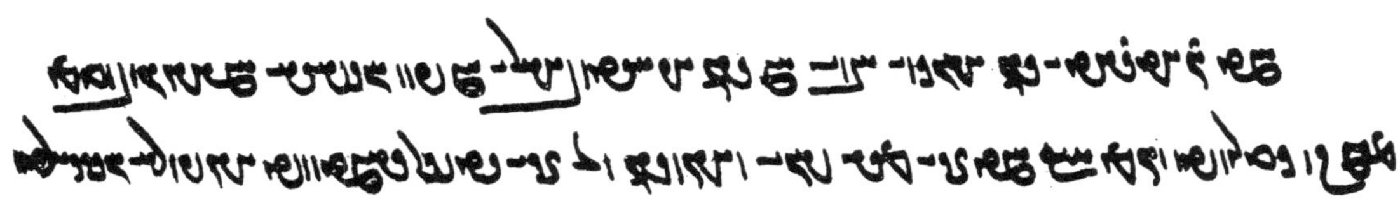

A daughter possessed the right to refuse to enter into a marriage of her father's choice[1], but still it may have caused trouble between father and daughter, so it is an interesting fact that the daughter's disobedience does not disqualify her for becoming her father's successor. We learn that a daughter who is appointed *ayōkēn* will inherit her father's fortune in full. If she has sisters, she will inherit the same portion as a *pātixšāy*-wife, which is double a daughter's share. If she is the only surviving offspring of her father, she will inherit half his fortune while the other half would be settled on her son, her father's true heir. Here would be a good opportunity for a woman to achieve independence, provided, of course, that the father was well-to-do, and one may well imagine that the advantages for her will outweigh the prospect of becoming *Mihrēn*'s wife.

From these passages, we may conclude that despite the fact that *ayōkēnīh* and *stūrīh* served the same purpose, and that the same person could undertake either one or the other, there can be no doubt that the *MHD* distinguishes rigorously between the two institutions. If *aparmānd* really means "full inheritance", it would certainly make a difference, as regards the size of the inheritance, whether the daughter became *stūr* (*21.15*) or *ayōkēn* (*89.17*). Since both institutions serve the issue of succession, it is not surprising that the term *yō hē pasčaēta* should appear in connection with both, but they do certainly not denote the same thing. It is, indeed, highly unlikely that they should have been used indiscriminately in a text which is characterized by its clear distinction between the complexities of its various regulations.

The system does not appear to be upset by the possibility that a daughter who carries her father's *ayōkēnīh* might only bear daughters. The *ayōkēnīh* can, theoretically, be carried on through generations of daughters until, eventually, the son and heir is born and can take his place as the *yō hē pasčaēta.*

This situation has been dealt with in

MHD 41.13-14

ka duxtdāt ī andar xānak ī pit ī māt andar apāyēt bahr ī māt pat x^{v}ēšīh hamaivēn duxt apar ōh manēt u ēn kū ka ān ī mas šōd kunēt ō ān ī ditīkar rasēt aivap nē uskārtan.

If the offspring of a daughter is needed in the house of her mother's father, the mother's share will be inherited by the daughter as her's absolute, and if the eldest daughter marries, it will be considered whether the next one will step in, or not.

This paragraph presents the case of a man who, throughout his life, has kept up the hope of acquiring a male heir, but who now finds himself with a sole female successor who has got a family of her own with no sons to spare. She may even be past the childbearing age, so his only possibility is to appoint a female grandchild as his *ayōkēn*. He might, of course, appoint a *stūr*, but the preferable solution seems to be the appointing of his granddaughter as *ayōkēn* judging from the length of the explanation.

MHD 24.3-7 corroborates this evidence of the granddaughter's obligation towards her maternal grandfather:

1. Also in *MHD 36.10-15*.

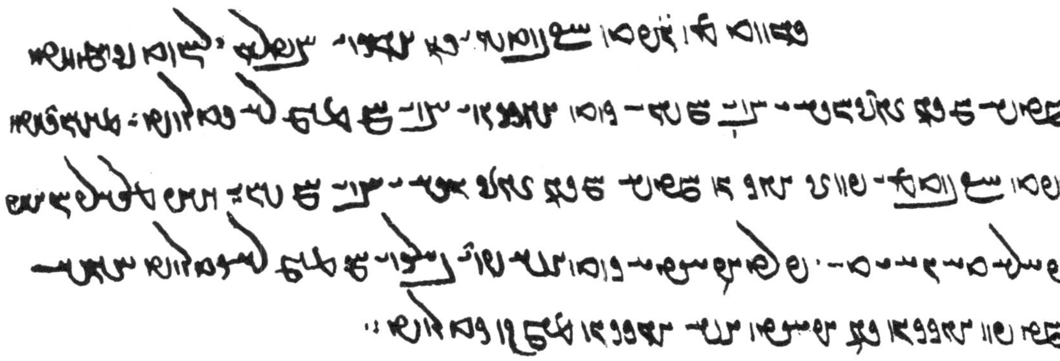

MHD 24.3-7

būt kē guft kū duxt ī andar xānak ī pitarān zāt ēstēt ka-š māt andar zindakānīh ī pit ī māt šōd ayōkēn ī pit ī māt apar nē manēt.

Māhvindāt guft kū duxt ī pat ān ayōkēn ka-š māt andar zindakānīh ī pit ī māt šōd aivap margarzān aivap paratācaiti kart a-š nēm bahrak ī māt apar nē manēt adak-iš ka pat ayōkēn andar apāyēt a-š ayōkēn apar ōh manēt.

One jurist has said that a daughter born in the house of her parents may not act as *ayōkēn* for her mother's father if the mother married during her father's lifetime.

Māhvindāt[1] said: "If a mother has married while her father was still alive, or if she has committed a *margarzān*-sin or a *paratacaiti*-sin[2], her daughter shall not inherit the halfpart of the mother's inheritance, but if necessary she will become *ayōkēn* for her mother's father, and shall inherit him as such."

Two legal views are here advanced. If the mother has married in her own father's lifetime, and her daughter has been born in the house of the mother's husband, then the daughter is under no obligation to become *ayōkēn* for her grandfather. According to *Māhvindāt*, however, she will act as *ayōkēn* for her maternal grandfather under certain circumstances. Evidently, the learned in law disagree as to the point when the female line is finally severed from its origin. In this respect, it is interesting to note that there is no question of a daughter's obligation towards a paternal grandfather. The ties of blood must have been felt to be very strong through the female line, so strong, in fact, that daughters' daughters could be called upon to act as intermediary successors to their grandfather. This must have given rise to a certain animosity on the part of fathers generally. When could a man be sure of having heirs for himself? His sons might die, and if his daughters had obligations towards their maternal grandfather, how would he secure his own succession? Even a *pātixšāy*-marriage would not be an insurance against dying without an heir. His wife would have obligations towards her father and brothers, his daughters, although they had obligations towards him, might also be called upon to oblige their grandfather, perhaps even at a time when their father could not foretell that he would need them himself. His best insurance would be to have several *pātixšāy*-wives, if he could afford it.

The family structure was decidedly patriarchal, but with an inherent conflict. It was, obviously, a woman's duty to provide successors for her *pātixšāy*-husband, but at the same time, she had an obligation towards her father, her brother, and even her maternal grandfather. So one cannot define the family structure as agnatic[3], since the succession was not secured by the nearest male relative of the deceased male, as he would not inherit automatically. On the contrary, the succession must be inherited in a direct line, from father to son, or, failing this, from father through daughter to a grandson, or even through two female intermediaries to the successor proper[4].

---

1. A jurist.
2. C. Bartholomae (1923) p. 34 ff. proposes that this sin is the sin of leaving her husband (cf. Avestan *paratacaiti* 3. sing. pres. = runs away).
3. As A. Perikhanian does (1983), p. 641 ff.
4. The same pattern of succession can be found in B.N. Dhabhar (1932) p. 198.

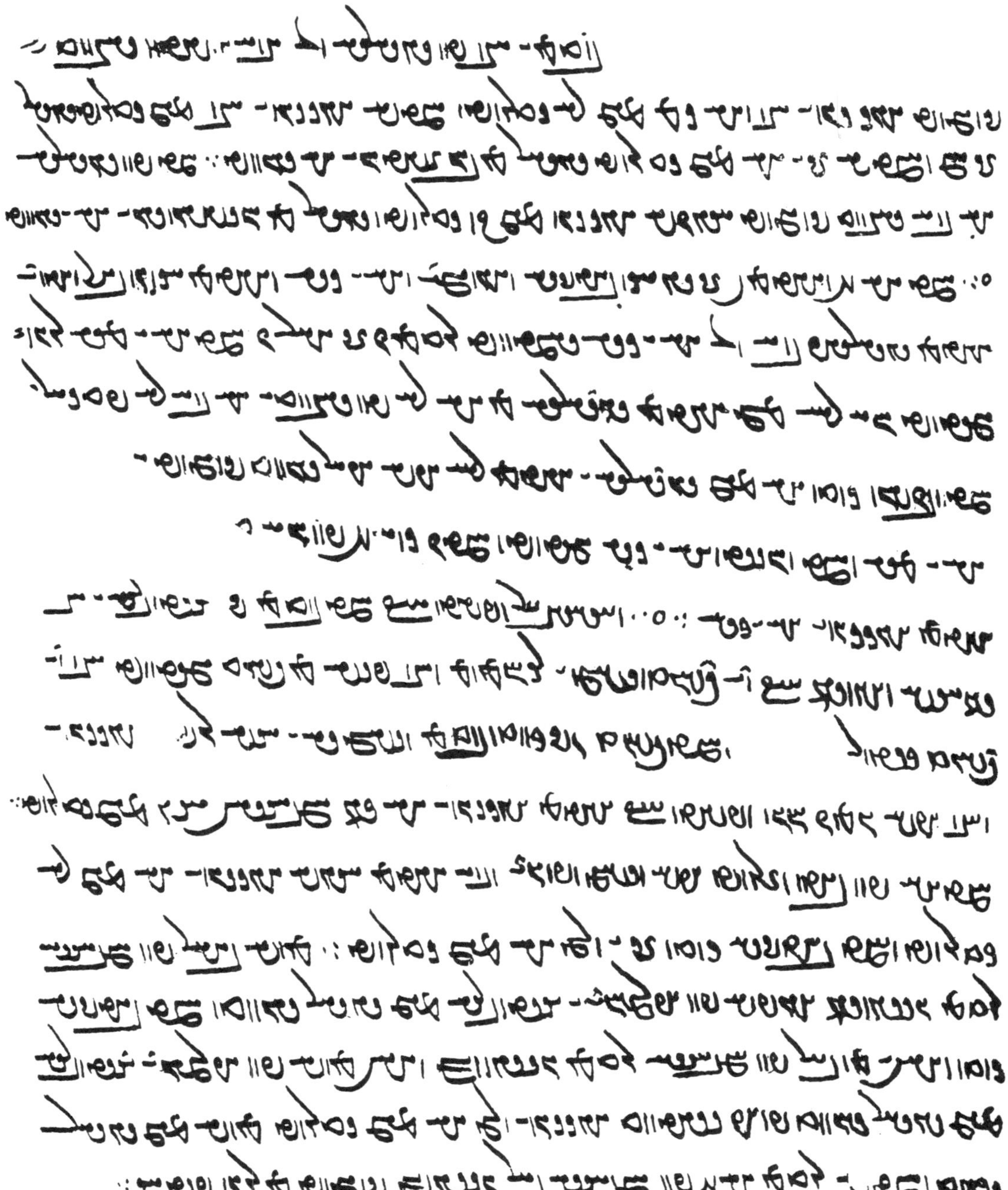

MHD 22.9 - 23.10

duxt ī pit pat sardārīh ō mart ī šahr dāt ēstēt ayōkēn ī pit u brāt kam apar nē manēt, ka-š ayōkēn ī pit apar manēt sardār ān māt u ka-š ān ī brāt manēt sardār hac nabānazdištān[1] ī brāt bavēt. ka pat sardārīh brāt bē dāt ēstēt adak-iš ayōkēn apar ōh manēt u sardār hac x^vēšāvandān ī brāt ī bavēt.

ka brāt 2 u x^vah 1 ān giyāk baxtīkīh kunēnd u brāt ī kas u x^vah hakanēn bahr kunēnd x^vah sardārīh-ic bē ō brāt ī kas rasēt apāk-ic ān pas-ic ka brāt ī mas pēš mīrēt ē rād cē x^vah sardārīh hac brāt nē pat dāt ī brāt bē nē patkār, ka bazišn[2] kart brāt apar sardārīh ī x^vah rād hac-iš apar būt ēstēt x^vah ayōkēn ī brāt ī mas u ka nax^{v}ist brāt ī kas mīrēt u ka-c har 2 pat ē x^vah ayōkēn ī brāt ī kas.

(*23.1*) Vayayār nipišt kū ka duxt ān dastavarīh ī pit andar kas kunēt kū tāi 10 sāl zan ī tō hom u pit pēš hac 10 sāl mīrēt pit tāi 10 sāl stūr (gumārišn)[3] u ka 10 sāl ...KWNt'[4] zanīh ī kas nēst u ayōkēn ī [u] pit, u-š ēn-ic ōgōn nipišt kū x^vah ayōkēn ī brāt andar hambāyīh adak apar manēt.

ka brāt pat baxt šavēt u-š zan u frazand u bē x^vah adak-iš ayōkēn ī brāt apar nē manēt u ka baxtīkīh kart ān ī ō brāt apar manēt. kē-š bahr pat hambāyīh apāk stānēt aivap-iš pat aparmānd ī dastavarīh apar sardār būt ka baxtīkīh kart u brāt 1 ī kē bahr pat hambāyīh apāk stat u brāt 1 kē-š pat aparmānd dastavarīh apar sardār būt frāc ayōkēn ī ō brāt apar manēt kē-š apar sardār būt u ka-š apāk brāt 2 pat hambāyīh bahr stat ēstēt hac pēš paitāk.

A daughter who has been placed by her father under the guardianship of a fellow-citizen may, nevertheless, become an *ayōkēn* for her father or brother. If she is appointed *ayōkēn* for her father, then her mother's guardian shall be hers also, but if she becomes *ayōkēn* for her brother, her guardian shall be one of her brother's next-of-kin. If she is placed under the guardianship of her brother, she will inherit his *ayōkēnīh*, her guardian in that case being one of her brother's relatives.

When there are two brothers and one sister and they divide their inheritance, the younger brother and the sister taking their shares jointly, then the guardianship over the sister is entrusted to the younger brother. It is further stated that: "Later, if the elder brother dies first the guardianship over the sister cannot be disputed, because it was not transferred by the elder brother, but if the younger brother by the division of the inheritance has lost the guardianship over the sister, she is the elder brother's *ayōkēn*, and if the younger brother dies first, or if both die at the same time, the sister is the younger brother's *ayōkēn*."

(*23.1*) *Vayayār* says: "If a daughter, with her father's consent, enters upon a ten-year marriage contract, and the father happens to die within this ten-year period, a *stūr* must be appointed for him for the remaining period; when the

---

1. Ms has *b'nzdšt'n*.

2. Ms has *wbcšn*.

3. The text is not legible, but *gumārišn* must be understood.

4. The text is not legible here either.

ten-year period expires, her marriage with her husband will be dissolved and she will become her father's *ayōkēn*."

He also says that a sister inherits the *ayōkēnīh* for her brother with whom she has entered into partnership.

If the brother dies, and he has a wife and children, she will not become her brother's *ayōkēn*. If the distribution of the inheritance has been completed, she will become *ayōkēn* for the brother with whom she is co-inheritor, or the brother who was her guardian according to the authority of inheritance. If the distribution of the inheritance has been concluded, and the brother with whom she was co-inheritor, and the brother who was her guardian according to the authority of inheritance both die, then she will become *ayōkēn* for him who was her guardian; if she happened to be co-inheritor with both brothers, the procedure will be as the above.

It is apparent from these passages that the daughters of the family have obligations towards their brothers as well as towards their father. The expression "has been placed under the guardianship of a fellow-citizen" may be taken to mean "was married to", but not necessarily so. However, the important fact expressed in this paragraph is that if the girl's father or her brother needs her as an *ayōkēn*, the guardianship over her will be reassumed by her family.

22.13 contains information about *hambāyīh*, partnership, which plays an important role in Zoroastrian family law. According to the paragraph here, a brother and sister can enter into a contract according to which they take joint possession of their inheritance. As this would, in most cases, consist of land, this solution would seem both practical and certainly more profitable. There may have been other reasons for Zoroastrian families to endeavour to keep their properties intact, but information on the subject of landownership is extremely scarce.

Partnership between brother and sister seems, in other instances too, to have been regarded as a very important relationship, in most cases implying guardianship too, even though the partner-brother were not the eldest son, because guardianship and partnership were both based on economic relationship.

In the paragraph treated here, however, there seems to be some doubt as to the procedure in case the elder brother might need his sister as *ayōkēn*; but she will only be his if the younger brother did not attain the guardianship. As cited in *23.1ff*, *Vayayār* imparts clearly that partnership, as the one treated above, is the most important of family relations. It must also have seemed the most obvious solution from an economic point-of-view, inasmuch as the *ayōkēn*-sister after her brother's death will have simply continued to manage her own and her brother's property until her son came of age to enter upon his inheritance. There is no mention anywhere of the award granted for the services of an *ayōkēn*, but it seems likely that she would be granted a share corresponding to that of a *pātixšāy*-wife, since, to all intents and purposes, she functions as such. Anyway, through the services of the *ayōkēn*, the property will stay in the hands of the family, whereas if a *stūr* has to be appointed, he must be paid a salary, and his son who will be the future heir to the property, could be expected to continue to feel loyalty towards his biological father and his family.

The problem of a lack of male heirs is treated from a different angle in *MHD 23.1*. A man who foresees that he may die without leaving any male issue has the possibility of giving his daughter away in marriage for a limited space of time. Thus, he avoids committing the sin of leaving his daughter unwed, while, at the same time,

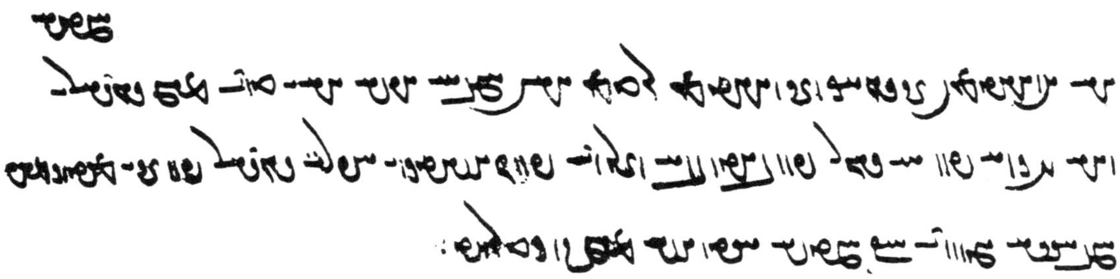

he circumvents any problems that may arise with his daughter's husband in case he himself might need his daughter as *ayōkēn* to continue his lineage.
Such a temporary marriage contract is mentioned in only a few passages of the *MHD*[1]. It is certainly a question whether a *pātixšāy*-marriage could be contracted in such a way, but I am inclined to believe that it could. *Zan* (wife) invariably denotes *zan ī pātixšāy* where nothing else is implied, and the only other possibility: That the daughter would undertake *stūrīh* for a limited period, would most certainly have been specifically pointed out. If this is so it lends support to my argument, in the chapter on *sardārīh,* that marriage contracts in Sasanian times, in contrast to later periods, could be made to meet individual requirements. The advantages of the above-mentioned temporary marriage contract would be that the daughter would be able to provide her husband with *pātixšāy*-children and thus secure his succession, while the obvious disadvantage to the husband would be that he could only have the disposal of his wife's dowry for ten years.
In the *MHD 23.5* we learn that the eldest son who would customarily act as guardian for his sister would also have a prior claim to her as *ayōkēn*. Legal opinion on this issue varies, however:

MHD 22.3-6

ka-š brāt 2 u x^{v}ah 1 ān giyāk u ān x^{v}ah apāk brāt ē hambāy u-š brāt ē dit apar sardār ī u brāt 2 har pat ē yāvar pat baxt bē šavēnd pat cāstak ī Aparak sardār, pat ān ī Mētōkmāh hambāyīh gōbēnd kū ka-š hast a-š apar ōh manēt.

In a family with two brothers and one sister in which the sister has become associate partner with one brother, and the other acts as her guardian, if both brothers die at the same time, then, according to the teachings of *Aparag* she will inherit the *(ayōkēnīh)* of the guardian, while, according to the teachings of *Mētōmāh*[2], that of the associate partner if he has some property.

The above passage makes it abundantly clear that the jurists disagree as to which of the said relationships was considered the most important. This, of course, reflects the complexity of the economic interrelationship in certain families. The sister in question was obviously bound economically to both her brothers. The guardian-brother had the right and the duty to look after her fortune, the fortune that had come into existence through her business partnership with her other brother with whom she had co-inherited their father. It would certainly be difficult to determine which brother was the one most closely connected with his sister. One must bear in mind, however, that the question is solely of which economic relation is considered the most important and legally binding, as it is the closest economic relation that requires the *ayōkēnīh.*
These differing points of view as to which brother has the legal right to claim his sister confirm the fact that the family into which the woman was born has the first claim to her services, not her husband's family.
Sisters and daughters seem to have been much in demand as intermediary successors, considering the detailed prescriptions put down in the law-texts. The cause of this must be sought in the prevailing social conditions. The mortality rate was certainly high, and in addition to this, the men were regularly exposed to the dangers of war. It must have been very difficult to secure an heir for every man. The avail-

1. See M. Macuch (1985), where these passages are treated.
2. A jurist.

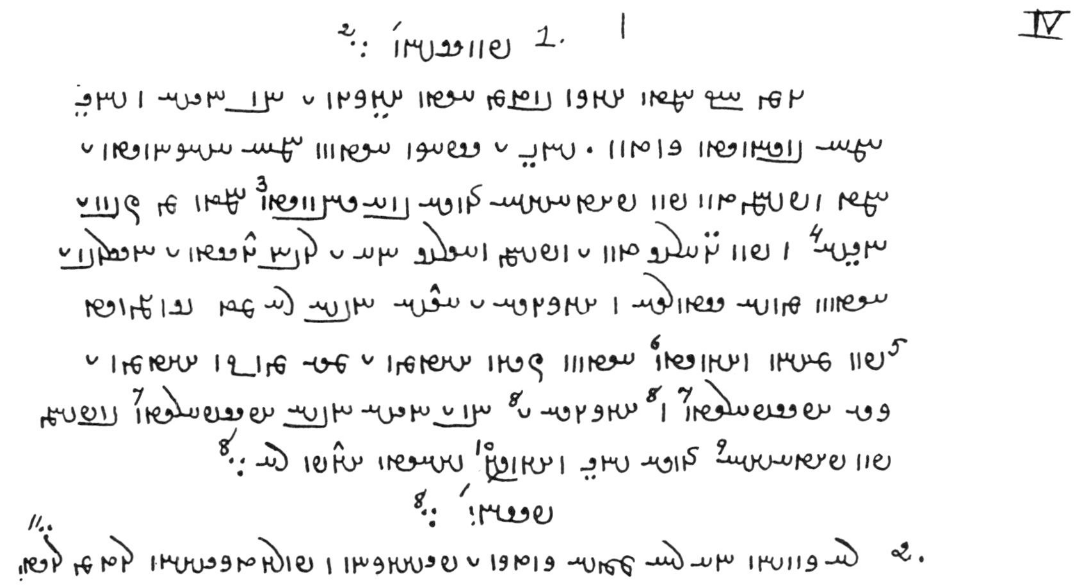

IV 1. *Written with red ink in* TD_2. 2. TD_2 *omits*; G *torn*.
3. G [illegible]. 4. G (*torn*) [illegible].
5. TD_2 *prefixes* 1.6. G [illegible]. 7. G [illegible]. 8. TD_2 *omits*.
9. G [illegible]. 10. [illegible]. 11. *Both omit*.

able men must have been obliged to enter into several marriages of different types to enable the women to fulfil their obligation to produce heirs.

From the evidence of these paragraphs on the institution of *ayōkēnīh*, we may conclude that the essential function of a daughter was to fulfil her obligation to her family. When she married and brought her share of the family fortune with her as dowry, her husband could by no means be sure that she would remain his wife, or that the property she brought with her would remain in his family. Her own family retained a prior claim to it. So, the family structure is not agnatic.

Judging from the intricate and closely interwoven economic ties within the family revealed in the rules of *ayōkēnīh*, with its insistence on the obligations of the daughters towards their male relatives, the Zoroastrian family emerges as a closely knit, if somewhat inscrutable, unit. Economic ties supersede the marital bond. The logical consequence of this family structure must, in fact, be the next-of-kin marriage, the *x^{v}ētōdah*, which will radically solve the problems arising out of the conflicting interests of a woman's own family and that of her husband.

AFS

The *AFS* does not, to any great extent, treat the problems of *ayōkēnīh*. In fact, only one brief paragraph in the *Farnbag Srōš* deals with the subject:

> **AFS IV**
>
> *pursišn:*
> ēn kū ka ēvak duxt hast ayōkēn ī pit x^{v}ēš u šōd hamē x^{v}ahēt kartan, šōd ī sacāk ētōn hamē vindēt ī ka x^{v}ēš tan pat pātixšāy zanīh bē dahēt ka hac hīr ī x^{v}ēš u pat gōhrīk tan ī x^{v}ēš nairīk ē ī rūvān dōst ī husrav ī ētōn kē-š stūrīh u ayōkēnīh ī kas aviš nē mat ēstēt pat miyān kunēt ētōn cigōn x^{v}ah ī mas kē ōh x^{v}ah ī kas apispārēt x^{v}at pat pātixšāy zanīh šōd kunēt šāyēt aivap nē?
>
> *passax^{v}:*
> nē kunišn ē rād cē-š kartak ī pēšēnikān u pōryōtkēšān apāk nēst.
>
> *Question:*
> This is the question: Will an only daughter who is *ayōkēn* for her father and who wants to take a husband for life be allowed to take a proper husband and give herself in a *pātixšāy*-marriage. Is she allowed, being a woman of good reputation and noble lineage, out of her own property, like one who is not obliged to take on *stūrīh* or *ayōkēnīh* for anyone, like an older sister who hands over to her younger sister, and assigns the *ayōkēnīh* of their father to her, and herself takes a *pātixšāy*-husband, will she be allowed to do this or not?
>
> *Answer:*
> This ought not to be done because the laws of the ancestors, and the first religious teachers do not allow it.

The most important message contained in this paragraph is that there is no way for a daughter to escape the responsibility and obligation to act as her father's *ayōkēn*, if he should need one. There is no indication that the obligation extends towards her brother too, however. But even if she should want to contract a very proper marriage with the purest intentions, herself being a good person and a stout believer, there is no way she may shirk her responsibility. One senses the compassion of the author, but the decision is clear-cut: She must obey the rules, and can

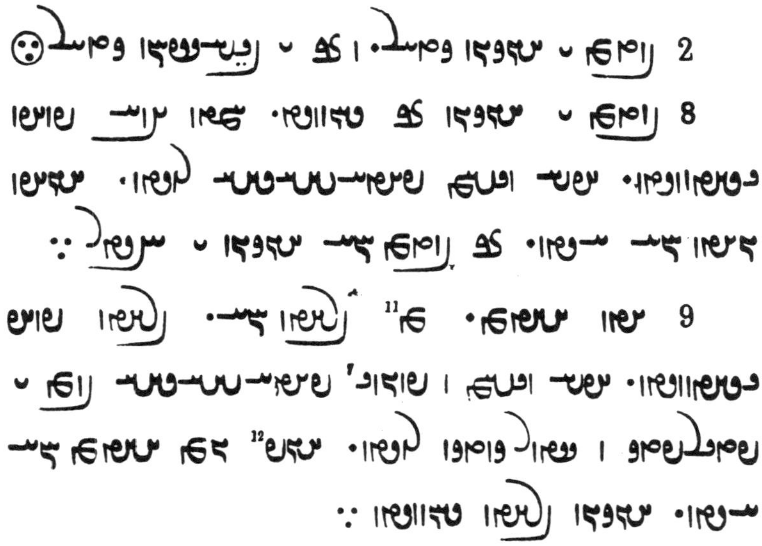

11. For [Pahlavi word]. 12. For [Pahlavi word].

thus only contract a marriage in which she will hold an inferior position in her husband's family, since he must, of course, provide himself with a *pātixšāy*-wife in order to secure heirs for himself.

In the same question, we are presented with the case of a family with no sons but two daughters in which the elder daughter cleverly pushes the obligation of acting as *ayōkēn* for their father on to the younger sister. This is apparently in accordance with the law. As long as one of them does it, the law is satisfied.

The *AFS* does not seem to be concerned with the details of the institution of *ayōkēnīh*, the principal message is put forward in bare outline. The differing opinions expressed in the *MHD* have evidently been discarded, and the point of view that has survived seems to be the one that gives the family an indisputable right to use their daughter as *ayōkēn*. We do not know, however, whether that right went as far as forcing her to divorce her husband.

Where the *MHD* treats people only in relation to the law, the *AFS* seems to be concerned with the moral standard and religious dedication of the members of the community, cf. the above-mentioned good, religious woman. This is one of the most striking differences between the two codes.

REA

The *REA* treats the problem of *ayōkēnīh* in far greater detail than the *AFS*, but it is still a collection of case studies rather than a full account of the intricacies of the institution. The rules are compiled so that we have to wait for the definition of *ayōkēnīh* until after we have been given an example of how the institution works interspersed with various other subjects. This method is foreign to the *REA*, which normally proceeds in an orderly and systematic manner.

The *REA* has two almost identical definitions of the phenomenon:

REA 31.2, 8-9:

pursišn 2:
duxt ī ayōkēn katār. (....)

passaxᵛ 8:
duxt ī ayōkēn ān bavēt, ka mart frāc ravēt, u-š zan pātixšāyīhā nēst, ēvāc duxt ē hast, ān duxt ē ayōkēn ī pitar.

9. hakar xᵛah, kē brāt ē, brāt frāc ravēt, u-š zan u frazand pātixšāyīhā pus ī patīriftak stūr kartak nēst, ēvāc ēn xᵛah ē hast. ayōkēn brāt bavēt.

Question 2:
Who is an *ayōkēn*-daughter?

Answer 8:
An *ayōkēn*-daughter is this: If a man dies, leaving no *pātixšāy*-wife, but only a daughter, then this said daughter becomes her father's *ayōkēn*.

9. If a sister has a brother who dies, leaving no *pātixšāy*-wife or -children, no adopted son, nor a designated *stūr*, but only this one sister, then she becomes her brother's *ayōkēn*.

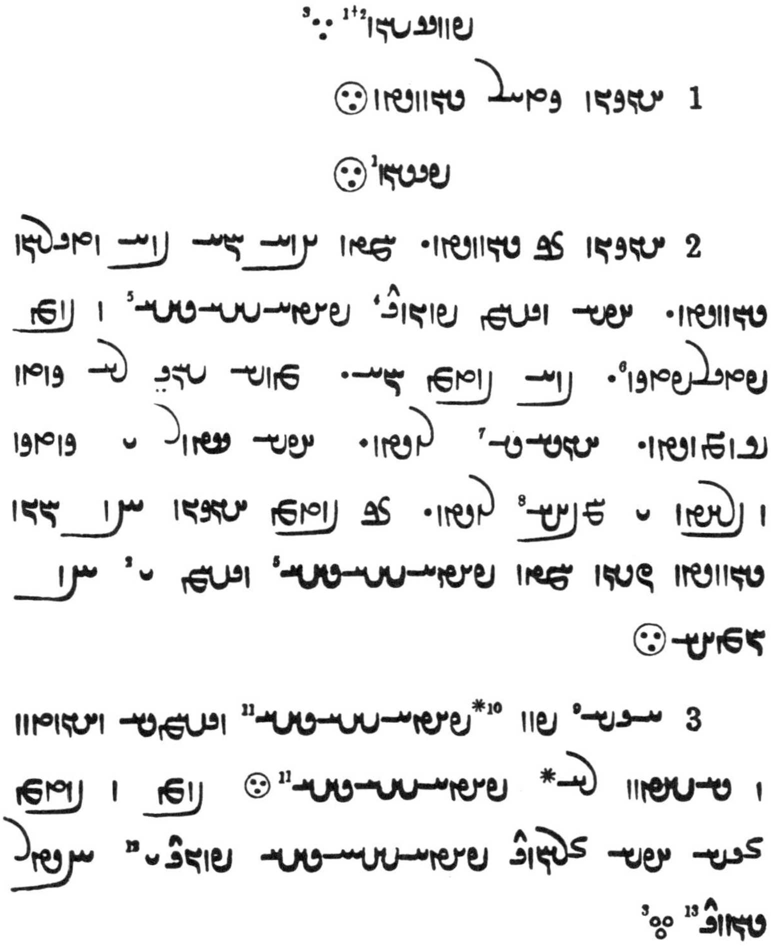

1. Written with red ink in TD. 2. G omits. 3. TD omits. 4. Better [illegible]. 5. For [illegible]. 6. TD leaves a blank space of half an inch after this; G torn; must have had a blank over which .. و اسم is inserted. 7. For [illegible]. 8. Better [illegible].

9. TD [illegible]. 10** G [illegible] ; TD omits. 11. Better [illegible]. 12. TD [illegible]. 13. TD [illegible].

REA 44.1-3:

pursišn 1:
ayōkēn katār bavēt.

passax[v] *2:*
ayōkēn ān bavēt, ka mart ē bē vitīrān bavēt, u-š zan frazand pātixšāyīhā u pus patīriftak bē duxt ē, kē-š šōd nē kart ēstēt, ēnyā-š nēst, u-š stūr ī kartak u brāt ī hambāy nēst, ān duxt ayōkēn pit ōgōn bavēt cigōn ka pātixšāyīhā zan ī pit hā.

3. kas pat pātixšāyīhā zanīh griftan u dāštan nē pātixšāyīhā. pus u duxt ī-š hac-iš zāyēnd pātixšāyīhā frazand ī pitar bavēnd.

Question 1:
What is an *ayōkēn*?

Answer 2:
An *ayōkēn* is this: If a man dies, leaving no *pātixšāy*-wife or -children, no adopted son, but only one daughter who is not married, and no one else, and who has no designated *stūr*, and no associated brother as partner in the inheritance, then this daughter will become her father's *ayōkēn* in the same way as if she were her father's *pātixšāy*-wife.

3. Nobody is entitled to marry her and keep her in a *pātixšāy*-marriage. The sons and daughters born of her will be her father's *pātixšāy*-children.

The two definitions, following hard upon one another, although they differ slightly, do not represent different views; they are presumably meant to supplement each other, and as they are recorded separately, they are probably quoted from two different sources. An *ayōkēn* is defined as a woman who cannot enter into a *pātixšāy*-marriage because she is under an obligation to provide her father or her brother with an heir. As compensation, she will be regarded as her father's *pātixšāy*-wife, which will imply certain economic advantages. All her children, daughters as well as sons, will be regarded as her father's/brother's children, and she will not be able to change her marriage status into that of *pātixšāy*-wife even after an heir has been born.

Curiously enough, the *REA* has adopted the view of the dissident jurists of the *MHD*, viz. that an *ayōkēn* must be unwed at the time of her appointment, as she is not allowed to divorce her husband in order to become an *ayōkēn*. This means that the *REA* supports the view that the relationship between husband and wife is seen as more important than the one between father-daughter and brother-sister. This is also reflected in the fact that she is not the first choice, even if she is unmarried. An adopted son, a designated *stūr,* or an associate brother all take precedence over her, not to mention a *pātixšāy*-wife who might contract a *cakar*-marriage and thus supply the missing heir. One may wonder what has wrought the change in the legal point-of-view. Laws are normally fairly conservative, but they may also be prescriptive, and in that case, a change must reflect a need in society for different measures.

In this case, the reason could be that the number of girls available for *pātixšāy*-marriages was dwindling because of the daughters' obligations towards their own families. This would, obviously, present a threat to the continuation of the Zoroastrian community. A young man who could not find a wife from his own community might well take a Muslim wife in order to secure a family of his own. If girls were so much in demand as bearers of the succession, it must mean that there was

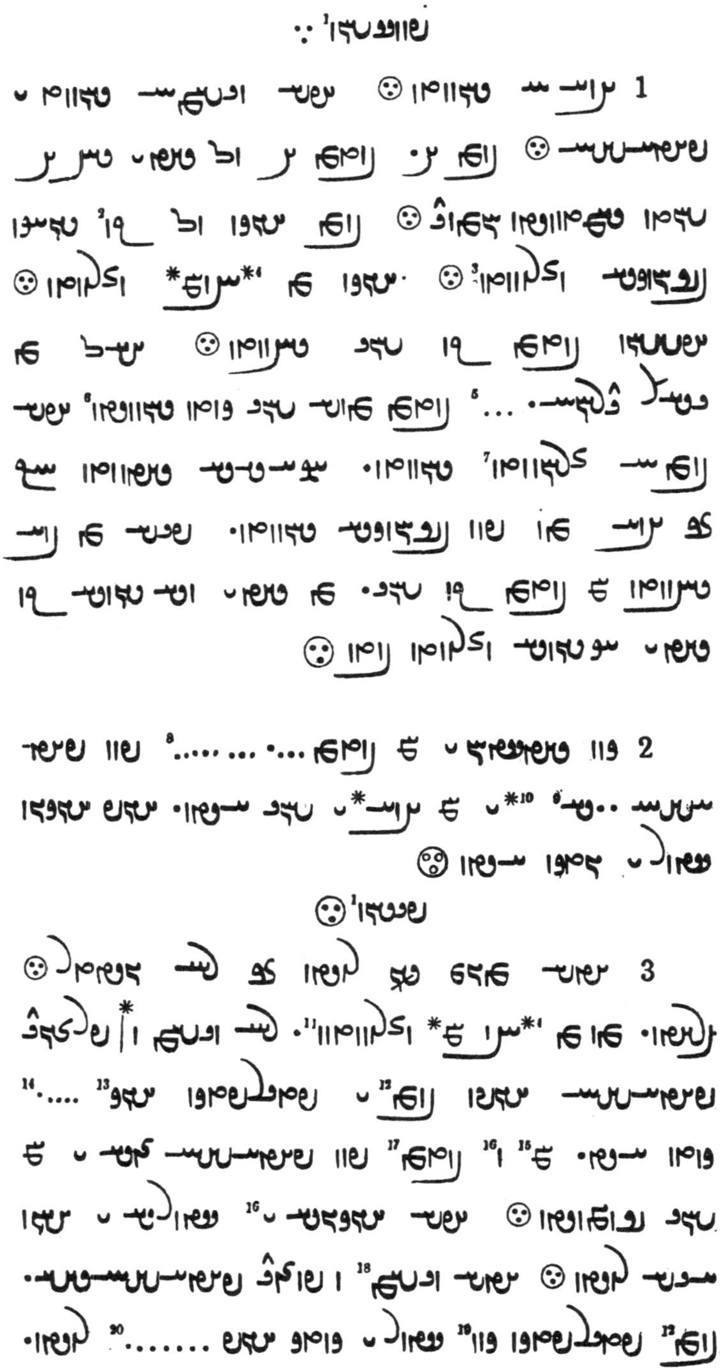

1. Written with red ink. 2. او is written above the word; better omit. 3. Better [illegible]. 4. For [illegible] (?); see Pûrs. V, 5. 5. [illegible] seems to be omitted here. 6. Better [illegible]. 7. Better [illegible].

8. The words [illegible] seem to be missing. 9. For [illegible]. 10** [illegible] repeated by mistake. 11. For [illegible] (?). 12. فس added above. 13. Better [illegible]. 14. [illegible] omitted. 15. ماه added above. 16. Better omit. 17. دخت added above. 18. زن added above. 19. [illegible] added above; [illegible] of the last word seems to be repeated by mistake; better have [illegible]. 20. [illegible] seems to be omitted.

a scarcity of young men. This would necessarily create a conflict between the individual family and the community as a whole. Families without an heir must have put pressure on their daughters to keep the family property intact and thus securing the livelihood of the whole family, whereas the community would be more concerned with the increase in number of Zoroastrian families, to strengthen the whole community. The family without an heir would therefore be encouraged to adopt a son or appoint a *stūr*.

Evidently, the priests did not want to go to such radical lengths as to eliminate the time-honoured institution of *ayōkēnīh* altogether, but by changing the rules as to when an *ayōkēn* would be required they gave the girls a chance to marry in a *pātixšāy*-marriage. The priestly class anxiously guarded the old customs, but in this case, they were lucky enough to be able to quote instances from the old laws when they wanted to change the laws in order to adapt them to the needs of the community.

The conclusion must be that the two paragraphs on *ayōkēnīh* were intended to strengthen the Zoroastrian community by regulating a custom, which had become so widely used as to threaten the establishing of new families, and thereby the whole community.

Despite the clear intention of these paragraphs on *ayōkēnīh*, we find a contradiction in the case described in

REA 1.1-6:

pursišn 1:
mart ē būt. u-š zan ē būt ī pātixšāy. pus 2 duxt 2 ō dāt ī 15 sāl rasēt hēnd. pus ēvak ō ōh giyāk bēkānukīh šut. ēvak hac āvām šut. u-šān duxt ōh šōd dāt. pas hac sāl drahnāy duxt kē-š šōd kart bavēt hac-iš pus ē zāt būt, ākāhēh āmat kū ān mart kē pat bēkānukīh būt, pēš hac bē dātan im duxt ōh šōd, hac dāt ī vēh dēnīh ōh dāt ī akdēnīh šut būt.

2. nūn dātistān ī im duxt pat pātixšāy zanīh ī im mart ī šōd hast, aivap ayōkēn stūr ī dūtak hast?

passaxᵛ 3:
hakar-iš ciš andar nēst ān rād yuvattar. brāt, kē hac āvām šut, rād zan u frazand pātixšāy aivap pus ī patīriftak ēvak kart hast, im [u] duxt pat pātixšāy zanīh ī im šōd ēstēt. u-š ayōkēnīh ī stūrīh ī an kas nēst. hakar-iš zan u frazand pātixšāyīhā, pus patīriftak u stūr ī kartak aivap .... nēst, im duxt pat ayōkēnīh stūr(īh) ī brāt ēstēt, u-š pātixšāy zanīh im šōd nēst. pus ī-š zāt andar dūtak ī im brāt zāt bavēt.

4. hakar im mart, kē-š šōd hast, sahēt kū im zan pat zanīh dārēt, adak-iš pat ayōkēnīh brāt zan apāyēt kartan, nikēcītan pat zanīh šōdīh dēnīkīhā xūp būt. ka yuvattar u adak nē xūp. cē im mart im zan pat pātixšāyīh zanīh dāštan nē pātixšāyīh.

5. u hakar dānēt kū pat pātixšāyīhā zanīh dāštan nē dastavarīhā, u-š pat pātixšāyīhā dārēt, pat giyāk tanāpūhl vinās, u pat sāl drahnāy margarzān.

6. hamē ka bē dānēt kū-š pat pātixšāyīhā zanīh dāštan nē dastavarīhā, u-š pat zanīh apāyišnīk adak-iš zamānīk pat ayōkēnīh ī brāt u cakarīh zanīh zan kunišn. u-š pat ayōkēnīh ī brāt dārišn. hac vinās apparnipišt apēcār.

Question 1:
A man had a *pātixšāy*-wife and two sons and two daughters who had attained the age of fifteen. One son went to foreign parts, and the other died. One

[illegible] [17] [illegible] [21] [illegible] [22] [illegible]

[illegible] [23] [illegible]

[illegible]

4 [illegible] [24] [illegible]

[illegible]

[illegible] [25] [illegible]

[illegible] [26] [illegible] [27] [illegible] [16] [illegible]

[illegible] [16] [illegible] [28] [illegible]

[illegible] [28]

5 [illegible] [29] [illegible]

[illegible] [29]

[illegible] [30] [illegible]

[illegible]

6 [illegible]

[illegible] [31] [illegible]

[illegible] [32] [illegible] [33]

[illegible]

[illegible] [34] [illegible]

[illegible] [1]

1 [illegible]

21. For [illegible]. 22. Better [illegible]. 23. [illegible] omitted. 24. Better [illegible]. 25. For [illegible] (?). 26. Better [illegible]. 27. دختر added above. 28. Better [illegible]. 29. Better add [illegible].

30. Better [illegible]. 31. Better [illegible]. 32. For [illegible]. 33. Better [illegible]. 34. For [illegible].

1 Written with red ink.

daughter was given away in marriage, and after one year this married daughter gave birth to a son. A message arrived telling that the son in foreign parts had left the law of the good religion for that of the evil religion before the said daughter was given in marriage.

2. Will the status of the said girl, from now on, be that of *pātixšāy*-wife to her husband or that of *ayōkēn stūr* to her own family?

Answer 3:
Unless other circumstances exist to alter the case then, if the brother who died had a *pātixšāy*-wife and -children, or an adopted son[1], the said sister shall stay in her *pātixšāy*-marriage with her husband. She will not assume *ayōkēnīh ī stūrīh* for anybody else. If he has no *pātixšāy*-wife and -children, nor an adopted son or designated *stūr* or ... (*gumārtak*? = appointed) she must take on the *ayōkēnīh stūrīh* for her brother, and she will no longer be the *pātixšāy*-wife of her husband. Her son will be regarded as born into her brother's family.

4. If the woman's husband is pleased to keep her in marriage, he must make his wife the *ayōkēn* of her brother and must explain about the marriage, which is then regarded by the religious law as all right. If it is done in any other way it is not good, because the man is not allowed to keep the woman in a *pātixšāy*-marriage according to the law.

5. And if he knows that it is not legal to have her in a *pātixšāy*-marriage, and yet he keeps her in such a marriage, he will immediately have committed a *tanāpuhl* (sin), and after a year a *margarzān* (sin).

6. When he knows that it is not legal to have her in *pātixšāy*-marriage, but he needs her for marriage, she should then be made his wife in a *cakar*-marriage for as long as she is *ayōkēn* for her brother. In that case he will be free of the above-mentioned sin.

REA 2.1-2:

pursišn 1:
hakar im duxt ayōkēn stūr dūtak hast pat rāh ayōkēnīh u stūr ī dūtak ī, x^vāstak ī andar im dūtak bē ōh duxt frazand rasēt aivap nē?

passax^v 2:
hakar-iš ciš andar nēst ān rād yuvattar. brāt ī vēhdēn, hac āvām šutak rād zan u frazand pātixšāyīh ī, pus patīriftak, stūr kartak, ēvak-ic nēst. hac im cim, dātistān ī im x^vah ētōn kū pat ayōkēn brātar ēstēt. hīr u x^vāstak pat x^vēšīh im brāt ēstēt, hamāk pat ayōkēnīh ī brāt bē ōh im x^vah rasēt, u-š pat ayōkēnīh u stūrīh brāt dārišn. ētōn-ic apārik x^vāstak andar im dūtak.

Question 1:
If the said *ayōkēn*-daughter is *stūr* of the family, will the family property go to this daughter and her children by way of the *ayōkēnīh* and the family *stūrīh*, or not?

1. B.T. Anklesaria (1962) inserts *stūr ī kartak* (designated *stūr*).

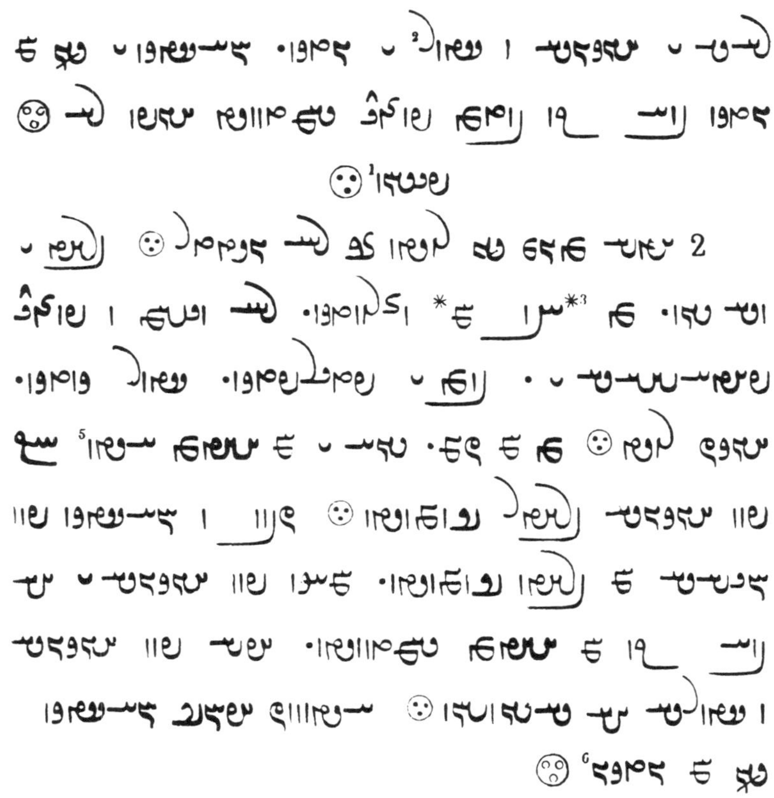

2. For [illegible]. 3. See P. 2, n. 4. 4. Better [illegible].
5. Better [illegible]. 6. Better [illegible].

Answer 2:

Unless other circumstances exist to alter the case then the law says the following: If the brother of the good religion died leaving no *pātixšāy*-wife or -children, nor an adopted son or designated *stūr* then the sister must take on the *ayōkēnīh* for her brother. His property and private fortune will all go to her on account of the *ayōkēnīh*, and she must keep it in *ayōkēnīh* and *stūrīh* for her brother. The same applies to other family property.

There are many curious aspects in the case presented here. First, it flatly contradicts the two paragraphs, discussed previously, in declaring that the married daughter must divorce her husband, and let her only son become her brother's heir. Secondly, the *ayōkēnīh* seems to be required for a limited period only. In the *MHD*, divorcing in order to take on *ayōkēnīh* is the rule rather than the exception. The question is whether the self-contradiction detected here in the *REA* reflects a difference of opinion among the jurists like the one we saw in the *MHD*, or whether it is of a different kind. The *REA* was compiled by one author with the declared purpose of answering vital questions regarding the faith and its social manifestations in a precise and unambiguous way. It is therefore highly unusual, in fact, this is the only example, to find diverging opinions in the *REA*. In *31.2* and *44.1,* we have precise and unambiguous answers to any doubts arising in connection with the institution of *ayōkēnīh*, and we must presume that this was the message the author wanted to convey. This is very much in accordance with the *REA* as a whole throughout which theoretical questions and answers are shaped so as to formulate general rules. *Question 1* is the only instance in the whole collection in which a specific case is being discussed. It is the only one which begins with *mart ē būt*, and it is the only example in which the expressions *ayōkēnīh ī stūrīh* and *ayōkēn stūr* occur. In the *MHD*, *AFS*, and elsewhere in the *REA* the two institutions are always mentioned separately, each with its specific significance. Another strange feature is that the case has been placed at the beginning of the text instead of in its natural context in connection with the definitions of *ayōkēnīh*.

These peculiarities point strongly in the direction of an interpolation; the spirit of this interpolation is wholly Zoroastrian, but must be a later contribution. It could be an interpolation from a different source that has kept the general rules from the *MHD* alive.

I conclude that the two views of the family with which we are familiar from the *MHD* have both survived, but that the author of the *REA* chose the view which he felt would fit his time best, but one scribe put in the other view also in order to complete the picture.

X^{V}ĒTŌDAH

The Middle Persian term *x^{v}ētōdah* is derived from the Avestan *xvaētvadatha*, explained by C. Bartholomae[1] as consisting of *xvaētu-* "kinsman, one's own", cognate with Latin *suus*, and **vadatha* "marriage". His definition of the term is: "der eine Sippenehe geschlossen, in die nächste Verwandschaft geheiratet hat", and "wofür die Sippenehe bezeichnend ist". The *xvaētvadatha* is attested in the younger *Avesta*[2], but not in the *Gathas*. Unfortunately, the examples of the term occurring in the Avestan scriptures do not convey any clue to the meaning of the word. From a passage in the *Vendidad*, however, it may be inferred that the term denotes some kind of act performed by a man and a woman. Corpse bearers, it is stated, may purify themselves with the urine of cattle or with the mingled urine of a man and a woman who have performed *xvaētvadatha*[3].

The Pahlavi texts, on the other hand, are wholly unequivocal about the connotations of the term. *X^{v}ētōdah* is quite obviously used about a union between father and daughter, or brother and sister, or mother and son. This has been vigorously repudiated by Parsee scholars who claim that this type of union was never practised among Zoroastrians[4].

The practice of consanguineous marriage was abandoned at some stage between the time of the *Pahlavi Rivāyats* and the *Persian Rivāyats*[5] when *x^{v}ētōdah* has come to signify marriage between cousins[6]. At some stage the Parsees have evidently adopted the incest taboos of the surrounding societies viz. the contentious assertion of the above-mentioned scholars. There can be no doubt, however, that this type of union did exist, but there is some uncertainty as to the origin, the where, and the when of the custom, nor do we know how widespread it was.

We find the earliest reference in Herodotus (III. 31). In the story of Cambyses's marriage to his sister Herodotus tells us that "the Persians did not normally cohabit with their sisters", and he expresses his own disgust at the idea. It is probably no coincidence that Herodotus gives this brother-sister marriage as a unique example of this type of marriage among the Persians, since he is obviously bent on blackening the character of Cambyses, and showing his depravity. On the other hand, if such marriages were at all common at the time he would surely have known about it since he travelled widely in Persia, and was governed by an insatiable curiosity. It would not have been quite like him to suppress juicy gossip of

1. C. Bartholomae: *Altiranisches Wörterbuch*, Strassburg 1904, p. 1860.
2. *Yasna*, 12.9; *Vispered* 3.3; *Vendidad* 8.13; *Yasht* 24.17.
3. See also L.H. Gray: "Marriage (Iranian) no.2, Next-of-Kin Marriage", in Hastings: *Encyclopaedia of Religion and Ethics* VIII (1915) p. 456-9.
4. E.g. D.P. Sanjana: "The Alleged Practice of Consanguineous Marriages in Ancient Iran". *The Collected Works of D.P.Sanjana*, Bombay 1932, p. 472-9; J.C. Katrak: *Marriage in Ancient Iran*, Bombay 1965, p. 58-71.
5. From 1478 began communications between the Zoroastrian communities in India and Iran. Letters containing advice on religious matters were sent to Indian priests. See M. Boyce (1979) p. 173; B.N. Dhabhar (1932).
6. J.M. Unvala: *Dārāb Hormazyār's Rivāyat*, Vol. I & II, Bombay 1922. (I. 308.15-16); B.N. Dhabhar (1932) p. 293.

this kind just to show up Cambyses as a demoralized madman; this might have been done in various other ways[1]. If, on the other hand, the phenomenon was common among the Magi and originated in the Magian tribe, he might not have known.

Several other Greek and Latin sources mention this type of marriage. According to Plutarch, (*Vita Art. 23*) Artaxerxes married his sister Atossa, and the young Cyrus loved his mother in an unnatural way, according to Aelian (*de. nat. anim. VI 39*). These examples are from the royal Achaemenian family, but the custom is also ascribed to the Persians in general by Diogenes Laertios, Strabo, and other late authors[2]. The Latin poet Catullus (*XC. 3 ff.*) comes up with a very interesting piece of information: "magus ex matre et nato gignatur oportet" (a Magus ought to be born by his mother and her son). Xanthus Lydus, cited by Clemens Alexandrinus (*Stromateîs III.2*), also spoke of consanguineous marriages as especially favoured by the Magi.

The origins of this next-of-kin marriage have been the focus of several scholars' attention. Two different theories were advanced by Moulton[3] and Feist[4] respectively. Moulton maintained that the custom was neither Indo-European nor Semitic, but Magian, and Feist held that the custom was certainly Indo-European substantiating this by showing the custom to have existed among the Balto-Slavic tribes and the Irish. Furthermore, he draws attention to the fact that the ancient Greeks allowed marriages between paternal half-brothers and -sisters[5].

L.H. Gray maintains that pure Zoroastrianism never knew of *xvaētvadatha*[6], but that it may have been practised by non-Zoroastrian Persians, and that Zoroaster abolished the custom. He supposes the custom to originate from the Magi who wanted to keep the priestly families pure and uncontaminated. In this, he is followed by Duchesne-Guillemin[7]. B. Spooner[8] suggests that the origin might be sought in Mesopotamia, but he does not quote any sources that might prove this supposition. Mazahéri[9] quotes two different theories, but does not commit himself to any of them: "C'est un phénomène sociologique qui nous intéresse, peu nous importe son origine préhistorique, aborigène ou allogène".

Gray's claim, mentioned above, cannot be proved satisfactorily. The *Gathas*, Zoroaster's original teachings, do not contain any reference to *xvaētvadatha*, but they have not all been preserved, so the question must be left open.

It seems plausible that the Indo-Europeans practised consanguineous marriages despite the fact that there is no notion of it among the Indians who, on the contrary, show a strong tendency towards exogamy, a few mythological examples ex-

---

1. About Cambyses's religion see Carl Clemen: *Die griechischen und lateinischen Nachrichten über die persische Religion*, Heidelberg 1920, p.64 ff.
2. All instances quoted by L.H. Gray (1915) p. 457.
3. J.H. Moulton: *Early Zoroastrianism*, London 1913, p .204-8.
4. S. Feist: *Kultur der Indogermanen*, Berlin 1913, p. 478.
5. M. Macuch in "Inzest im vorislamischen Iran", *Archäologische Mitteilungen aus Iran* 24 1991, p.141-154 suggests the origin of *x*^{v}*ētōdah* as part of a fertility cult.
6. L.H. Gray (1915) p. 458.
7. J. Duchesne-Guillemin (1973) p. 94; see also S. Shaked: "Dualism in Transformation" *School of Oriental and African Studies*, London 1994.
8. B. Spooner: "Iranian Kinship and Marriage". *Iran* IV, 1966, p. 51-9.
9. A.A. Mazahéri (1938) p. 113 ff.

cepted. It remains an open question whether, in early times, the consanguineous marriage was only practiced in royal families. In the case of Persia our earliest references are, as we have seen, to the Achaemenian dynasty, whereas references to the Magi and people in general are found only in Hellenistic sources. We know from other countries that royal persons married their next-of-kin e.g. Ptolemaic Egypt, but then, in Egypt common people married their next-of-kin too[1].

The reason why the consanguineous marriage became particularly associated with the Magi in the Hellenistic period may be simply that the Magi, as a priestly caste, had been practising this custom for a long time. It may even have been common practice among Indo-European priests. The frequent references in the Hellenistic texts may, on the other hand, reflect a reaction on the part of the Magi to the uncertain position held by Zoroastrianism in this period. Iran was governed by the Seleucids, and, although they did not try to impose their own religion upon the Persians, they did try to spread Greek ideas and customs, so the Zoroastrians must have felt the lack of a leader of their own religious belief. During the Seleucid period the religion was guarded by the Magi[2] at a time when contact between the various groups of Zoroastrians scattered all over the empire must have been scanty. Under these circumstances, the notion of *xvaētvadatha* must have come to the fore. It is small wonder that, in a world which is insecure and devastated by wars, people turn their attention inwards, and try to keep their families as pure and intact as possible. As Gray says[3] "...which (*xvaētvadatha*) is perhaps nothing but endogamy carried to its extreme". Priestly classes and ordinary people, at least landed families, under pressure from without may endeavour, like royal families, to keep the power within the family.

There is another side to the problem of consanguineous marriage, the material side; how to keep the family property intact? Exogamy means the disappearance of part of the family property, whichever way one looks at it, either in the form of a dowry or the cost price of a spouse. The account will never balance; no family will ever be in the same financial position as before they started marrying off their children, some will be left poorer, others will be wealthier than before. This fact alone may have been sufficient to further endogamy as next-of-kin marriage in a society in which the concept of incest was elastic.

A man who had married off his daughter giving her marriage portion could not, particularly in times of unrest and stress, be sure that she would stay around to support him if the necessity should arise. Also, Iranian inheritance law did not operate with the idea of primogeniture so the inheritance, apart from the part of the patrimony that was given to the daughters as dowries, had to be divided equally between the brothers. This meant, of course, that the property would be cut up unless the brothers continued living together, and it would certainly seem an economic advantage for a brother and sister to marry. In Islamic times when consanguineous marriages were forbidden, this must obviously also have been seen as an advantage since marriages between the sons and daughters of brothers were much encouraged[4]: Two brothers living together off the same property inherited from

---

1. R. Middleton: "Br-Si and Fa-Da Marriage in Ancient Egypt", *American Sociological Review* XXVII, 1962, No. 5, p. 602-11.
2. B. Hjerrild: "The Survival and Modification of Zoroastrianism in the Seleucid Times", *Religion and Religious Practice in the Seleucid Kingdom*, Aarhus 1990, p. 144-7.
3. L.H. Gray (1915) p. 458.
4. Cf. B. Spooner (1966) p. 57 ff. on FaBrDa marriage.

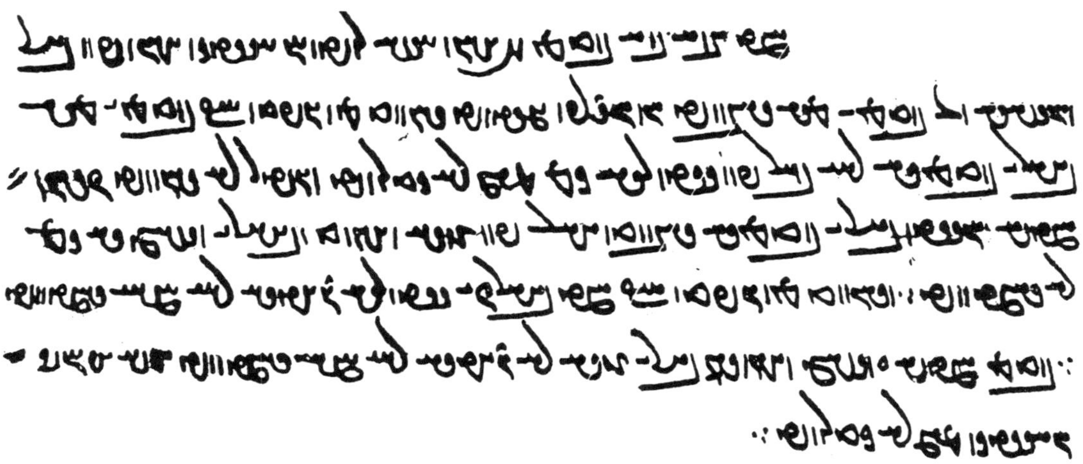

their father often married their children to each other to save money going out of the family and to keep the property intact. The Zoroastrians then just carried this view to its logical conclusion. The consanguineous marriage must have been seen as the ideal solution where the property consisted in land and cattle rather than in business or trade. Families who earned their living working for others would not have had the same incentive to practise this type of union.

A third important reason for the propagation of the consanguineous marriage, especially in difficult times, would have been the Zoroastrian religious tenet that every member of the community must marry and procreate. One could not just let a daughter stay at home, unmarried. If a decent husband of the right faith could not be found, it would certainly be a better solution to marry her to her brother or even her father.

The above reasons hold for both the period between the Achaemenians and the Sasanians, and for the period after the Arab invasion. Since no incest taboos existed, the Zoroastrian was authorised by law to close his family against the surrounding world if circumstances warranted such a procedure.

Few references to the above exist from the Seleucid period, but the few we do have certainly point in the direction I have suggested.

Society in the Sasanian period was entirely different. Zoroastrianism was state religion, and the state was powerful. There was no political reason for practising consanguineous marriage, but the wish to keep land and property within the family was still an important consideration. Also, one might imagine families in remote districts, finding it difficult to come across suitable husbands and wives, deciding that marriage between their offspring would be a convenient way of avoiding the sin of remaining single.

MHD

In the *MHD,* consanguineous marriage is mentioned only in a few instances; in none of them is the term *x^{v}ētōdah* employed, but the fact is nonetheless unequivocal.

MHD 44.8-14

ka mart bē duxt 2 an kas nēst x^{v}āstak u xān pat bahr u x^{v}ēšīh ō duxt ī mas dahēt; an-handarz mīrēt, būt kē guft kū duxt ī mas bahr ī duxtīh rād bahr pat stūrīh kam apar nē manēt u yuvattar nē bavēt cigōn ka-š nax^{v}ist bahr ī duxtīh dāt, pas pat zanīh kart u bahr ī zanīh kam nē rasēt. u būt kē guft kū [ka][1] bahr-ic ī stūrīh duxtīh rād hamē rasēt.

duxt ka-š zan kunēt bahr ī zanīh nē duxtīh rād hamē rasēt u-š aparīk x^{v}āstak apar nē manēt.

One jurist has said of a case where a man has no heir but only two daughters, and the man gives property and the ownership of his house to the elder as her share and personal possession, and he dies intestate, that the daughter, even though she has received a daughter's share, nevertheless succeeds to the share connected with the position of *stūr*, in the same way as if he had first given her her daughter's share and then had married her in

1. If kept, the sentence will miss the main clause.

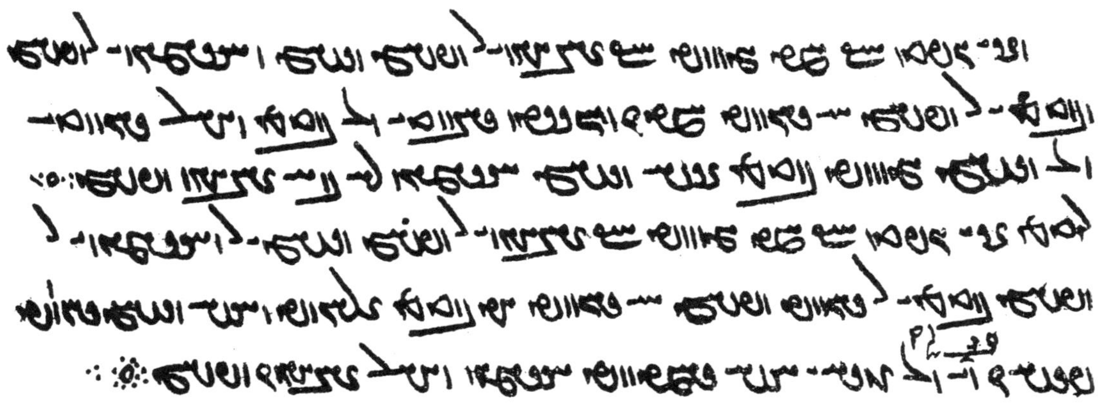

which case she would nevertheless get a wife's share. Another jurist has said that she would certainly also have the share of a *stūr* because of her being his daughter.

If a man marries his daughter the share of a wife will never go to her because she is his daughter, and she will not inherit other property[1].

The case cited in this paragraph is not centred round the problem of *x^{v}ētōdah*. The subject is rather a person's suitability as *stūr*, and, as is so often the case in the *MHD*, two legal opinions are being advanced. The point of the paragraph is to establish how and when a daughter may be called upon to be her father's *stūr*, and to establish a procedure in the bestowing of certain advantages on one of two daughters. In this case, the father had bestowed both land and house on his eldest daughter, presumably the share transferred to her as her marriage portion. The father then dies without having appointed a *stūr* to provide an heir to the estate. The first opinion that is given is that the elder daughter should be chosen as *stūr*, even if she had already received property that would be her personal property. The fortune she would receive in *stūrīh* was not her own, but she was able to enjoy the proceeds, until the heir she produced could take over. The problem in this case is that there seems to be no provision for the younger daughter, but the tradition for choosing the elder daughter as *stūr* must have been so strong that it must prevail. The fact that she received the property as *bahr* "share" might also mean that the younger daughter's share had been taken care of. The case is compared with a situation where a daughter marries her father. In that case, she would first have obtained her daughter's share, and later on also a wife's share. The diverging opinion is in agreement with the first with regard to *stūrīh*, but not with regard to the rule of inheritance concerning a daughter cum wife: A daughter would get a daughter's share, and only that whether she became her father's wife or not. These two completely contrasting juridical views reflect the difficulties in differentiating intertwining roles in the family, and the question of which role, daughter or wife, should take precedence over the other, seems then to have been an unsolved problem. That the jurists advance opposite opinions might lead to the supposition that consanguineous marriages, although legal, were not too common, because if they had been frequent we would suppose that the important inheritance rules had been regulated more strictly, but it is a noticeable fact that the existence of consanguineous marriages is taken for granted.
Diverging opinions occur also in

MHD 104.9-14

u ān ī guft kū ka gōbēt kū zarrēn ī man x^{v}ēš zan u asēmēn ī man x^{v}ēš [u] duxt ī man x^{v}ēš ē bavēt, ka-c nax^{v}ist dāt ī ō duxt u pas dāt[2] ī ō zan gōbēt duxt ī-š zan asēmēn nē bē zarrēn x^{v}ēš. apāk ān ī guft kū ka gōbēt kū zarrēn ī man x^{v}ēš zan ī man u asēmēn ī man x^{v}ēš duxt ī man (bavēt) x^{v}ēš ē bavēt. hakar duxt zāyēt u kas zan bavēt pēš-ic tāi ō zanīh ī kas rasēt asēmēn u pas zarrēn-ic x^{v}ēš.

And a jurist said: "If a person declares: 'The golden object of my own shall be the personal property of my wife and the silver object of my own shall be the personal property of my daughter', also if he first mentions the daughter's gift

1. M. Macuch (1993) p. 347; F. Schirasi-Mahmoudian (1975) p. 62.

2. Corrected from *YHWWN-t*.

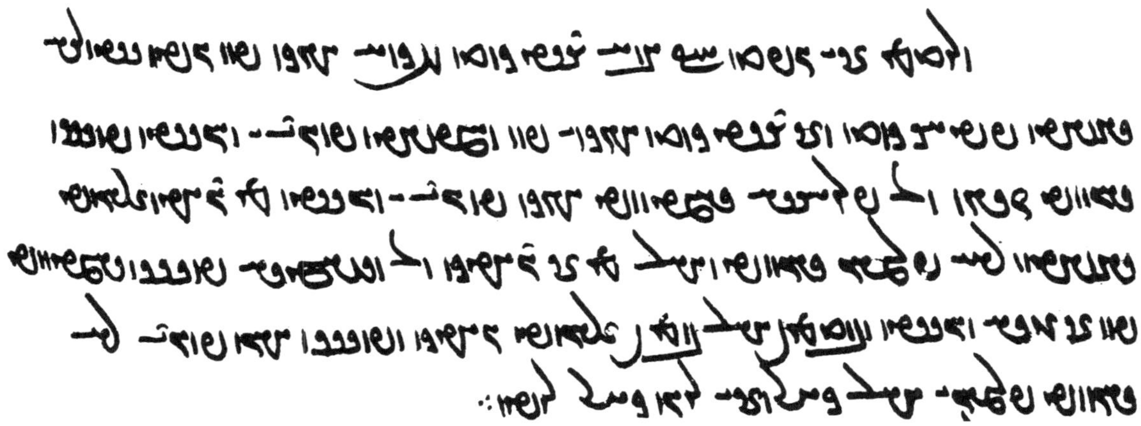

and then the gift to the wife, the daughter who is also his wife shall not own the silver object, but shall own the golden one". In connection with this has also been said: "If a man declares: 'The golden object of my own shall be my wife's personal property and my silver object shall belong to the daughter that will be', when a daughter is born, and she becomes his wife, the silver object will come to her, before the marriage to her father, and after the marriage also the golden one".

In the first part of *104.9-12* the opinion is advanced that a daughter who is also wife shall not come to own the gift of silver that is declared a daughter's property, but only the gift of gold that is declared the wife's property. This means that the role of wife takes precedence over that of daughter. The woman in question had become wife and had left her position as daughter. Presumably then the daughter/wife would get a wife's share as her lawful inheritance, but not a daughter's as well. This interpretation of the rules governing the inheritance of a daughter/wife differs from both the viewpoints stated in *MHD 44.8-14*. The second part of the paragraph (*12-15*), however, advances the same point as we have seen in the comparison in *44.8-14*. The daughter had a daughter's share, in this case the silver object, when she was still only a daughter, and after marrying her father she became entitled to the golden object, too. In brief, we are presented with three possible ways of dealing with the inheritance problem of a daughter/wife: The daughter gets only a daughter's share, she gets only the wife's share, or she will get both. This is indeed one of the subjects in the *MHD* on which opinions differ widely. There are three possibilities, each of them with legal authority behind them. This ambiguity may have been founded on the supposition, stated above, that the occurrence of consanguineous marriages was fairly rare in this period.
There are two paragraphs in the *MHD* dealing with consanguineous marriage between brother and sister:

MHD 105.5-10

u apāk ān ī guft kū mart dastkart 2 har ēvak pat yūt stūrīh dāšt paitāk kart u ān dastkart ēvak ī pat nāmcišt frazand ī nax^{v}ist pusak bavēt cigōn ō purnāyīh rasēt ēvak frazand ī nax^{v}ist hac duxt zāyēt dāštan rād framān bavēt u pas hac ān duxtak ō zanīh [ī] pusak rasēt pat ān zanīh nax^{v}ist duxt 1 pas pus 1 zāyēt (u) duxtak u pusak an frazand nē bavēt framān ī pas kār u ān ī pēš kār nēst.

In connection with this, one jurist has stated that in a case where a man reveals that two estates are being held in separate *stūrīh*, one of them being intended for the first-born child of his son (if it is a boy)[1], when he comes of age, the other for the first child born of his daughter, and the son subsequently marries the daughter, and they have one daughter and afterwards a son, and they have no other children, then only the last half of the testamentary disposition will come into force.

---

1. C. Bartholomae (1923) p. 17, inserts "sofern es ein Sohn wird". His emendation is necessary for the inner logic of the statement. A second *pusak* can easily have been omitted by mistake. M. Macuch (1993) p. 654 interprets this differently.

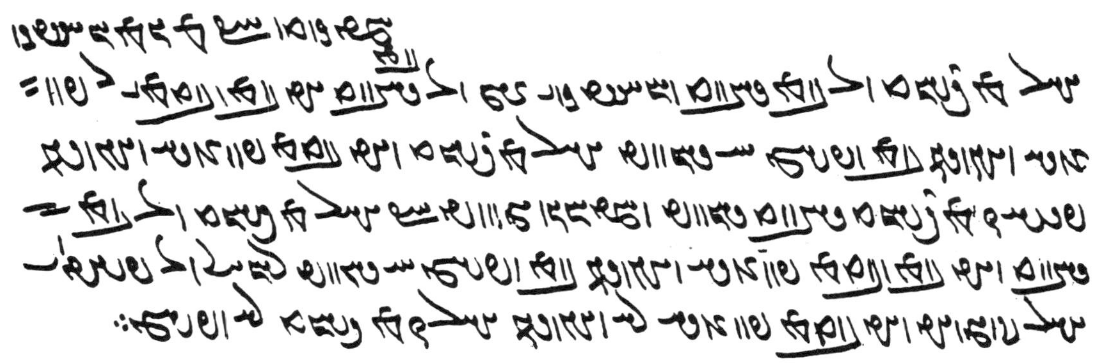

Like the paragraph treated above this one deals with legal problems that may arise in a family in which ties of kinship are intermingled with those of marriage[1]. The problem here is that the first-born of the son and daughter is their first child as they are married to one another. As there was no stipulation in the father's will as to the sex of the first-born of his daughter, the second part of the father's testamentary disposition will come into force, but not the first, since the first-born of the son was a girl. Bartholomae's emendation is essential because if the sex of the son's first child was not required to be male, then the first part of the declaration would be just as valid as the second part, as a daughter would have done quite as well.

The meaning is quite clear: The couple's first-born child, a daughter, will succeed to the *stūrīh* according to her grandfather's will, but the second child, a boy, will not get the other *stūrīh*. The text offers no information about the vacant *stūrīh*.

One is left with the suspicion that this was certainly not what testator had intended. Presumably, he would have wanted the two *stūrīh*-estates to have been settled on the two children of his son and daughter who had married one another. The case story here looks suspiciously like a legal exercise in how to interpret a given text, illustrating what the consequences of an inadequately phrased declaration might be. When making a legal declaration one should make absolutely sure that every contingency has been taken into account to secure that one's intentions are not being obstructed by unfortunate phrasing or through lack of foresight. The example used here is a case of consanguineous marriage, because, as the former paragraph shows, such a union, if not foreseen, may complicate the normal inheritance pattern.

The following passage in the *MHDA* is also a legal example. The text offers a choice of two phrasings which are equally well suited to express testator's wish: namely that his son will marry his daughter.

MHDA 18.7-12

ka kart kū-m ēn x^vāstak pas hac 10 sāl ō pus dāt u x^vāstak [ī] i-m ō pus dāt hakar pus [u] duxt ī man pat zanīh gīrēt pus x^vēš ē bavēt pas hac 10 sāl u hakar duxt pat zanīh gīrēt pēš-ic hac 10 sāl dāt bavēt u ka ōgōn gōbēt kū pas hac 10 sāl ō pus dāt u hakar pus [u] duxt pat zanīh gīrēt pus x^vēš ē bavēt apāc ō pašt ī pas ēstāt u hakar duxt pat zanīh nē gīrēt pas-ic hac 10 sāl nē x^vēš.

If a man declares: "This property will be given by me after ten years to my son, and if my son takes my daughter in marriage, this property of mine bequeathed to my son will be his absolute after ten years"; it will be his also if he marries her before the period is out. If he says the following: "After ten years it will be given to my son, and if he takes my daughter in marriage it will be his absolute", then it will be subject to the last promise, and it will not be his absolute after ten years if he does not marry the daughter.

This paragraph forms part of the law text concerned with conditional gifts, and the chapter deals with different ways of expression in legal declarations. The property in question is stipulated as *stūrīh*, and bequeathed to the son as such, but in the event of marriage between the brother and sister, the property will be transferred

1. See J.P. de Menasce: "La '*Rivāyat d'Ēmēt i Ašavahištān*'". *Studia Iranica* (cahiers 3), 1985, p. 138-9.

XX

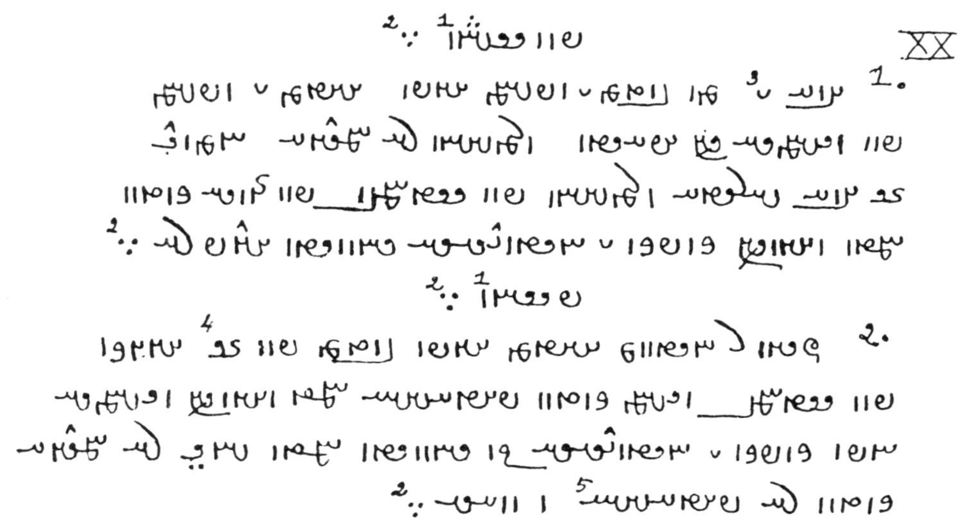

XX 1. *Written with red ink in* TD_2. 2. TD_2 *omits*. 3. *Thus* TD_2; *G torn; better* [Mandaic]. 4. TD_2 *adds* [Mandaic] *at the end of the line*. 5. *G* [Mandaic].

to the son's absolute ownership. If, however, the condition is not fulfilled, then the promise of transference of ownership will not be fulfilled either.

These passages in the *MHD* are interesting in that they are the only references to consanguineous marriage in a Sasanian source. The term *x^vētōdah* is not employed, but the fact is made abundantly clear, although, of course, we cannot know whether the sisters and brothers were half-siblings.

The first two paragraphs discussed above are very similar. They use the marriage between father/daughter, and brother/sister as case studies, which must mean that this type of union cannot have been purely fictitious, and that it was accepted by the law. It also indicates that the legal experts must have been aware that problems in family law, especially with reference to inheritance, might arise in consequence of such a union. We may infer from these passages that the consanguineous marriage was treated like any other legal phenomenon, and there is no indication that it was confined to a particular social class, or that it was treated as something peculiar or in any way singular.

The same applies to *MHDA 18.7-12*, but here, in addition, we are given some hidden information. The father in question sets up an award if his son and daughter will marry each other. He wants them to marry, and in order to induce them, especially the son, he is prepared to give them considerable pecuniary advantages. This might also give a hint that the couple may not have been particularly keen to comply with his wishes.

This does not, of course, make any sense if the above examples are taken to describe purely fictive cases, but I base my suggestions on the fact that case studies will serve no purpose if they have no basis in reality. So, I suggest that if the examples had been felt to be fictive, they would not have been used at all.

All these paragraphs of the *MHD* convey a certain pragmatic attitude towards the phenomenon. They are concerned with legal problems just like the rest of the text and make no attempt to bring the desirability or religious implications of such a union into focus. This is not to say that there may not have been religious considerations behind the decision to enter into this type of marriage, but the focus of this law text is the problems of inheritance.

AFS

The *AFS* and *REA* law texts differ considerably from the above on this issue. The two texts stress the religious aspects of *x^vētōdah*, raising this type of marriage to a sacred ritual that will secure great rewards in the hereafter for the performers. Both texts are, furthermore, extremely keen to propagate this type of union, as I shall hope to show in the following.

AFS 20.1-2

pursišn 1:
mart ī kē duxt ī x^vēš aivap x^vah ī x^vēš pat zanīh andar apāyēt ōišān nē hamdātistān hēnd ān mart pātixšāy ōišān pat stahmb pat zanīh kartan ? ka kunēt kirpak ī x^vētōdahīh bavēt aivap nē ?

passax^v 2:
cigōn man dānam: x^vah aivap duxt pat ān aivēnak pat stahmb zan kartan pātixšāy, ka kunēt zanīh xūp kirpak ī x^vētōdahīh ō bavēt ka šōd nē hamdātistān kartan nē pātixšāy u vinās.

CXLIII

[illegible]

[illegible]

[illegible]

CXLIII 1. Written with red ink in TD_2; G omits. 2. Both omit. 3. G [illegible]. 4. TD_2 [illegible]. 5. G [illegible]. 6. G [illegible]. 7. Thus TD_2; for [illegible] (?); G torn. 8. TD_2 [illegible]. 9. TD_2 [illegible]. 10. Thus both; for [illegible] = [illegible] (?). 11. G [illegible]; TD_2 [illegible]. 12. TD_2 [illegible]. 13. G [illegible]; TD_2 [illegible]. 14. TD_2 [illegible]. 15. TD_2 omits. 16. Written with red ink in TD_2. 7a. For [illegible]. 16a. For [illegible]. 17. TD_2 [illegible]. 18. TD_2 [illegible]. 19. Thus both. 20. Thus TD_2; G torn. 21. TD_2 adds . . 22 TD [illegible]; G torn. 23. G [illegible]. 24. TD_2 [illegible]; G (torn) [illegible]. 25. TD_2 prefixes 1. 26. TD_2 [illegible]. 27. Thus both; for [illegible]. 28. G [illegible]. 29. TD_2 [illegible]. 30. [illegible]. 31. G [illegible]. 32. TD_2 [illegible]. 33. TD_2 [illegible]. 34. G [illegible]. 35 TD_2 [illegible]. 36. G [illegible]. 37. TD_2 [illegible].

Question 1:
If a man is obliged to marry his daughter or his sister, and they do not consent. Is this man authorised to force the marriage through? If he does this, will the meritorious deed of *x^v^ētōdah* be his or not?

Answer 2:
As I understand it: He is authorized to force his sister or his daughter to marry him, and if he does so the marriage is valid, and his will be the meritorious deed of *x^v^ētōdah*. If, however, he is unwilling to do so, he is not authorised to go through with it, and it will be regarded as a sin.

In the answer to *question 20*, the author's favourable attitude to *x^v^ētōdah* is apparent. The alliance was commendable, even if the women were against it. As long as the prospective bridegroom was in favour of the marriage, it was enough. He, of course, was also the one who reaped the rewards in the life hereafter. But it was not only the women who might be against a union of this kind. A man might also hesitate to marry his sister, as we see in the following:

AFS 143.1-4

pursišn 1:
mart ē hāvišt kē x^v^ahar ī x^v^ēš andar hanjamān pat zanīh bē patīrēt u-š ān cim rād cand sāl hac šōd kartan patīrān dāšt[an] u-š avdom x^v^at pat zanīh nē kart. cē pat zanīh bē ō mart ē dāt nūn pat patigriftan ī x^v^ētōdah āšnāk u pat nē kartan x^v^ast āfrās īn kū-š pat yazišn kartan ī kasān cē framāyēt.

passax^v^ 2:
hakar-iš hac bunīh kār ī-š x^v^ah pat zanīh kunišnīh u x^v^ētōdah rāyyišnīh rāhkārīhā patigrift aš hac ān patigīrišn kirpak būt; ka hac ān frāc cigōn x^v^ēškārīh u tuvān būt u nē hamāi rāyēnēt aš pas hac panzdah sālakīh ī ziyānak har daštānmāh ē rād dēnīkīhā andar-iš tōzišnōmand u kirpak ī x^v^ētōdah nē rāyēnītan ān kirpak ī x^v^ētōdah patīrān dāštan rād ī vinās ī garāy u ka-š fratōm kirpak ī x^v^ētōdah nē rāyēnēt u ān patīrišn u pašt drōzišnīh ī-š hac bunīh rād pat-iš ērangōmandtar u candīh ī dāštanmāh u cand ī zamān vinās vicārišnīh rād dānistan apāyēt.

3. zan hilēt būt kē margarzān guft u būt kē x^v^ārtar bē ān ī x^v^ētōdah garāntar.

4. u pas ka-š bē ō mart ē dāt u hakar mart nēvak u zan pat-iš hamdātistān būt aš hac dātan ērang ē nē dānam cē nūn pat patīrānīnītan ī vinās ī hac patīrān dāštan ī ziyānak bōzišnōmand hangārišn bē-š pat ān ī pēš tōzišnōmand apāyēt būtan u hakar x^v^at hac bunīh patigriftan ī ān kār dastavarīhā u-š pas tuvān ī pat rāyēnītan nē, u-š darmān ī tuvān ayāftakīhā apardāt bavišn ka-š hu-ēmētīh ī ētōn bē dānistan būtan aš pat hamdātistānīh ō mart ē ī dahm ī passacak dātan; aš andar rāyēnišn vināskārīh ē nē dānam u-š pat-ic dastavarīhā kunišnīh ān-ic bōzišn šnāsom ī pat *Skātōm* gōbēt: pātixšāy katār-ic-ē dahmān ī sardārān ō katār-ic-ē dahmān ī kasān ān ī x^v^ēš. nāirīk. pat ahlāyīh bē dātan.

Question 1:
Take a man, a disciple, who in the congregation has promised his sister marriage, and for this reason has kept her, for several years, from taking a

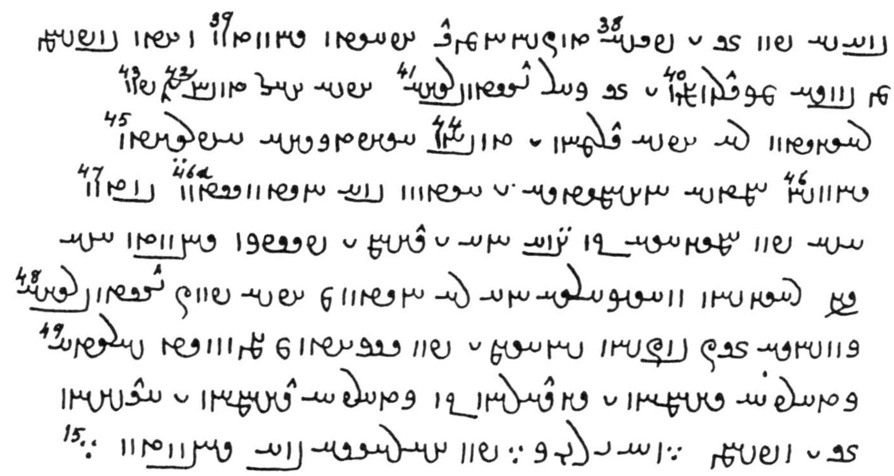

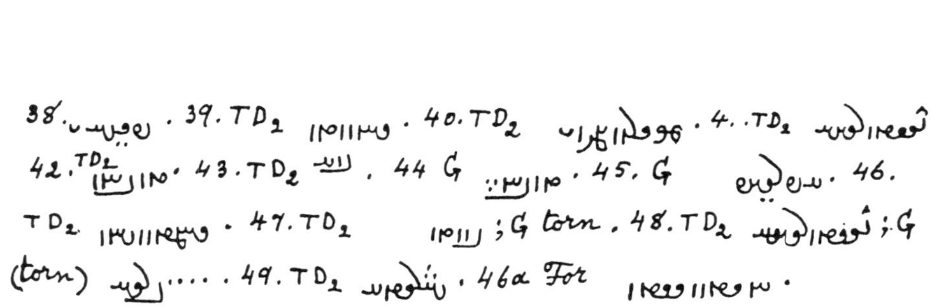

husband, and then finally does not marry her[1] but gives her in marriage to another man who knew about the promise of *x^{v}ētōdah*, and of his (the brother's) desire not to fulfil it (the promise). The question is, what does the teaching say about his performing ceremonies for other people?

Answer 2:
If, from the beginning, he did indeed promise his sister to marry her, and perform the *x^{v}ētōdah*, he acquired by this a meritorious deed; if, later, although it was his duty, and he was able to do it, he did not carry it through, he will have to atone for it according to the religion for as many menstruation periods she has had after her fifteenth year; it is a grave sin not to carry out the meritorious deed of *x^{v}ētōdah*, not to fulfil his promise of performing the meritorious deed of *x^{v}ētōdah*; and since he neither performed the meritorious deed of *x^{v}ētōdah* nor fulfilled his promise and the contract which was of his own (doing) in the first place, he deserves damnation in a high degree; the number of menstruation periods and the length of time must be determined in order to decide on the magnitude of the sin.

3. One jurist has said that a man who divorces a wife is *margarzān*, and another, that a man who does so is utterly contemptible, but that the breaking of a *x^{v}ētōdah* is a graver sin.

4. And later, if he gave her to another man, a good man, and she herself agreed to it, then I cannot really see that there can be much blame attached to the act of giving her away; he must be considered redeemed from the sin of withholding the woman (from marrying another man), but he certainly deserves to do penance for the former sin; if from the beginning, he himself accepted the act according to the law, and later found that he was not able to carry it through and consequently, striving to find an acceptable alternative, decided to give her to a man who, to the best of his knowledge, was pious and decent, then I do not think that he has committed a sin by acting as he did; also, with regard to the lawful action I accept the excuse with reference to what is said in "*Skātōm*"[2]: Any one of the guardians of the right faith is authorized by law to give his own woman to anyone of the right faith.

In this passage from the *AFS,* we are confronted with the problem of an unwilling bridegroom who has promised to marry his sister, but has given up the idea, and who, after some delay, has found her another husband among the true believers. We are presented with two opposing views on the case, one harsh and strict towards the man who broke his promise, the other, the author's own, a more lenient view. *143.2* argues that the sin is twofold: 1) It is a sin to break a promise of *x^{v}ētōdah*, because such a union is considered meritorious, not only in this life but also in the hereafter. 2) The delay while the brother is trying to make up his mind means that his sister, having attained marriageable age, is wasting valuable time and possibility of reproduction. This has always been considered a sin among Zoroastrians in accordance with their belief in the necessity of reproducing life, but at this time, which saw a consolidation of the Arabic regime, it had become an

1. B.T. Anklesaria (1969) p. 40, 119 translates differently, as he does not accept the meaning of *x^{v}ētōdah*, which he translates "self-dedication": "*There is* a disciple man who promises his sister in *the* assembly *for giving away* as wife; for that purpose, *he* prevented her from taking *a* husband, *for* some years; finally, he himself not handing *her* over as wife..."

2. A lost *Nask* of the *Avesta*. A. Christensen (1936) p. 316 has *Sahādhum*.

even graver sin. Since the Zoroastrian communities were in need of numbers, the sin was considered to be not only against the right faith, but, indeed, against society. It is noteworthy that the pragmatic attitude towards *x^{v}ētōdah* of the Sasanians has been replaced by a religious attitude. In this text, the *x^{v}ētōdah* is brought forward as a holy union presumably because the religious authorities wanted to induce people to perform it. The significance of the fact that the man in the example was a disciple of the priests cannot be determined. It is certainly not counted as an aggravating factor, but the question remains open whether he was presented as a disciple because this type of union was practised particularly among the priestly classes. This might be so, but I infer from the text's omission of rules concerning this, that the possibility existed also for ordinary people at this time, as in other periods as well.

141.3 quotes the very strict view of one authority who claims that divorce is so grave a sin that it deserves the punishment of death and that the breaking of a promise of *x^{v}ētōdah* is an even greater sin. What sort of punishment it deserves is, however, not mentioned.

The passage illustrates what is manifest in the *MHD*, namely that there are different opinions as to the interpretation of the rules of the law, but here we have the personal opinion of *Aturfarnbag* which is much more tolerant than that of the authority he quotes. He does, however, advocate some sort of punishment for the breaking of a promise of *x^{v}ētōdah*. On the other hand, he finds it a redeeming feature that the brother takes the trouble of procuring a good Zoroastrian husband for his sister, and he offers an excuse for the man, presenting him as someone who found himself unable to go through with the marriage, not someone who was unwilling to do it. In this difference of opinion between the quoted authority and *Aturfarnbag* it is easy to detect the latent conflict of how best to preserve the Zoroastrian community: One point of view is that the best way of doing it must be to adhere to very strict rules in order to define the community sharply and clearly, the other is the one represented by *Aturfarnbag* who was evidently of the same religious conviction, but held that the same goal could be reached by tolerance and understanding. As can be seen from the passage quoted, *Aturfarnbag* kept his eye on the main issue: That the woman was actually married to a man of the right faith, so no harm was done to the community. The sin, in that respect, was thus negligible, and by showing tolerance towards the brother, one would avoid antagonizing him, whereas the adherence to the strict rules would almost certainly make his continued life in the community very difficult indeed. *Aturfarnbag* seems to have realized the necessity of keeping up a subtle balance between the rules of the law which must be kept in order to distinguish the Zoroastrians from the surrounding Islamic society, and the intelligent and tolerant interpretation of them which was vital in order not to antagonize the members of the community.

REA

The subject of *x^{v}ētōdah* is allotted much space in the *REA* in which this type of union seems to rank high in the hierarchy of religious deeds. *Question 17* begins by posing the problem of whether it will be more meritorious to build a bridge across a river than spending the same amount of money on other meritorious deeds. The answer is carefully disposed between material good deeds and moral good deeds, which take precedence over the former. Among the former are the building of fortresses, the tilling of the land, the establishing of water supplies, irrigation etc., and among the latter are counted the raising of families, help given to

[illegible][1]

1 [illegible]
[illegible]
[illegible]
[illegible]
[illegible]
[illegible]
[illegible]
[illegible]
[illegible]

2 [illegible]
[illegible]
[illegible]
[illegible]
[illegible]

[illegible][1]

3 [illegible]
[illegible]
[illegible]
[illegible]
[illegible]
[illegible]
[illegible]
[illegible] 4 [illegible]
[illegible]
[illegible]
[illegible]

1. Written with red ink. 2. Better [illegible]. 3. For [illegible].
4. For [illegible]. 5. For [illegible] (!). 6. For [illegible].
7. For [illegible]. 8. Better [illegible]; see p. 83, n. 10; p. 84, l. 4.
9. For [illegible] (!). 10. MS. has [illegible]. 11. MS. has [illegible].

the believers, support of the priestly classes, and finally the observance of religious commandments and rituals.
It is in the last part of the list that we find the practising of *x^vētōdah* listed as number two among rituals such as the *nōk nāvar*, the reciting of the *Avesta* from beginning to end, the ritual of *Gāhānbārs*, i.e. the preparation of food and offerings, libations to the Sacred Fire, the ritual of *dvāzdahomāst*, the praise of the *Amahraspandān*, and other daily, monthly or other perennial religious obligations.
The *x^vētōdah* is a type of marriage and thus closely connected with the good deed of raising a family of faithful Zoroastrians, one of the above-mentioned moral good deeds, and yet we do not find it listed among these. The *x^vētōdah* is singled out and takes its place among the purely religious acts and rituals. The explanation of this remarkable fact must be sought in its close connection with the treatment of the union in general.

REA 22.1-4:

pursišn 1:
mart ē kē-š x^vah ē hast, u-š andar hangām ēt guft bavēt, kū: man ēn x^vahar pat zanīh gīram, aivap-iš hac mātar u pitar patigrift bavēt, kū: x^vahar pat zanīh gīram. pas nē kunēt, vahānak ē rād rōckār pat-iš bē vitīrēt. pas, mart ē ān mart frāc gīrēt u gōbēt, kū: x^vahar ēn, pat kirpak ī man, pat zan(īh) gīr tāi -tān drahm aviš daham. gīrēt, drahm frāc gīrēt.

2. ēn mart kē brāt drahm dāt hac-iš kirpak ī x^vētōdahīh bavēt aivap nē? cigōn, hakar ēn guft, ī pēš būt, nē dānēt, mart nē gōbēt, kū. hac patīrišn ē kartak hast. adak-iš dātistān bē vartēt aivap nē?

passax^v 3:
hakar-iš ciš andar nēst ān rād yuvattar. ētōn paitāk kū ān pēš gōbišnīh patīriftārīh ē ī raftakīhā būt, ka-š andar ān hangām x^vētōdahīh pat kunišn nē rāyēnēt, u-š pas, pat hamkirpakīh ī ēn mart, kē-š drahm aviš dāt, bē rāyēnēt, ān sax^{v}an patīrišn ī pēš raft būt rād, ka gōbēt, ka-c nē, adak-iš yuvattarīh ē pat-iš nēst.

4. im x^vētōdahīh, im kirpak rāyēnēt bavēt, u rāyēnītār u drahmdātār hakanēn hamkirpak hēnd. u-šān har dōān kirpak ī x^vētōdahīh varzišnīh bavandakīhā x^vēš.

Question 1:
A man who has a sister said to her a while ago: "I will take this sister of mine in marriage"[1], or he accepts her from his mother and father saying: "I take my sister in marriage". He does not do so, after all, and time passes. Later, another man comes up to him and says: "As a good deed of mine I will give you money to take your sister in marriage". The brother takes her and receives the money.

2. Has the man who gave the brother money performed the meritorious deed of *x^vētōdah* or not? If he does not know what he (the brother) said earlier, and he (the brother) does not say: "A declaration has, by agreement, already been given", does the judgement then change?

1. N. Safa-Isfehani (1980) p. 156 interprets differently.

Answer 3:
If no other impediments exist, the former declaration was clearly an acceptance (of marriage) which has not come to pass.[1] He has not carried out the *xᵛētōdah* within the given time; later he performs it through the joint meritorious deed with the man who gave him the money, the former word of acceptance, whether it be told or not, making no difference.

4. This *xᵛētōdah*, this meritorious deed is certainly performed jointly, and the man who performed it, and he who gave the money have carried out together the meritorious deed. The merit of the accomplishment of the *xᵛētōdah* will go to the account of both of them.

As also stated by de Menasce[2], this chapter is very clear in its intention: The merits of *xᵛētōdah* do not go to the man who actually performs it only, but also to him who facilitates it by giving financial support to the union. The benefit to the latter is not diminished by the fact that a promise of *xᵛētōdah* had already been given before he offers his assistance, whether he knows about it or not.
There are other interesting features in this text. The brother seems to have given his promise without involving his parents, and we are given no reason to believe that he is his sister's guardian. The reason may be that the text is not concerned with this problem, but it might also be that this marriage is regarded as a holy union, in which case the parents' permission is not needed at all. Also, the carrying out of the actual marriage act is described in very vague terms. This appears to be a common feature in all cases of *xᵛētōdah.* In view of the offer of financial assistance in this case, we might have expected poverty to be given as the reason. But no reason is brought forward, only that time passes. In fact, poverty could not have been the reason as the family would number the same members as before the marriage, at least as long as no children were born. We may simply have here an example of commonsensical pragmatism. Let us imagine a family who have decided that, for religious or financial reasons, it would be convenient for the son of the house to marry his sister. The official betrothal is arranged, and the sister consequently prevented from looking elsewhere for a husband, her marriage portion being bound to the family. There seems to be no real spur to put the marriage into effect as by inference we must suppose that no love passion existed between the brother and sister. The family simply go on as before. Not until the man who needed to perform a good deed with a view to his after-life came up with his promise of financial reward was the reluctant couple induced to marry, at last.
REA 24.1-3 poses a case where a *xᵛētōdah*-marriage is hindered by a man running off with the bride-to-be:

REA 24.1-3:

pursišn 1:
mart ē kē-š xᵛah ē bavēt, hac pitar u mātar, pat hamdātistānīh ī xᵛah, frāc patīrēt, kū: xᵛah pat zanīh gīram. u pēš hac ān kū gukāi apar gīrēt, u-š bē

1. J.P. de Menasce (1985) p. 139 reads: “Si rien ne s’interpose (et) fait une différence, il est évident que la déclaration antérieure était une ‘réception’ ferme”; N. Safa-Isfehani (1980) p. 158 has: “If there is nothing else implied in this question which would require another answer, it is obvious that the former verbal acceptance is bygone”.

2. J.P. de Menasce (1985) p. 140.

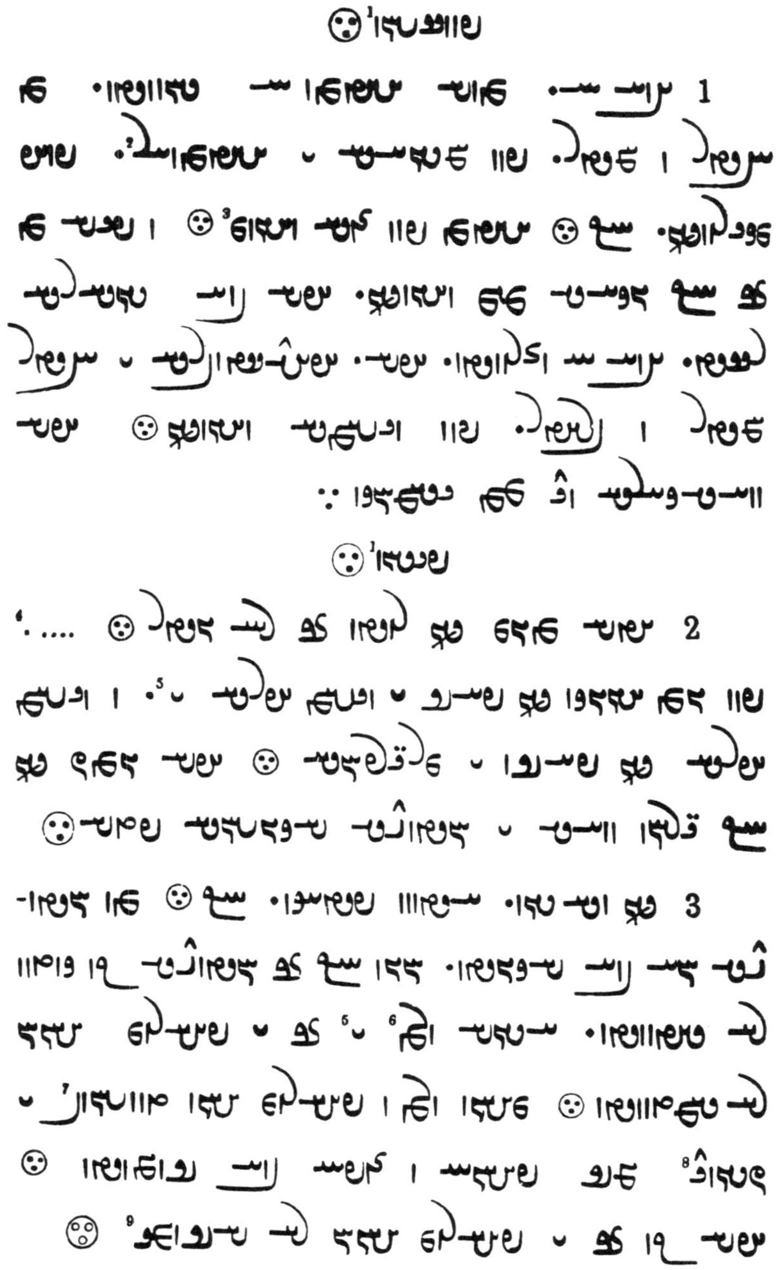

1. **Written with red ink.** 2. For . 3. in the MS.

4. omitted by mistake. 5. Better omit. 6. **Better** .

7. For (?). 8. Written in Avestan characters thus in the MS. for . 9. For .

sardārīh rasēt, mart ē šavēt[1], u-š apēdastavarīh ī pitar mātar u brātar, pat zanīh gīrēt. u-š vināskārīh tāi cē sāmānak.

passax^v 2:
hakar-iš ciš andar nēst ān rād yuvattar. (vināsī) pat ēn aivēnak andar pādak ī zan aparīh [ī], u zan aparīh andar pādak ī margarzānīh. u-š ēn-ic andar kū gerān vinās ī x^vētōdah škēnišnīh pat-iš.

3. andar vēh dēn, ētōn paitāk, kū: kē x^vētōdah ē bē škēnēt, ōgōn kū ān x^vētōdah ō kartan nē āyēt, adak-iš ō [i ī] ān ī pahlom ax^vān nē rasēt. miyān ōi u pahlom ax^v *tnwsnnb*[2] ī cand[3] damīk pahnāy u zopāy bē ēstēt. u-š ō ān ī pahlom ax^vān nē hilēnd.

Question 1:
A man has a sister and, with the consent of his sister, receives her from his father and mother[4] with the words: "I take my sister in marriage"; however, before he can procure witnesses so that she will come under his guardianship, a man comes along (lit. goes) and marries her without the consent (authority) of her father, mother, and brother. To what degree amounts the sinful act of this man?

Answer 2:
If there are no redeeming features in the case a sin of this kind is counted as of the same degree as the abduction of a woman, and the abduction of a woman is a sin of *margarzān*-degree. In this case, furthermore, is involved the grave sin of breaking a *x^vētōdah*.

3. In the good religion, it is revealed that he who breaks a *x^vētōdah,* in such a way that the *x^vētōdah* will not be accomplished, will never reach the blessed existence. Between him and the blessed existence there will be a ... wide and deep as the earth itself, and he will never achieve the blessed existence.

The meaning of the above paragraph is unequivocal, except for one corrupted word, which is inessential for my purpose, inasmuch as it is used in a simile. As pointed out in de Menasce[5]: Like any other marriage contract, the *x^vētōdah*-marriage contract requires witnesses and can be instituted by the parents. In *22* there was no mention of the consent of any other family member, the brother acted on his own; but in this case the parents actually take the initiative to the drawing up of the contract, and the bride-to-be has herself consented to the match. It is normally so in questions of marriage that the bride's consent is required, and certainly that of the guardian. In this case, it seems that not only the guardian, i.e. her father, is involved but also her mother. Presumably, this fact is emphasized to show the extraordinary boldness of the interloper. The family is presented as completely united in their effort to bring this union about, nobody being averse to the changed pattern of their relationship.

1. N. Safa-Isfehani (1980) p. 175 has *rasēt*, which is not established in the Ms.
2. Corrupt. N. Safa-Isfehani (1980) p. 178 translates "distance" but does not offer any explanation of her choice.
3. B.T. Anklesaria (1962) p. 98 holds the view that *cand* is written in Avestan characters in Ms.
4. N. Safa-Isfehani (1980) p. 176 reads differently: "[Assume] a man who has a sister from [his own] father and mother, with the consent of his sister agrees to take her as his wife...".
5. J.P. de Menasce (1985) p. 141.

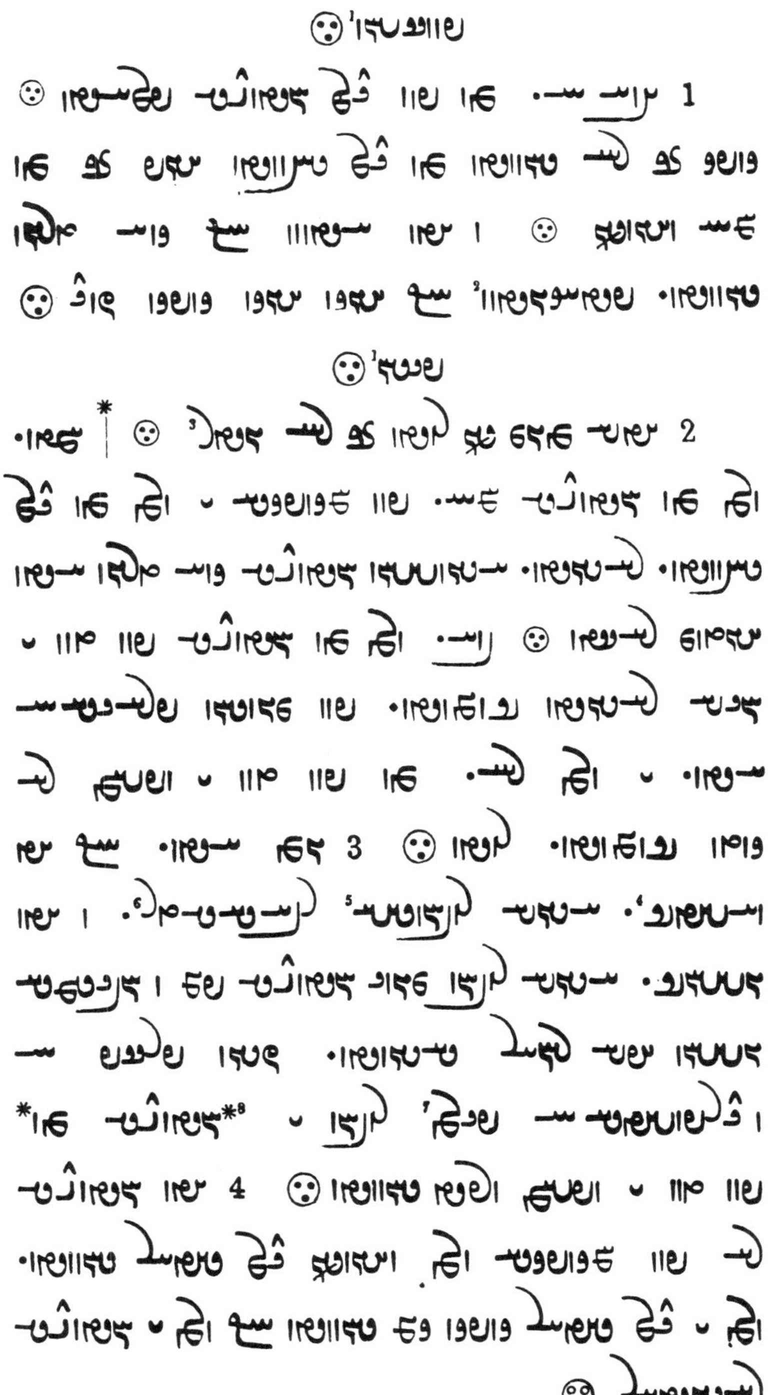

1. Written in the MS. with red ink. 2. For [illegible]. 3. [illegible] in the MS.

4. MS. has [illegible]. 5. For [illegible]. 6. For [illegible].

7. For [illegible]. 8** Better [illegible].

We may, however, infer from this that there must have been problems of exactly that nature. The answer is concerned only with the degree of the sin of the interloper, but the crucial question seems to be a completely different one. We are told that the sister has agreed to marry her brother, but that the actual ceremony was postponed until witnesses could be procured. The text does not specify the duration of this period of waiting, only that in the course of it the sister marries someone of her own choice. The whole sequence is presented in a very short form in order to give the impression that the interloper actually snatches the bride from under the nose of her brother. The facts, however, seem to be that the sister was not abducted against her will, nor was she raped, the crime treated being the breaking up of planned marriage, or worse a planned *x^vētōdah*-marriage. The woman must have been ready and willing, she must have known the man, at least slightly, and must have preferred marriage with him to one with her brother. We may even suspect that her consent to the marriage with the latter may have been given under pressure. What she did was to contract a *x^vasrāyūn*-marriage (*REA question 43*), a marriage approved by the law, and, accordingly, the man had honourable intentions, the woman married him willingly, so if she had not been promised to her brother everything would have been all right. An engagement seems to have been considered fully as binding as marriage, at least in this type of marriage, because the punishment for breaking the union was the same as the one mentioned for the abduction of a woman.

The sin amounted to a *margarzān*-sin, which was originally punished with death; here the penalty imposed was exclusion from paradise. The conclusion must be that the sin was punished after death, not with death. The Zoroastrians may not have been allowed by the Muslim authorities to pass death sentences.

After the description of the awful fate befalling a breaker of the *x^vētōdah*, chapter *27.1-4* gives a description of the blessed fate of one who performs this marriage:

REA 27.1-4:

pursišn 1:
mart ē, kē pat drahm x^vētōdah framāyēt, kirpak ān rād bavēt kē drahm dahēt aivap ān kē hamāi kunēt. u hakar ētōn kū har dō bavēt paitākēnītan kū ēvak kirpak cand?

passax^v 2:
hakar-iš ciš andar nēst ān rād yuvattar. ka, ōi kē x^vētōdah hamāi pat hamkirpakīh ī ōi kē drahm dahēt rāyēnēt, adak-išān x^vētōdah har dō hast ēvtōm rāst. bē, ōi kē x^vētōdah pat tan ī x^vēš rāyēnēt ēstēt, pat mēnōgān frāyīh ē hast, ī ōi rād kē pat tan ī x^vēš nē kart ēstēt, nēst.

3. ēn hast, kū hakar vahištīk, adak-iš ruvān gāh vuzurgīhātar, u hakar dušoxīk, adak-iš ruvān mēnōg x^vētōdah pīm u ...... dušox hac-iš apāc dārēt, cigōn frasp ē u drubuštīh ē pēramon ruvān ī x^vētōdah kē pat tan ī x^vēš varzēt bavēt.

4. hakar x^vētōdah nē pat hamkirpakīh ōi kunēt drahm dātār bavēt, ōi ī drahm dātār kirpak kēm bavēt kū ōi ī x^vētōdah rāyēnītār.

Question 1:
A man orders a *x^vētōdah* by giving money; does the merit belong to the one who gives the money, or to the one who actually performs it? And if it is so that it belongs to both of them, will you explain how much of the merit will belong to each of them?

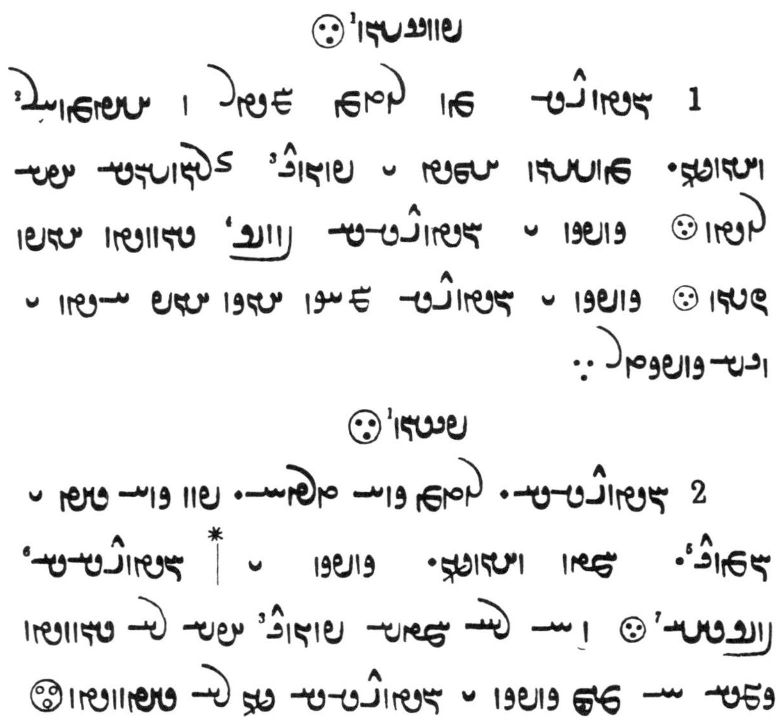

1. Written with red ink. 2. For [illegible]. 3. For [illegible]. 4. MS. adds [illegible]. 5. For [illegible]. 6. For [illegible]. 7. For [illegible].

Answer 2:
If nothing else is implied, because of which it should be different: When a man performs the *x^{v}ētōdah* in a joint meritorious deed with the man who gives the money, then the *x^{v}ētōdah* is strictly equal for both of them, but the one who performs the *x^{v}ētōdah* with his own body has in the spiritual existence a surplus which is not for him who did not do it with his own body.

3. It is like this that if he is destined for paradise, then his soul will be in a more exalted place, and if he goes to hell, then the heavenly *x^{v}ētōdah* will protect his soul from the torments and ...[1] of hell like a roof over, and fortifications round the soul of the person who practised the *x^{v}ētōdah* with his own body.

4. If he does not perform the *x^{v}ētōdah* in joint meritorious deed with him who gives the money, then this man will acquire smaller merit than will the man who accomplishes the *x^{v}ētōdah.*

The performing of *x^{v}ētōdah* is certainly here brought to a level of the highest meritorious deeds. It is considered so important that a person who, with a gift of money, persuades two people to perform a *x^{v}ētōdah*-marriage will have a better after-life in the spiritual existence. The man who performs the act will fare even better: The torments of hell will pass him by even if he is destined to be in hell because of his sins. The woman, on the contrary, seems to be rewarded neither in this life nor in the hereafter, so why then marry her brother if she does not want to, just to secure for him a better after-life?
The above passage shows that the theologians promised great rewards for the man who marries a near kinsman. The lawgivers evidently take upon themselves the responsibility of meting out God's rewards to men; they seem to know in detail what human actions will please God. This is, alas, a phenomenon known all too well from the history of the Christian church; it is, indeed, a well-known means by which any institutionalised religion may grasp and maintain power. The Zoroastrian community of this time was in desperate need of finding drastic means of keeping as many believers as possible within the fold. But was this way the right one? From a practical, pragmatic point of view, at least, it is brilliant. The wealthy benefactor gets his reward in heaven, he who receives the money likewise, but he also gets the financial support that enables him to stay within the Zoroastrian community himself, and to keep his sister or his mother within it too. It is a great pity that we have no means of verifying how often it worked. Was the price too high? According to the punishment suggested for the breaking of such contracts (*question 24*) some people, at least, must have found the price too high, so, consequently, one had to have both the inducement of rewards and the fear of retribution, to make the scheme acceptable.

REA 28.1-2:

pursišn 1:
x^{v}ētōdah kē apāk mātar u x^{v}ahar kunēt, kē-šān ēmēt ī frazand zāyišnīh hac-iš nēst, kirpak ī x^{v}ētōdahīh bavandak bavēt aivap cigōn?

kirpak ī x^{v}ētōdah hamāk ēvak aivap hast ī vēš kirpaktar?

1. The word is unidentifiable due to the corruption of the spelling. B.T. Anklesaria (1962) p. 105 emendit to *ax^{v}ašīh*, "unhappiness".

passax^v 2:
x^vētōdahīh, apāk har sē, pat har dāt ī hēnd, ka kunēt, kirpak ī x^vētōdahīh bavandakīhā u ē rād ka-š frazand hac-iš nē bavēt kēmīh ē apar kirpak ī x^vētōdahīh andar nē apāyēt.

Question 1:
If one performs *x^vētōdah* with one's mother or sister from whom there can be no hope of children being born, will the *x^vētōdah* then be considered all right? will the merit of the performance of *x^vētōdah* always be the same, or are some more meritorious than others?

Answer 2:
The performance of *x^vētōdah* with the three (mother, sister, daughter) at whatever age, is always a perfect, meritorious deed, so consequently even if no children are born of the union, the value of the meritorious deed of performing *x^vētōdah* will not be diminished.

28.1-2 is quite tricky from the point of view of interpretation. As de Menasce[1] rightly remarks: "... la naissance d'enfants, qui était très certainement la raison d'être première du *x^vētōdah* n'ajoutait pas au merite intrinsèque de l'acte." Why do we find a paragraph to the effect that the procreation of children does not add to the merit of the deed? The answer may be found on two levels: The theological and the practical, and in a combination of the two. Theologically speaking, it must have been difficult to maintain that an act which was looked upon by God with so much benevolence would only be meritorious if it resulted in the bringing forth of children, a process which, after all, is not completely under human control. In other words, if the act was performed by young people of fertile age, but did not result in the birth of any children, would this detract from the value of the deed? The only possible answer to such a question must be that the act itself is meritorious independently of the outcome in the way of children.

The pragmatic answer could be as follows: If an only son marries his mother who is past the age of childbearing, the result would be that the family stood in danger of dying out. If, however, there were several sons, and the mother was married to one of them, her part of the inheritance would, conveniently, stay in the family. An unmarried sister past the age of child-bearing would almost certainly have been married before since, according to Zoroastrian law, it was regarded as a sin to remain single, having attained marriageable age. This means that either she would be a widow with an inheritance from her late husband, or a divorcee with her marriage portion paid back. In both cases, her money would be a welcome addition to the family income. If, moreover, the bride-groom, i.e. the brother, had himself been married before, and had already provided himself with an heir, the above solution must have seemed very attractive. The same considerations would apply in cases of a father marrying a daughter.

However great the redeeming quality of the *x^vētōdah* might be, there were sins so fatal that not even the *x^vētōdah* could wipe them away. One of them being sodomy:

1. J.P. de Menasce (1985) p. 142.

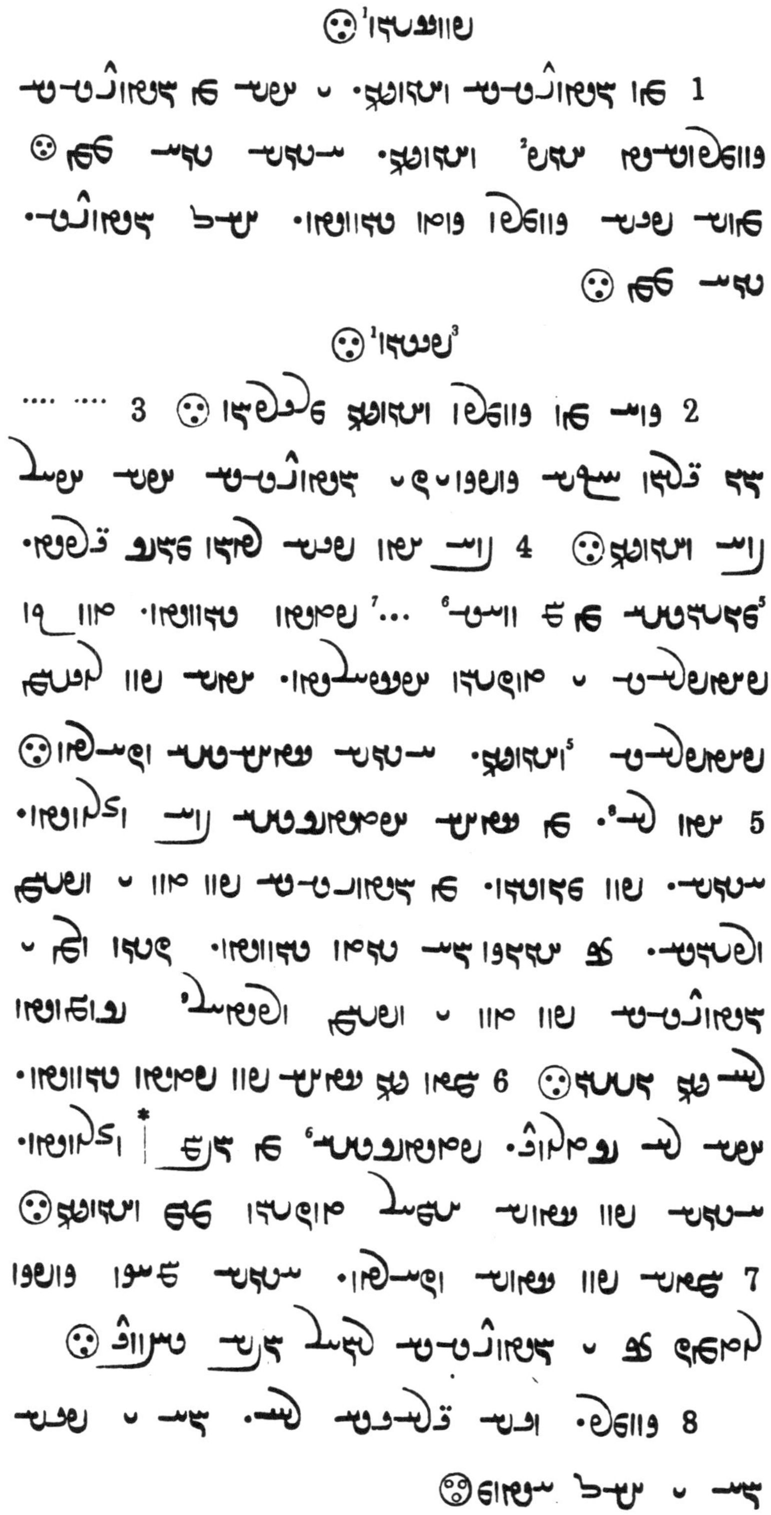

1. Written with red ink. 2. For [Pahlavi]. 3. Repeated with black ink. 4. [Pahlavi] seems to be omitted. 5. MS. prefixes ∴. 6. MS. adds ∴. 7. [Pahlavi] omitted.

8. For [Pahlavi] (?). 9. Better [Pahlavi].

REA 29.1-8:

pursišn 1:
kē x^vētōdahīh kunēt, ī u-š hac x^vētōdahīh kūnmarzīhēt aivap kunēt adak-iš dātistān cē? kē-š pēš kūnmarz kart bavēt, pas x^vētōdah, dātistān cē?

passax^v 2:
har kē kūnmarz kunēt margarzān.

3. .... ōgōn garān kū-š kirpak-ic-ī x^vētōdahīh hac-iš appar bē kunēt.

4. bē hakar pēš Ratān māndak garzēt, mēnišnīhā hac im vinās, patīt bavēt, tan ō pātifrās ī tōzišn apispārēt, hakar-iš pat sar pātifrās gīrēt adak-iš gētīhīhā vicārt.

5. hakar nē, hac gētāh apatītīkīhā bē šavēt, adak-iš, pat mēnōgān hac x^vētōdahīh pat tan ī x^vēš varzišnīh, ān aivēnak ē sūt bavēt, cigōn ōi ī x^vētōdahīh pat tan ī x^vēš varzītār ēstēt rād andar dušox.

6. ka andar gētāh pat patīt bavēt u-š nē ōzanēnd, patītīkīhā hac āvām šavēt, adak-iš pat satōš āmār tōzišn apar kunēt.

7. ka-š pat satōš vicārt, adak-iš hamāk kirpak apāk-ic ān ī x^vētōdahīh apāc aviš dahēnd.

8. kūnmarz, vēš garāyīh rād. ē ī pēš ē ī pas ētōm.

Question 1:
If a man having performed *x^vētōdah* submits to or commits sodomy, what punishment should he receive? And what will the judgement be on a man who practises sodomy and then performs the *x^vētōdah*?

Answer 2:
Everybody who commits sodomy commits a *margarzān*-sin.

3: (this sin) is so grave that it annuls the meritorious deed of *x^vētōdah*.

4: But if he repents his sin before the *Rats*, and if the *patīt* (confession) is given with all his heart, and if he submits his body to punishment in atonement, and if he instantly agrees that he should receive capital punishment, then he will be redeemed in the material world.

5. If not, and he leaves this world, unrepentant, then in the spiritual world, because he has performed the *x^vētōdah* with his own body, he shall benefit in hell like the person who performed *x^vētōdah* with his own body.

6. If he makes confession in this world, and is not killed, and dies having made his confession, then he will have to make his reckoning in the *Satōš*.

7. When he has been redeemed in the *Satōš*, all his meritorious deeds, including that of the *x^vētōdah*, will be given back to him.

8. The same applies to sodomy, because of its extreme gravity, whether performed before or after.

The only interesting feature in this chapter is that there seems to be a limit to the power of the *x^vētōdah*. Sodomy must, of necessity, be regarded with revulsion by Zoroastrians the basic creed of whom was that life must be generated. Therefore, a sexual union that never results in the procreation of children cannot really be tolerated. Nevertheless, after due penance all the merits accruing from the performance of *x*[v]*ētōdah* will be awaiting the soul.

There is one more interesting point, though, in the meting out of punishment. A person who has committed sodomy, but confesses[1] his sin and submits to punishment, will have expiated his sin already in this world, and will accordingly be able to enjoy the merits of *x*[v]*ētōdah* in the next.

The second possibility is that he neither confesses nor is punished, in which case the merit of *x*[v]*ētōdah* will help avert the tortures of hell, even though he has to stay there. The third possibility is that he confesses, but does not receive any punishment, in which case he will have to submit to the punishment during the *Satōš*[2], after which he is purified of the sin. In the *Pahlavi Rivāyat* accompanying the *Dātistān ī Dēnīk,*[3] it is also stated that if a man is not beheaded for a *margarzān*-sin in this life, he will be so in the *Satōš*. One may wonder what lies behind the curious fact that there seems to be a choice between punishment in this life and punishment after death. In the Sasanid period, such a choice would have been inconceivable. The sin was obviously considered of so grave a nature that only capital punishment would expiate it; what then made the theologians leave a choice for the sinner? The confession was, apparently, a crucial point. Without it, the sinner would find himself in hell, but without being submitted to torture because of the *x*[v]*ētōdah.* If he did confess, he would have to undergo punishment, but not in hell. The priests, evidently, regarded the confession as a mitigating circumstance, which may have meant that the confession constituted an important part of the influence of the priesthood upon laymen, such as we know it from the Roman Catholic church. As the priests were the ones who knew exactly how punishment after death would be meted out, their power must have been great.

Having extorted the confession, the next step would be to decide on the punishment. We are at a loss to understand why punishment could be postponed until after death. One reason might be that the Islamic authorities would not allow the Zoroastrian community to give out death sentences, and the sinner would therefore have to undergo punishment of his own free will. If he did not he knew that he would have to undergo it during the three days following his death. This may have seemed preferable to the sinner himself as well as to his family. The postponing of the punishment may have had other advantages, not only to himself but also to the community at large. As we have seen, it was of paramount importance to keep every available member of the community, so that as many families as possible were active, working units, and so that no property was left without an owner. So, in cases where the crime was so serious that it could not be condoned, one might postpone the punishment until after death for the benefit of the community as a whole.

The last question in the *REA* dealing with the *x*[v]*ētōdah* is

1. *patīt* = "confession", see Jes P. Asmussen: *X*[v]*āstvānīft, Studies in Manichaeism*, Copenhagen 1965, ch. 2, p. 26 ff.; also J.J. Modi: *The Religious ceremonies and Customs of the Parsees*, Bombay 1986, p. 93.

2. *satōš*: The state of a person who has just expired. The soul will remain at the head of the dead body for three days. See J.J. Modi (1986) p. 73, 174; H.S. Nyberg (1974).

3. A.V. Williams (1990) Chapter 15a 5ff.

REA 30.1-2:

pursišn 1:
mart ē, kē-š mēnišn pat x^vētōdahīh bavēt, ān ī kē-š apāk tuvān āyēt kartan pat vistarg dārēt, pat kāmak vicārtan atuvānīk, dātmasīh aivap vimārīh rād. adak-iš kirpak ī x^vētōdah bavēt aivap nē?

passax^v 2:
kirpakīh x^vētōdah ētōn bavēt, ka-c pat kunišn kart. ka-š mēnišnīkīhā, u-š kartan nē tuvān, ka-c atuvānīkīh rād. ō kartan nē rasēt ān pat kirpak, ī pat kunišn bavandakīhā nē kunīhēt, nē pat kartan hangārišn, bē-š adak-ic mēnišnīkīhā rād, vazurg ruvān frayāt ō bavēt.

Question 1:
A man has the intention of making a *x^vētōdah*-marriage. Accordingly he takes to bed a woman with whom he can perform it, but he is unable to follow up his desire with action because of great age or illness. Will he be accorded the merit of the performance of *x^vētōdah* or not?

Answer 2:
The merit is the same whether the *x^vētōdah* is carried out or only intended, but not carried out; when this meritorious deed is not accomplished, or not performed completely in action, it shall not be considered accomplished, but will, nevertheless, be of great help for the soul because of the good intention.

This text clarifies, without any doubt, the intention and nature of the institution of *x^vētōdah*. It is certainly meant as a physical relationship established with the intention of producing children. The good intention to fulfil this is accorded some merit, but the full merit in the life hereafter is accorded only those who actually perform the act with their own body. The Zoroastrians needed children born of men and women of the right faith who would rear their children to become steadfast believers and supporters of the Zoroastrian community. However, the lack of children did not belittle the merit of the *x^vētōdah*, whereas the lack of sexual union does. The reason for this can only be guessed at, impotency and infertility being beyond human control. Impotency may have been a ground for divorce, the wife being justified in leaving the marriage. The ensuing *x^vētōdah* would give small merit, thus discouraging an impotent man from embarking upon it, and thereby hinder the woman from becoming available for other suitors.
Still there is a certain emphasis on the sexual act itself. We see this very clearly expressed in the *Pahlavi Rivāyat* accompanying the *Dādestān ī Dēnīk*[1]. One may wonder why this sexual union is considered so powerful that it will kill demons and other evil creatures. The power issuing from it is remarkably like that of the *hierogamos* known from many other cultures, having the power to spread fertility, make crops grow, and incite humans as well as cattle to procreate. Here in the Middle-Persian version the power seems to be reversed, so that instead of creating it kills, but the principle is the same: A magic power that kills evil, parallel to the magic, creative power of the hierogamos, because good will grow where evil disappears. Seen in this light it becomes easier to understand why the *x^vētōdah* is considered a holy ritual (*vide REA 17*); it is a ritual. The fact that the ritual was discovered to have considerable advantages for the community only enhances its value.

1. A.V. Williams (1990) vol. II p. 14 (8f 3 ff.) in the translation.

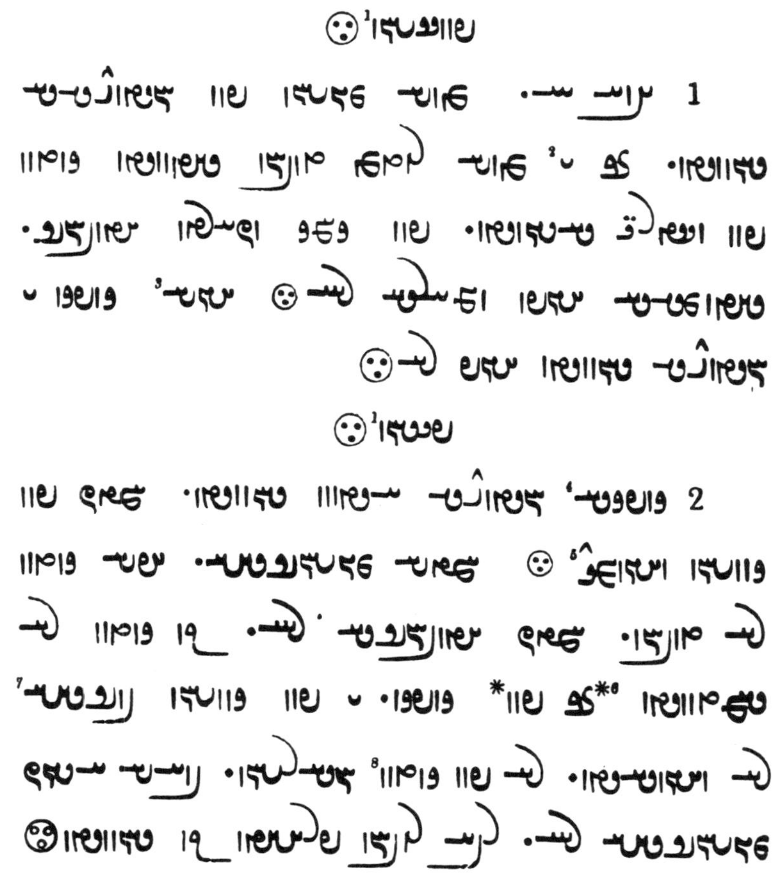

1. Written with red ink. 2. Better omit. 3. For [illegible]. 4. Better [illegible]. 5. For [illegible]. 6** For [illegible]. 7. For [illegible].
8. For [illegible].

If we compare the different notions of the institution of *x^{v}ētōdah* over the comparatively long period of time treated here, we discover that the idea behind it has remained steadfastly the same throughout, only the usage has changed.
The reference in the *Vendidad* to the purifying effect of the urine of a couple who have performed *x^{v}ētōdah* conveys the idea that the union is holy, and that its magic powers could be transferred to others. In the *Vendidad,* the union is neither advocated nor recommended, so we may conclude that the union must have been regarded as a very special one by the religion, but we can have no notion how widespread it may have been. It may have been practised only by the priestly classes, judging from the Latin sources, but this is by no means certain.
During the Sasanian reign this type of marriage existed, as witnessed by the *MHD*, but we do not know whether the union was considered holy or not. The Sasanian legislators and jurists concentrated their attention on the practical problems ensuing from marriages of this kind, but as the marriage has specific religious significance both before and after the Sasanian period, it seems fairly safe to conclude that it had so too in this period.
The treatment of the *x^{v}ētōdah*-marriage in the *Rivāyats* differs widely from the practical and pragmatic treatment it receives in the *MHD*. Its character of holy union, and its meritorious qualities are emphasized. It is hailed as a great spiritual achievement, and the practical problems connected with it are not touched upon at all. And there must, surely, have been many problems in marrying off closely related people to each other; but since the priests wanted very badly to have people of the right faith multiply they advocated this union strongly, and invented promises of rewards in paradise for those who performed it, and punishment for those who broke the union. From a psychological point-of-view, it is easy to see why people should be reluctant to enter into this type of union. Few people are attracted sexually, at least beyond childhood, to members of their own family; it is not in the least exciting to find ones mate among people one knows all too well.
The goal of the Zoroastrian priests, however, was to keep the families united, the faith pure, and thereby to keep the Zoroastrian community intact and strong.

CONCLUSION

The above analysis of four institutions under Zoroastrian family law have, according to my interpretation, revealed the following main points:

Throughout the Sasanian epoch, the law shows the same pragmatic attitude. Laws were created to further the basic aims of the Zoroastrian faith. Within the sphere of the family, this meant: To secure a patriarchal family structure, and to perpetuate a man's lineage. The Zoroastrian religion was not under challenge from other beliefs, but was, on the contrary, protected by a close collaboration between the religious and secular powers, so the intention of the law was to show people how the rules set down in the law were to be applied, and to provide a basis for the disentangling of complicated legal questions.

The examination of the institution of guardianship, in particular, shows that every contingency within the sphere of family economy had been taken into consideration, and had its specific rules and regulations, whether it be inheritance, marriage, income, or succession.

The examination reveals another interesting feature, namely the fact that women seem to have had a moderately independent status in so far as they were allowed, in certain cases, to manage their own economic affairs, and certainly that they seem to have had rather a large say in the question of whom they should marry. The usual focus of a patriarchal society on securing male heirs and successors, and the consequent demand on its women to provide these, does not seem to have weakened the position of women. On the contrary, since the succession was direct and could be transferred through a female to her son, her position must have been fairly strong. With the Zoroastrians, succession would not automatically be transferred to the nearest male relative, such as a brother or a brother's son, and their family structure could therefore not be said, as others have maintained, to be of the agnatic kind. The importance of women as bearers of the succession, on one hand, constituted an inherent problem in a patriarchal society because of the inevitable conflicts and competitions between a woman's husband and her own family, or her *cakar*-husband, over the right to her children. On the other hand, this only enhanced the value of women.

During the two centuries elapsing between the compilation of the *MHD*, and the composition of the *AFS*, in which Zoroastrian minority communities were established throughout the area, the intention of the law has changed considerably. This fact emerges clearly from my comparison and analysis of the two texts. The law, as it appears in the *AFS*, is now employed to preserve the families of true believers, and to encourage these to stay within the Zoroastrian community.

The rules of succession are substantially the same in the *MHD* and the *AFS*, but in the latter, the rules have become adapted to the overall goal of keeping as many families as possible within the fold of the true believers. The importance of keeping up the religious duties even as part of a person's family obligations seems to be emphasized to a marked degree. The promotion of consanguineous marriages may be seen as part of this endeavour.

A hundred years later, the Zoroastrian community must have found itself in even greater difficulties, as witnessed by the rules laid out in the *REA*. In this, we find detailed definitions of the various institutions, and it seems to have been difficult for the remaining groups of believers to get hold of a priest to witness marriage contracts, and to install guardians. As in the *AFS*, the *REA* emphasizes the religious aspect of the life of the community, but the latter goes further in laying stress on the hereafter. Failing to act according to the rules of the law becomes a grave sin, which would affect even the life after death. Personal guidance from a priest had become difficult to obtain, and consequently clear rules, laid down in script were necessary to deter deviators, and hinder apostasy. Continuing a deviating legal opinion from the *MHD,* the *REA* supports the notion that a woman belongs to her husband and not to her own family. The reason for this, in the light of the above, must be that if it became too complicated to establish lasting *pātixšāy*-marriages between young couples there would be a greater risk of creating more apostasy.

What we are left with, after this detailed analysis and comparison of the three law texts, is thus not a uniform picture of Zoroastrian law. Despite the fact that it is a law based on religious beliefs, purporting the same basic ideas throughout several centuries, the law is seen to be ever changing to adapt to radical changes in the surrounding society, with the laudable aim of securing the survival of the Zoroastrian community.

INDEX

List of quotations

MHD

MHDA

AFS

REA

Some legal terms

from the Zoroastrian laws of wills and succession

Ayōkēnīh

This term denotes a woman (*ayōkēn*) whose duty was to procure an heir/successor for her father or brother who had died or would die without one. To effect this she must marry according to a special contract which made the children of the union her father's/brother's legal heirs. She and her husband would not inherit each other and the husband would not be the woman's guardian.

Cakarīh

The purpose of the *cakar*-institution was to procure an heir/successor for a man who had died or would die without one. With this end in view his *pātixšāy*-wife (see below) could enter into a *cakar*-marriage as *cakar*-wife. Her husband in this second marriage would become her *cakar*-husband and their children would be their biological father's *cakar*-children. Legally, they would be the *pātixšāy*-children of their mother's *pātixšāy*-husband and thus his successors/heirs.

Gātār ("lover")

The expression *gātār kartan* ("to take a lover") was used when a woman chose her own husband without her guardian's consent and without coming under her husband's guardianship (see also *x^{v}asrāyūn*).

Hambāyīh

Partnership in business or property. The term is used of the partnership of heirs in cases where the inheritance had not been divided but was kept as a joint possession.

Pātixšāy ("authorised")

A term applied to the husband and wife married according to the principal marriage contract. The wife was married with the consent of her guardian, and the guardianship was transferred to her husband. Husband and wife would inherit each other and their children (*pātixšāy*-children) were legal heirs/successors of the husband who would also normally be their guardian.

Sardārīh ("guardianship")

Guardianship was always a part of the *pātixšāy*-marriage; the husband was guardian of his wife and children, which meant that he had the authority to manage the economic affairs of the family. In case of the demise of the head of the family when there were still minors in the household, the guardianship would be transferred to a *sardār ī būtak* ("natural guardian"): The *pātixšāy*-son, the adopted son (disputed), the *stūr* designated by will, or the brother who was business partner (*hambāy*). In the AFS and the REA *sardār ī kartak* denotes a guardian designated by will and *sardār ī gumartak* a guardian appointed by the authorities.

Stūrīh

A proxy (*stūr*) whose function was to provide the man for whom he/she was *stūr* with an heir, and to be curator of the property that went with this function. When a son had been born and come of age he would be the successor and heir to the *stūr*-property. There were three types of *stūrs*: *Stūr ī būtak* ("the natural *stūr*") which includes *pātixšāy*-wife and –daughters, *stūr ī kartak* who was designated by the testator's will, and *stūr ī gumartak* who was appointed by the authorities.

X^vasrāyūn

The term for a woman who married a man of her own choice without the consent of her guardian. The marriage was legally valid (see also *gātār*).

X^vētōdah

Marriage between blood-relations: Father – daughter, mother – son, brother – sister.

ABBREVIATIONS

AFS: The *Pahlavi Rivāyat* of *Aturfarnbag* and *Farnbag Srōš*

BSOAS: Bulletin of the Society of Oriental and African Studies

MHD: J.J. Modi: *Mâdigân-i-Hazâr Dâdistân*; also used in the analysis of the law book as a whole

MHDA: B.T. Anklesaria: The Social Code of the Parsis in Sassanian Times or *Mādigān i Hazār Dādistān*

MIS: Middle Iranian Studies (ed. by W. Skalmowski & A. van Tongerloo, Leuven 1984)

MSS: Münchener Studien zur Sprachwissenschaft

REA: *Rivāyat i Emēt i Ašavahištān*

(...): Indicates words or letters restored in the manuscript

[...]: Indicates words or letters omitted from the manuscript

BIBLIOGRAPHY

Anklesaria, B.T.

- *Rivâyat-î Hêmît-î Ašavahištân*. Vol.I, Bombay **1962**.
- *The Pahlavi Rivāyat of Aturfarnbag and Farnbag Srōš*. I (Text and Transcription), II (Introduction and Translation), Bombay **1969**.

Anklesaria, T.D.

- *The Social Code of the Parsis in Sassanian Times or Mādigān i Hazār Dādistān*. Part II, Bombay **1912**.

Asmussen, J.P.

- *X^vāstvānīft, Studies in Manichaeism*, Copenhagen **1965**.

Bartholomae, Chr.

- *Altiranisches Wörterbuch*, Strassburg **1904**.
- *Über ein sasanidisches Rechtsbuch*, Heidelberg **1910**.
- "Beiträge zur Kenntnis des sasanidischen Rechts": *Mitteliranische Studien* IV, *WZKM* 27 (**1913**), p. 347-74.
- *Die Frau im sasanidischen Recht*, Heidelberg **1924**.
- *Zum sasanidischen Recht*, Heidelberg:
  - I, **1918**
  - II, **1918**
  - III, **1920**
  - IV, **1922**
  - V, **1923**

Boyce, M.

- *Zoroastrians*, London **1979** (reprinted 1986).
- *A History of Zoroastrianism,* Brill **1975**.
- *The Letter of Tansar*, Roma **1968**.
- "The Pious Foundations of the Zoroastrians". *BSOAS* 31, **1968**.

Bulsara, S.J.

- *The Laws of the Ancient Persians as found in the "Mâtikân ê hazâr Dâtastân" or "The Digest of a Thousand Points of Law"*, Bombay **1937**.

Carlsen, B. Hjerrild

- "The *cakar* Marriage Contract and the *cakar* Children's Status in the *Mātiyān i hazār Dātistān* and *Rivāyat i Ēmēt i Ašavahištān*". *MIS*, Leuven **1984**, p.103-114.
- "Who is the *bayāspān* Daughter?". *MIS*, Leuven **1984**, p.115-121.

Christensen, A.

- *L'Iran sous les Sassanides*, Copenhague **1936**.

Christensen, P.

- *The Decline of Iranshahr*, Copenhagen **1993**.

Clemen, C.

– *Die griechischen und lateinischen Nachrichten über die persische Religion*, Heidelberg **1920**.

Dhabhar, B.N.

– *The Persian Rivayats of Hormazyar Framarz and Others*, Bombay **1932**.
– *Essays on Iranian Subjects*, Bombay **1955**.

Duchesne-Guillemin, J.

– *Religion of Ancient Iran*, Bombay **1973**.

Feist, S.

– *Kultur der Indogermanen*, Berlin **1913**.

Frye, R.N.

– *The Heritage of Persia*, London **1962**.
– *The Golden Age of Persia*, London **1975**.
– "Zoroastrian Incest". *Orientalia Iosephi Tucci Memoriae Dicata*, Roma **1985**, p.445-455.

Gray, L.H.

– "Marriage (Iranian) no.2 Next-of-kin Marriage". In Hastings, *Encyclopaedia of Religion and Ethics* VIII (**1915**), p. 456-459.

Harmatta, J.

– "Inscriptions des Vaiselles Sassanides". *Mémorial Jean de Menasce*, Louvain **1974**.

Hjerrild, B.

– "Zoroastrian Divorce". *Acta Iranica* Vol.XII, Brill **1988**, p.63-68.
– "*Ayōkēn*: Woman between Father and Husband in the Sasanian Era". *Medioiranica*, Leuven **1993**, p.79-86.
– "The Survival and Modification of Zoroastrianism in the Seleucid Times". *Religion and Religious Practice in the Seleucid Kingdom*, Aarhus **1990**, p.140-151.

Isaios

– Wyse, W. (Ed.): *The Speeches of Isaeus*, Olms, Hildesheim **1967** (1904).

Katrak, J.C.

– *Marriage in Ancient Iran*, Bombay **1965**.

Klingenschmitt, G.

– "Die Erbtochter im zoroastrischen Recht nach dem *Mādiyān ē hazār dādistān*". *MSS 21* (**1967**), p. 59-70.
– "Neue Avesta-Fragmente". *MSS 29* (**1971**), p. 111-175.

Kotwal, F.M.P.

– "The Supplementary Texts to the *Šāyest nē-Šāyest*". *Det Kongelige Danske Videnskabernes Selskab, Historisk-filosofiske Meddelelser* 44,2, København **1969**.

Lambton, A.

- *Theory and Practice in Medieval Persian Government*, (Variorum Reprints), London **1980**.

MacKenzie, D.N.

- *A Concise Pahlavi Dictionary*, London **1971**.
- "The Model Marriage Contract in Pahlavi", *K.R. Cama Oriental Institute Golden Jubilee Volume*, Bombay **1969**, p.103-112. Addendum. D.N. MacKenzie and A. Perikhanian.

Macuch, M.

- *Das sasanidische Rechtsbuch "Mātakdān i Hazār Dātistān"*. (Teil II), Berlin **1976**.
- "Der *dastwar*, "auctor", im sasanidischen Zivilprozess". *Archäologische Mitteilungen aus Iran* 21 (**1988**), p.177-188.
- "Die Zeitehe im sasanidischen Recht - ein Vorläufer der šī'itischen Mut'a-Ehe in Iran?". *Archäologische Mitteilungen aus Iran* 18 (**1985**), p.187-203.
- "Inzest im vorislamischen Iran". *Archäologische Mitteilungen aus Iran* 24 (**1991**), p.141-154.
- *Rechtskasuistik und Gerichtspraxis zu Beginn des siebenten Jahrhunderts in Iran*, Wiesbaden **1993**.
- "Herrschaftskonsolidierung und zoroastrisches Familienrecht: zum Verhältnis von Kirche und Staat unter den Sasaniden". *Iran und Turfan*, Harrassowitz **1995**, p. 159 ff.

Manu

- G. Bühler: "The Laws of Manu". *Sacred Books of the East*, Vol. XXV, Oxford **1886** (reprint Delhi 1967).

Mazahéri, A. A.

- *La Famille Iranienne aux Temps Anté-Islamiques*, Paris **1938**.

de Menasce, J.P.

- *Feux et fondations pieuses dans le droit Sassanide*, Paris **1964**.
- "Le 'Rivāyat d'Ēmēt i Ašavahištān'". *Revue de l'histoire des Religions* 162 (**1962**), p.69-88. Reprint: *Studia Iranica*, Cahier 3 (**1985**), p.125-144.
- "Problèmes des Mazdéens dans l'Iran Musulman". *Festschrift für Wilhelm Eilers*, Wiesbaden **1967**, p.220-230.

Middleton, R.

- "Br-Si and Fa-Da Marriage in Ancient Egypt". *American Sociological Review* XXVII (**1962**), No.5, p. 602-11.

Modi, J.J.

- *Mâdigân-i-Hazâr Dâdîstân.* A Photozincographed Facsimile of a Ms. belonging to the Mânockji Limji Hoshang Hâtariâ Library in the Zarthoshti Anjuman Âtashbeharâm, Poona **1901**.
- *The Religious Ceremonies and Customs of the Parsees*, Bombay 1937. Reprint: Bombay **1986**.

– “The Mobadân Mobad Omîd bin Ashavast, referred to by Hamzā Isphahani. Who was he?”. *Studia Indo-Iranica, Ehrengabe für Wilhelm Geiger*, Harrassowitz/Leipzig **1931**.

Moulton, J.H.
– *Early Zoroastrianism*, London **1913**.

Nyberg, H.S.
– *A Manual of Pahlavi*:
  - Part I: Texts, Wiesbaden **1964**
  - Part II: Glossary, Wiesbaden **1974**

Pagliaro, A.
– “IX *χ^varan* ‘riunione, assemblea, festa’, arm. *χoran*”. *Rivista degli Studi Orientali XXVI*, **1951**, p.47-51.

Perikhanian, A.
– “On some Pahlavi Legal Terms”. *Henning Memorial Volume*, London **1970**, p. 349-357.
– *Sasanidskij Sudebnik*, Erewan **1973**. English translation: *The Book of a Thousand Judgements*, Costa Mesa & New York **1997**.
– “Iranian Society and Law”. *Cambridge History of Iran* 3 (2), Part 5, Cambridge **1983**, p.627-680.

Sachau, E.
– *Syrische Rechtsbücher*, Berlin:
  - Vol.I, **1907**
  - Vol.II, **1908**
  - Vol.III **1914**

Safa-Isfehani, N.
– *Rivāyat-i Hēmīt-i Ašavahistān*. A Study in Zoroastrian Law, Harvard **1980** (Harvard Iranian Series 2).

Sanjana, D.P.
– “The Alleged Practice of Consanguineous Marriages in Ancient Iran”. *The Collected Works of D.P. Sanjana*, Bombay **1932**, p.472-79.

Schirasi-Mahmoudian, F.
– *Rechtsnormen der Vormundschaft und der sekundären Erbnachfolge im sasanidischen “Rechtsbuch der tausend Entscheidungen”, “Mātagdān-ē hazār Dātastān” (“Mādayān-ē hazār Dādestān”)*, Diss. Berlin **1975**.

Schmidt, H.P.
– *Some Women's Rites and Rights in the Veda*, Poona **1987**.

Shaked, S.
– “Dualism in Transformation”. *School of Oriental and African Studies*, London **1994**.
– *Bibliotheca Orientalis* XLV, No. 1-2 (**1988**).

Shaki, M.

- "The Sassanian Matrimonial Relations". *Archiv Orientální* 39 (**1971**), p.322-345.
- "The Concept of Obligated Successorship in the Mādiyān ī hazār Dādistān". *Monumentum Nyberg, Acta Iranica* 5 (**1975**), p.227-242.
- "Two Chapters of the Rivāyat ī Emēd ī Ašavahištān". *Oriental Studies*, Tblisi **1983**, p.45-53.

Simonsen, J. Bæk

- *Studies in the Genesis and Early Development of the Caliphal Taxation System*, København **1988**.

Skalmowski, W.

- "On Middle Iranian *dstkrt(y)*". *Medioiranica, Orientalia Lovaniensia Analecta*, Leuven **1993**, p. 157-62.

Spooner, B.

- "Iranian Kinship and Marriage". *Iran* IV (**1966**), p.51-59.

Spuler, B.

- *Iran in früh-islamischer Zeit*, Wiesbaden **1952**.

Tamm, D.

- *Romerret*, København **1980**.

Unvala, J.M.

- *Dârâb Hormazyâr's Rivâyat*. Vol.I & II, Bombay **1922**.
- *King Xusrav and his Page*, Wien **1917**.

Westrup, C.W.

- *Mand og Kvinde*, København **1941**.

Widengren, G.

- "Recherches sur le féodalisme iranien". *Orientalia Suecana* Vol. V (**1956**), p.79-182.

Williams, A.V.

- *The Pahlavi Rivāyat Accompanying the Dādestān ī Dēnīg*:
    - Part I: Transliteration, Transcription and Glossary.
    - Part II: Translation, Commentary and Pahlavi Text, Copenhagen **1990**.

Summary

The present dissertation on Zoroastrian family law is based on an examination of four legal institutions: Guardianship (*sardārīh),* the levirate marriage (*cakarīh*), a daughter stepping in as intermediate successor until her son comes of age (*ayōkēnīh*), and marriage between near relatives (*x*^{v}*ētōdah*). Three law texts from different periods constitute the source material: The *Mātiyān ī hazār Dātistān (MHD)* dating from the first quarter of the 7th century, The *Pahlavi Rivāyat of Aturfarnbag and Farnbag Srōš (AFS)* from the first half of the 9th century and the *Rivāyat ī Ēmēt ī Ašavahištān (REA)* from the first half of the 10th century.

The *MHD* dates back to the Sasanian period, when Iran was a strongly centralized state, and the secular powers collaborated with the Zoroastrian State church. The priests were also jurists, since the law was based on Zoroastrian religion and ethics. The Arab invasion and subsequent occupation of the empire brought about the collapse of this system of government. Eventually most Zoroastrians converted to Islam for tax reasons, or at the prospect of improved economic circumstances. There seems to have been little religious persecution, and those who stuck to their religion were treated as "People of the Book" and as such were permitted to keep their own family law. The *AFS* and the *REA* are law texts established by these religious minority communities.

Zoroastrian family law seems to have been exceptionally complex. The family structure was patriarchal, and the rules of the law were made to ensure that every man would have a successor to carry on the family name until the end of time. At the same time, an essential part of the successor's function was to perform the rites for the soul of the dead *paterfamilias*. The order of succession was direct, from father to son, and in default of a son, through a daughter to the daughter's son, or in certain cases to a son of the *paterfamilias's* wife by another man. Testator might also secure the succession by adopting a son, or by designating a *stūr* whose task it was to produce a son who would become testator's lawful son, when he reached his majority.

The close scrutiny of these law texts reveals considerable, if sometimes subtle, changes in legal practice between the time of the *MHD* when Zoroastrianism was the established religion and the two later law texts, composed at a time when the Zoroastrian religion was practised in minority communities only. I have examined these changes with a view to demonstrating that the changes in legal practice reflect changes in the political and economic conditions under which the Zoroastrian minority groups lived at the time of the *AFS* and the *REA*. These later laws serve essentially to uphold and protect the Zoroastrian minority communities in adversity under Arab rule, whereas the *MHD* texts reflect general social conditions and domestic economy in Zoroastrian society as such.

Chapter 1 deals with "guardianship" (*sardārīh*). In the so-called *pātixšāy*-marriage, the husband was guardian of his wife, and husband and wife would inherit each other. Their sons would be heirs to, and successors of their father. The notion of guardianship testifies to the fact that the family was kept under strict patriarchal control. Even so, and despite the fact that women were normally placed under male guardianship, it was possible for them under certain circumstances to dispense with a guardian. They had a certain freedom of choice in the question of marriage. A young woman could choose to marry somebody without her father's/guardian's consent, in a so-called *x*^{v}*asrāyūn*-marriage. If her guardian did not approve of her choice, and she insisted on continuing this marriage, the relationship between guardian and ward would be dissolved, and her father would no longer benefit from her income, while she would not inherit him. In my opinion, these rules and their attending practical problems all have to do with the economic relations of the parties concerned. E.g. a daughter had the right to refuse to contract a marriage arranged by her father, but she could not refuse to accept a *stūrīh* on her father's orders, because this was a financial transaction, and thus within his range of authority.

A man might voluntarily limit his own authority as guardian by taking his wife as his business partner, which gave her the right to dispose of part of their joint property, a practical measure in cases where a man had to be absent from his home for a long period. The fact that this possibility existed must certainly indicate that before the law women were regarded as persons in their own right. On the other hand, only the husband could take the initiative in making such an agreement, and only a man could instigate a divorce.

Guardianship might temporarily be transferred to another person, and by the death of the *paterfamilias* it would be transferred to a grown-up son, if one existed, if not, to somebody else. The lady of the house might evade such a contingency by finding herself a cohabiter, which again indicates that women enjoyed a certain amount of independence.

In the *AFS* the institution of guardianship is the object of a great deal of attention, and in the main, the rules are the same. Still, some significant changes seem to have taken place. On one hand we find attempts to tighten the father's authority over his daughter, on the other hand the rights of women were strengthened, inasmuch as they might obtain guardianship over their daughters. There is not a single instance of female guardianship in the *MHD*. Thus two apparently contradictory aims are reflected: The strengthening of men's control over their household, if possible, and the strengthening of women's authority, if necessary. The Zoroastrian minority communities could not afford to have their members feel hidebound by too strict rules, and thus running the risk of their defecting. At the same time they felt obliged to continue a system, which would mark a clear distinction between their community and the surrounding society.

The *REA* begins with a definition of three types of guardian: 1) the natural guardian (*sardār ī būtak*), i.e. a grown-up son of the dead *paterfamilias*, 2) a guardian designated by testator's will (*sardār ī kartak*), or 3) a guardian appointed by the religious authorities (*sardār ī gumārtak*). The text specifies down to the last detail what type of person should be chosen for guardianship, and it discusses the procedure one should adopt when appointing a guardian. Since it was apparently not always possible to command the presence of a priest, alternatives are given, in order of priority. Great attention is also paid to possible measures against apostates, in order that their possible guardianship over minors may be transferred to members of the community who are true believers. The legal rules here clearly reflect the unsettled conditions of the time, with the number of Zoroastrians dwindling, as many of them converted to Islam.

Chapter 2 treats of the *cakar*-institution. The purpose of this institution was to procure a successor for a man who did not have any son, and sometimes also if he had. His *pātixšāy*-wife might, to that end, contract a special marriage (*cakar*) with another man, either while her *pātixšāy*-husband was still alive, or after his death. The offspring of this connection would become her *pātixšāy*-husband's legitimate heirs. There were no economic obligations between the partners in a *cakar*-marriage, except that the wife must be given her day-to-day requirements, while she would be obliged to take part in the daily housework. The *MHD* reflects the obvious problems attached to this institution. A *cakar*-husband without an heir of his own would naturally want to adopt his own son as his successor, but if this were allowed, the whole idea of the institution would be forfeited. Certain differences of opinion among the jurists show that, from time to time, exemption from the rules was granted.

The *AFS,* on the other hand, declares the right of the biological father to adopt his *cakar*-son, and also that he has certain legal claims on his son. There is a strong emphasis on the religious aspects of the institution: Would a *cakar*-son's good deeds benefit his *cakar*-father or his mother's *pātixšāy*-

husband in the afterlife? According to the authors of this law text, one quarter of the good deeds will benefit the *cakar*-father, three quarters in case he is responsible for his son's upbringing, and the remaining quarters will benefit the *pātixšāy*-father. During the Sasanian period, Zoroastrians and their laws were concerned with the things of this life, whereas in the 9th century they turned their attention to the hereafter, as their possibilities for expansion and success here on earth gradually diminished.

The *REA* reflects this phenomenon too. Here deviations from the prescribed rules were judged as sins of various degrees.

Chapter 3 deals with the institution of *ayōkēnīh* (a daughter stepping in as intermediate successor). This is yet another way of securing the succession for a man who was dead, or would be likely to die without leaving an heir. If such a man had a daughter, she could marry by a special contract, which would make her offspring her father's legitimate heirs. She might do the same for a brother. This way of continuing a man's lineage is also known from ancient Greece and India. The very existence of this institution proves that to the Zoroastrians the idea of lineal succession was very firmly established. A man from the agnatic circle might equally well have carried on the succession, but to the Zoroastrians this was not an option. A daughter who was married already could be forced to terminate the *pātixšāy*-contract with her husband in order to assume the responsibility of providing her father or brother with an heir. This fact indicates that a woman's obligation towards her father was greater than her duty to her husband, as was her obligation towards a brother, especially towards one who was also her business partner, i.e. he and she shared their inheritance. My interpretation of the rules about *ayōkēnīh* from the Sasanian period is that the internal economy of a family constituted such a strong bond that it took priority over the marriage bond, and also, that a woman had greater obligations towards the family she was born into than towards the one she had married into. Thus, conflict seems to be a built-in element in the patriarchal family structure: The parental generation had certain claims on the offspring of their daughters, while, at the same time, the younger generation was expected to found a new family, based on the patriarchal system, with its own lineal succession. This conflict is reflected in divergent legal opinions.

The *AFS* does not devote much space to this institution, but contents itself with stressing, yet again, a daughter's duty towards her father. There is, however, a certain suggestion of regret that an *ayōkēn* cannot contract a *pātixšāy*-marriage. Despite the expressions of regret, the performance of ones religious and moral duty is, as always in this text, the essential point.

The *REA* gives a definition of what an *ayōkēn* is. This is an interesting point, as it seems to suggest the gradual disappearance of the old, general knowledge. The text differs from that of the *AFS* in that it states quite firmly that a wife's duty towards her husband is greater than the obligation she owes her father or brother. Interestingly, the *REA* continues the debate begun in the *MHD*. In my view, the reason for this must be sought in the fact that the number of young women who were potential *pātixšāy*-wives had decreased dramatically by this time, making it necessary for the minority communities to help establish new *pātixšāy*-marriages with all the means at their disposal.

Chapter 4. Deals with the *x*^{v}*ētōdah*- marriage. This was a connection between close relatives, i.e. a marriage between father/daughter, mother/son or brother/sister. This type of marriage had obvious religious and economic advantages. A closely-knit family unit like this would safeguard its members against apostasy, while at the same time securing the family fortune on family hands. There was no dowry or bride price to be paid, and no daughters-in-law to be paid their share of the inheritance. As the Iranians did not operate with the right of primogeniture, this type of marriage might also be a way to avoid the splitting up of land into small unprofitable units. In the Middle

East marriage between first cousins is very common, precisely to avoid the splitting up of family property.

In the *MHD* the attitude towards this type of marriage is entirely pragmatic. The problems treated here are purely legal ones, as for instance, how a daughter who was the wife of her father should be treated with respect to inheritance.

The two later texts reveal a different attitude. They both emphasize the religious aspect, and this type of union seems to have taken on the character of a holy ritual established to secure the reward in the hereafter of the parties involved. In these two texts this type of marriage is encouraged by the promise of rewards, but, at the same time, one may read between the lines that the parties who had promised to marry a close relative often showed great reluctance to fulfill their promise. So, for this type of marriage, a breach of promise was regarded as a serious sin.

I am convinced that the attempts, recorded in these texts, to promote this type of union reflect the difficulties of the Zoroastrian community of the time of keeping the families of believers together, and finding suitable spouses for the young people from outside the family. This served to distinguish the community of true believers from the surrounding society, by which means they presumably hoped to preserve purity of the community of the true faith until better times.

It is my hope that the close analysis of these texts will have shown that despite their differences, the three law texts work towards the same goal: the promotion and preservation of the Zoroastrian religious ethics. In the Sasanian period the laws were principally concerned with the secular problems of the community, and the family within the community in a purely pragmatic way, but always with a view to the furthering and maintaining of the Zoroastrian religion. In the later texts, the *REA* and the *AFS,* the same purpose is apparent; but these texts also reflect the fundamental changes in society, both economically and politically. The laws must now help to keep families and the Zoroastrian community together. To achieve this goal, the law is forced to slacken some rules and make others more stringent, while increasingly emphasizing the religious aspect.